PRENTICE HALL
LITERATURE

PENGUIN  **EDITION**

Reader's Notebook
Adapted Version

Grade Eight

PEARSON

Prentice Hall

Upper Saddle River, New Jersey
Boston, Massachusetts

ISBN 0-13-165376-8

2 3 4 5 6 7 8 9 10 10 09 08 07 06

ACKNOWLEDGMENTS

Grateful acknowledgment is made to the following for copyrighted material:

Arte Público Press
"Baseball" by Lionel G. García from *I Can Hear The Cowbells Ring.*

Brent Ashabranner
"Always to Remember: The Vision of Maya Ying Lin" by Brent Ashabranner from *Always to Remember.*

Black Issues Book Review
"Zora Neale Hurston: A Life in Letters, Book Review" by Zakia Carter from *Black Issues Book Review,* Nov–Dec 2002; www.bibookreview.com.

The Christian Science Monitor
"Lots in space: Orbiting junk, from old satellites to space gloves, has scientists worried for spacecraft— & engineers working on ways to clean it up." By Peter N. Spotts From *The Christian Science Monitor, Oct. 9, 2003. Pg. 11.* Copyright Christian Science Monitor Oct. 9, 2003. Copyright © 2004 ProQuest Information and Learning Company. All rights reserved.

Curtis Brown London
"Who Can Replace a Man?" by Brian W. Aldiss from *Masterpieces: The Best Science Fiction Of The Century.* Copyright © 2001 by Orson Scott Card and Tekno Books. All rights reserved.

Neil Simon & Albert I. Da Silva
The Governess by Neil Simon from *The Collected Plays of Neil Simon, Volume 2.* Copyright © 1974 Neil Simon and Albert I. Da Silva. **CAUTION NOTICE:** Professionals and amateurs are hereby warned that *The Governess* is subject to a royalty. It is fully protected under the copyright laws of the United States of America and of all countries covered by the International Copyright Union (including the Dominion of Canada and the rest of the British Commonwealth), the Berne Convention, the Pan-American Copyright Convention and the Universal Copyright Convention as well as all countries with which the United States has reciprocal copyright relations. All rights, including professional/amateur stage rights, motion picture, recitation, lecturing, public reading, radio broadcasting, television, video or sound recording, all other forms of mechanical or electronic reproduction, such as CD-ROM, CD-I, information storage and retrieval systems and photocopying, and the rights of translation into foreign languages, are strictly reserved. Particular emphasis is laid upon the matter of readings, permission for which must be secured from the Author's agent in writing.

The Dramatic Publishing Company
from *Anne Frank & Me* by Cherie Bennett with Jeff Gottesfeld from Anne Frank & Me. Copyright © 1997 by Cherie Bennett. All rights reserved.

Farrar, Straus & Giroux, LLC
"Charles" by Shirley Jackson from *The Lottery.* Copyright © 1948, 1949 by Shirley Jackson and copyright renewed © 1976, 1977 by Laurence Hyman, Barry Hyman, Mrs, Sarah Webster and Mrs. Joanne Schnurer.

Gale Group
"Summary of The Tell-Tale Heart from Short Story Criticism" from *Short Story Criticism: Criticism Of The Works Of Short Fiction Writers.* Copyright © 2000. All rights reserved.

Richard García
"The City Is So Big" by Richard García from *The City Is So Big.*

Harcourt, Inc.
"For My Sister Molly Who in the Fifties" from *Revolutionary Petunias & Other Poems,* copyright © 1972 and renewed 2000 by Alice Walker. "Choice: A Tribute to Martin Luther King, Jr." by Alice Walker from *In Search Of Our Mother's Gardens: Womanist Prose.* Copyright © 1983 by Alice Walker. Reprinted by permission.

Harold Ober Associates, Inc.
"Cat!" by Eleanor Farjeon. Copyright © 1938 by Eleanor Farjeon, renewed 1966 by Gervase Farjeon. Reprinted by permission of Harold Ober Associates Incorporated. All rights reserved.

(Acknowledgments continue on page V52)

Contents

READING INFORMATIONAL MATERIALS
Advertisements

UNIT 3 Nonfiction

MODEL SELECTION
"Making Tracks on Mars: A Journal Based on a Blog" by Andrew Mishkin

"Harriet Tubman: Guide to Freedom" by Ann Petry

"Baseball" by Lionel G. García

from I Know Why the Caged Bird Sings by Maya Angelou

from Always to Remember: The Vision of Maya Ying Lin
by Brent Ashabranner

READING INFORMATIONAL MATERIALS
Textbooks

UNIT 4 Poetry

UNIT 5 Drama

UNIT 6 Themes in Literature

INTERACTING WITH THE TEXT

As you read your hardcover student edition of *Prentice Hall Literature,* use the ***Reader's Notebook*** to guide you in learning and practicing the skills presented. In addition, many selections in your student edition are presented here in an interactive format. The notes and instruction will guide you in applying reading and literary skills and in thinking about the selection. The examples on these pages show you how to use the notes as a companion when you read.

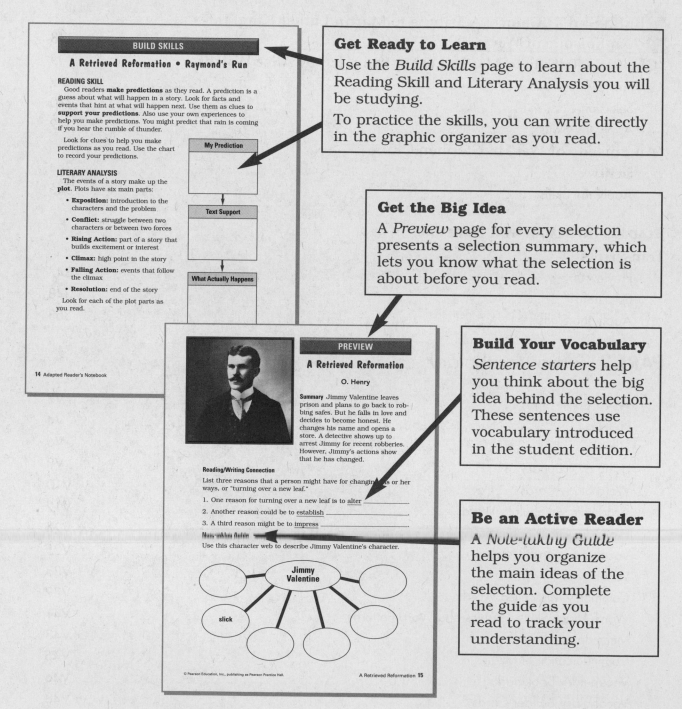

Get Ready to Learn

Use the *Build Skills* page to learn about the Reading Skill and Literary Analysis you will be studying.

To practice the skills, you can write directly in the graphic organizer as you read.

Get the Big Idea

A *Preview* page for every selection presents a selection summary, which lets you know what the selection is about before you read.

Build Your Vocabulary

Sentence starters help you think about the big idea behind the selection. These sentences use vocabulary introduced in the student edition.

Be an Active Reader

A *Note-taking Guide* helps you organize the main ideas of the selection. Complete the guide as you read to track your understanding.

Content shown in the notebook example images:

BUILD SKILLS

A Retrieved Reformation • Raymond's Run

READING SKILL
Good readers **make predictions** as they read. A prediction is a guess about what will happen in a story. Look for facts and events that hint at what will happen next. Use them as clues to **support your predictions**. Also use your own experiences to help you make predictions. You might predict that rain is coming if you hear the rumble of thunder.

Look for clues to help you make predictions as you read. Use the chart to record your predictions.

My Prediction

LITERARY ANALYSIS
The events of a story make up the **plot**. Plots have six main parts:

- **Exposition:** introduction to the characters and the problem
- **Conflict:** struggle between two characters or between two forces
- **Rising Action:** part of a story that builds excitement or interest
- **Climax:** high point in the story
- **Falling Action:** events that follow the climax
- **Resolution:** end of the story

Look for each of the plot parts as you read.

Text Support

What Actually Happens

PREVIEW

A Retrieved Reformation

O. Henry

Summary Jimmy Valentine leaves prison and plans to go back to robbing safes. But he falls in love and decides to become honest. He changes his name and opens a store. A detective shows up to arrest Jimmy for recent robberies. However, Jimmy's actions show that he has changed.

Reading/Writing Connection
List three reasons that a person might have for changing his or her ways, or "turning over a new leaf."
1. One reason for turning over a new leaf is to <u>alter</u> _____
2. Another reason could be to <u>establish</u> _____
3. A third reason might be to <u>impress</u> _____

Note-taking Guide
Use this character web to describe Jimmy Valentine's character.

Jimmy Valentine

slick

A Retrieved Reformation **15**

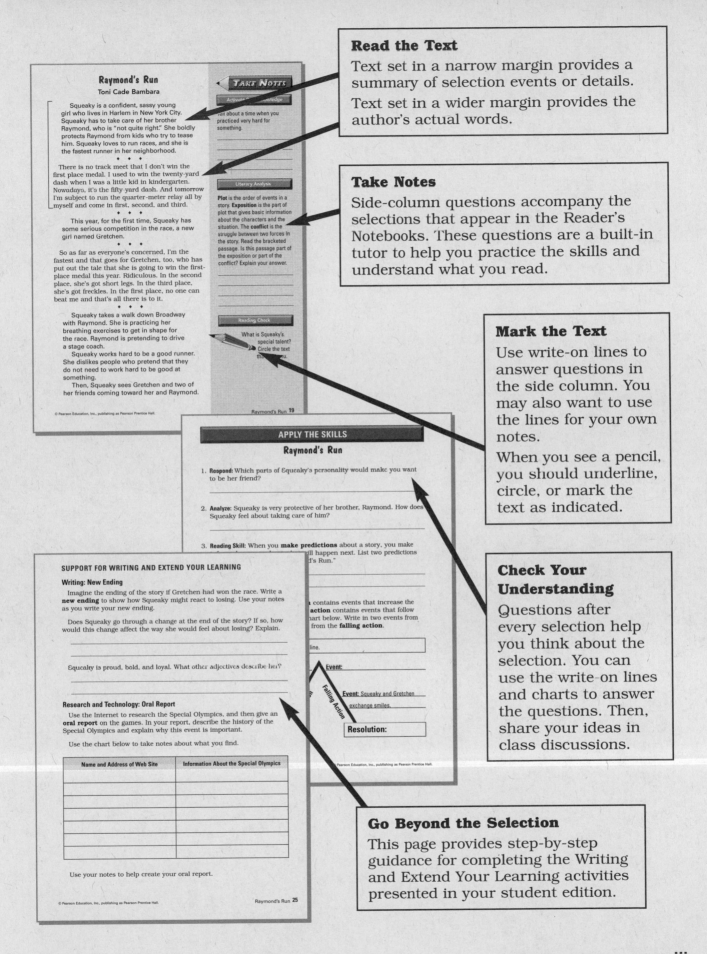

Read the Text

Text set in a narrow margin provides a summary of selection events or details.

Text set in a wider margin provides the author's actual words.

Take Notes

Side-column questions accompany the selections that appear in the Reader's Notebooks. These questions are a built-in tutor to help you practice the skills and understand what you read.

Mark the Text

Use write-on lines to answer questions in the side column. You may also want to use the lines for your own notes.

When you see a pencil, you should underline, circle, or mark the text as indicated.

Check Your Understanding

Questions after every selection help you think about the selection. You can use the write-on lines and charts to answer the questions. Then, share your ideas in class discussions.

Go Beyond the Selection

This page provides step-by-step guidance for completing the Writing and Extend Your Learning activities presented in your student edition.

PART 1

SELECTIONS AND SKILLS SUPPORT

The pages in your *Reader's Notebook* go with the pages in the hardcover student edition. The pages in the *Reader's Notebook* allow you to participate in class instruction and take notes on the concepts and selections.

BEFORE YOU READ

Build Skills Follow along in your *Reader's Notebook* as your teacher introduces the **Reading Skill** and **Literary Analysis** instruction. The graphic organizer is provided on this page so that you can take notes right in your *Reader's Notebook*.

Preview Use this page for the selection your teacher assigns.

- The **Summary** gives you an outline of the selection.
- Use the **Reading-Writing Connection** to understand the big idea of the selection and join in the class discussion about the ideas.
- Use the **Note-taking Guide** while you read the story. This will help you organize and remember information you will need to answer questions about the story later.

WHILE YOU READ

Selection Text and Sidenotes You can read the full text of one selection in each pair in your *Reader's Notebook*.

- You can write in the *Reader's Notebook*. Underline important details to help you find them later.
- Use the **Take Notes** column to jot down your reactions, ideas, and answers to questions about the text. If your assigned selection is not the one that is included in the *Reader's Notebook*, use sticky notes to make your own **Take Notes** section in the side column as you read the selection in the hardcover student edition.

AFTER YOU READ

Apply the Skills Use this page to answer questions about the selection right in your *Reader's Notebook*. For example, you can complete the graphic organizer that is in the hardcover student edition right on the page in your *Reader's Notebook*.

Support for Writing and Extend Your Learning Use this page to help you jot down notes and ideas as you prepare to do one or more of the projects assigned with the selection.

Other Features in the *Reader's Notebook* You will also find note-taking opportunities for these features:

- Learning About the Genre
- Support for the Model Selection
- Support for Reading Informational Materials

from The Baker Heater League

Nonfiction is different from fiction in these ways:

- Nonfiction deals with real people, events, or ideas.

- Nonfiction is told through the voice of the author. The author is a real person. The author's view is the **point of view** of the writing.

Many things affect the outcome of nonfiction writing. Two examples are these:

- **Mood:** the feeling the reader gets from the work

- **Author's style:** all of the different ways that a writer uses language. Rhythm, language, and ways of putting things in order are all part of the author's style.

Purpose	Mission	Examples
To persuade	• written to convince audiences of a certain idea or opinion	• speeches • editorials
To inform	• written to present facts and information	• articles • reference books • historical essays • research papers
To entertain	• written for the enjoyment of the audience	• autobiographies • biographies • travel narratives

The 11:59

Fiction is a story that comes from the author's imagination. It tells about characters and events. Fiction has these basic parts:

- **Setting:** the time and place of the story

- **Plot:** the events that move the reader through the story. The plot includes a **conflict**, or problem. The **resolution**, or outcome, comes at the end of the story.

- **Characters:** the people or animals that take part in the action in a story. The **character's traits**, or qualities, can affect his or her thoughts and actions.

- **Point of view:** the view from which the story is told to the reader. The **first-person point of view** is used when the story is told from the view of a character. The **third-person point of view** is used when the story is told from the view of a person outside the story.

- **Theme:** a message about life that the story tries to show

Type	Description	Characteristics
Short stories	short works that can usually be read in one sitting	• contain plot, characters, setting, point of view, and theme • usually focus on one main plot around one conflict
Novels	longer works	• contain plot, characters, conflict, and setting • may also contain **subplots**, independent stories or conflicts related to the main plot
Novellas	shorter than novels, but longer than short stories	• may contain characteristics of short stories and novels
Historical fiction	works of fiction that take place in a real historical setting	• uses information about real people and events to tell invented stories

from The Baker Heater League

Patricia C. McKissack and Fredrick McKissack

Summary This nonfiction selection explains how railroad workers called *porters* shared tales with one another. The porters would gather around a potbellied stove, called a Baker heater, to tell their stories. Legends such as those of Casey Jones and John Henry grew out of these stories.

Note-taking Guide

Use the chart below to record the different facts and legends you learned while reading "The Baker Heater League."

Facts	Legends
About 1870, John Henry joined a steel-driving team for the C & O Railroad.	John Henry was so strong that he could drive steel with a hammer in each hand.

The Baker Heater League
Patricia C. and Fredrick McKissack

This nonfiction selection explains how railroad workers called porters shared and passed on stories. The porters would meet one another in train stations across the United States. When they were not working, the porters sat around a potbellied stove, called a Baker heater, and told stories. The porters became known as "The Baker Heater League."

The selection describes how the porters told stories that were based on the actions of real people. One story was about a real engineer named Casey Jones.

◆　◆　◆

John Luther Jones, better known as Casey Jones, was an underline engineer on Cannonball Number 382. On the evening of April 29, 1900, Casey and his black fireman, Sim Webb, prepared to take the Cannonball from Memphis to Canton. The scheduled engineer was out ill. The train left at 12:50 A.M., an hour and thirty minutes late. Casey was determined to make up the lost time.

◆　◆　◆

When Casey's train crashed, he refused to jump to safety. Instead, he stayed on the train, saved many lives, and then died. He became a railroad hero.

Another railroad hero was based on a real person named John Henry.

◆　◆　◆

The real John Henry, believed to be a newly freed slave from North Carolina, joined the West Virginia steel-driving team hired to dig out the

---

Vocabulary Development

engineer (en ji NEER) *n.* someone whose job it is to control the engine on a ship or train

---

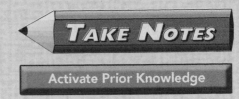

TAKE NOTES

Activate Prior Knowledge

What lessons could you learn from family members who tell stories about jobs they have done?

_____

_____

Nonfiction

One of the purposes of nonfiction writing is **to inform**, or to present facts and information to the reader. Read the information in the bracketed paragraph. Who are the people the author talks about? Circle their names in the text.

Nonfiction

Nonfiction is written **to persuade**, **to inform**, or **to entertain** readers. What do you think is the author's purpose for writing about John Henry?

_____

_____

Stop to Reflect

Why do you think the porters wanted to share their stories with one another?

_____

_____

Read Fluently

Sometimes a new word is formed by joining two separate words together. The new word is known as a compound word. Read the underlined sentence. The word *storyteller* is formed by joining the words *story* and *teller*. Each of those words can stand alone, but they form a new word when joined together. Circle another compound word in the last paragraph.

Nonfiction

What **character traits**, or qualities, would have made the porters look up to Daddy Joe as a hero?

_____

_____

_____

Reading Check

Who is described as "the most terrific Pullman porter who ever made down a berth"? Circle the text that tells you.

Big Bend Tunnel for the C & O Railroad, <u>circa</u> 1870. Many stories detail the life and adventures of this two hundred-pound, six-foot man who was so strong he could drive steel with a hammer in each hand. John Henry's death occurred after competing with a steam drill, winning, and then dying.

◆　◆　◆

The porters also told stories about Daddy Joe, a real-life porter, who became a legend. Although they exaggerated Daddy Joe's actions, the stories showed what qualities the porters admired.

◆　◆　◆

<u>Whenever a storyteller wanted to make a point about courtesy, honesty, or an outstanding job performance, he used a Daddy Joe story.</u> And a tale about him usually began with: "The most terrific Pullman porter who ever made down a berth was Daddy Joe."

◆　◆　◆

The porters also liked to tell funny stories about new workers who made foolish mistakes. As soon as one story was over, someone would begin a new one.

◆　◆　◆

Amid thigh-slapping laughter, another tale would begin with: "Did you hear the story about the flagman?" Of course they'd all heard the story a hundred times. But each teller added or subtracted something until the tale was his own. That's how the tales stayed fresh and original.

Vocabulary Development

circa (SER cuh) *adj.*　around; used before a date to show that the date is uncertain

courtesy (KER tuh see) *n.*　polite behavior

The 11:59

Patricia C. McKissack

Summary Lester Simmons, a retired porter, hangs out every night at the porter house, telling stories to the other railroad employees. One night, he tells the young porters about the mysterious 11:59 Death Train. Lester's story becomes real. He tries to escape the train.

Note-taking Guide

Use this web to recall the different stories that Lester tells.

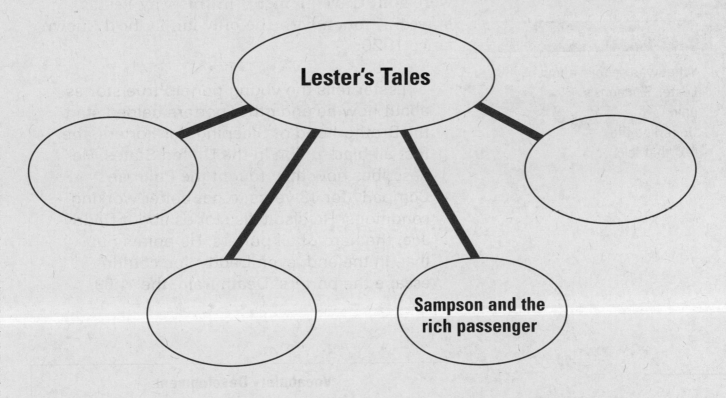

Lester's Tales

Sampson and the rich passenger

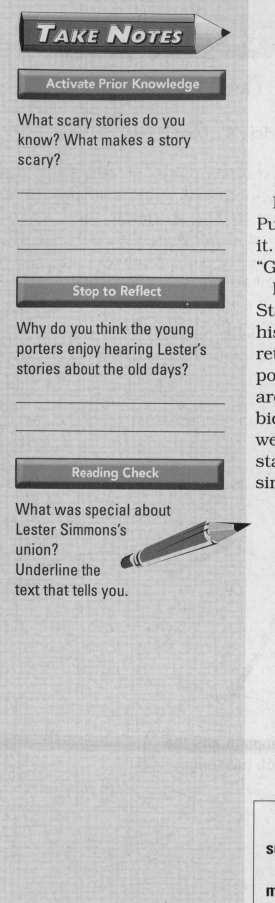

Activate Prior Knowledge

What scary stories do you know? What makes a story scary?

_____

_____

_____

Stop to Reflect

Why do you think the young porters enjoy hearing Lester's stories about the old days?

_____

_____

Reading Check

What was special about Lester Simmons's union? Underline the text that tells you.

The 11:59
Patricia C. McKissack

This fictional story is set in St. Louis in the 1950s. Its main character is an old man who has retired from his job as a Pullman porter after thirty years of work.

◆ ◆ ◆

Lester Simmons was a thirty-year retired Pullman car porter—had his gold watch to prove it. "Keeps perfect train time," he often bragged. "Good to the second."

Daily he went down to the St. Louis Union Station and shined shoes to help <u>supplement</u> his <u>meager</u> twenty-four-dollar-a-month Pullman retirement check. He ate his evening meal at the porter house on Compton Avenue and hung around until late at night talking union, playing bid whist, and spinning yarns with those who were still "travelin' men." In this way Lester stayed in touch with the only family he'd known since 1920.

◆ ◆ ◆

Lester tells the young porters true stories about how he and other porters helped start the Brotherhood of Sleeping Car Porters, the first all-black union in the United States. He describes how they fought the Pullman Company for 13 years to get better working conditions. He also tells stories about Daddy-Joe, the hero of all porters. He points out that, in the end, even Daddy Joe couldn't escape the porters' Death Train, the 11:59.

◆ ◆ ◆

Vocabulary Development

supplement (SUP luh muhnt) *v.*   add something, especially to what you earn or eat, in order to improve it
meager (MEE ger) *adj.*   very small in amount

"Any porter who hears the whistle of the 11:59 has got exactly twenty-four hours to clear up earthly matters. He better be ready when the train comes the next night . . ." In his creakiest voice, Lester drove home the point. "All us porters got to board that train one day. Ain't no way to escape the final ride on the 11:59."

Silence.

"Lester," a young porter asked, "you know anybody who ever heard the whistle of the 11:59 and lived to tell—"

"Not a living soul!"

Laughter.

◆ ◆ ◆

Then Lester tells the story of how his old friend, Tip Sampson, got his nickname. Tip once waited on a rich woman who rode a train from Chicago to Los Angeles. He was hoping to get a big tip from the woman. At the end of the trip, however, all she gave him was one dime. Lester started teasing Sampson by calling him Tip, and the nickname stuck. One of the porters tells Lester that Tip recently "boarded the 11:59," or died. Lester realizes that he is one of the last old-time porters left in St. Louis. Then he starts walking home a little before midnight.

◆ ◆ ◆

Suddenly he felt a sharp pain in his chest. At exactly the same moment he heard the <u>mournful</u> sound of a train whistle, which the wind seemed to carry from some faraway place. Ignoring his pain, Lester looked at the old station. He knew nothing was scheduled to come in or out till early morning. Nervously he lit a match to check the time. 11:59!

"No," he said into the darkness. "I'm not ready. I've got plenty of living yet."

Vocabulary Development

mournful (MAWRN fuhl) *adj.*   very sad; depressing

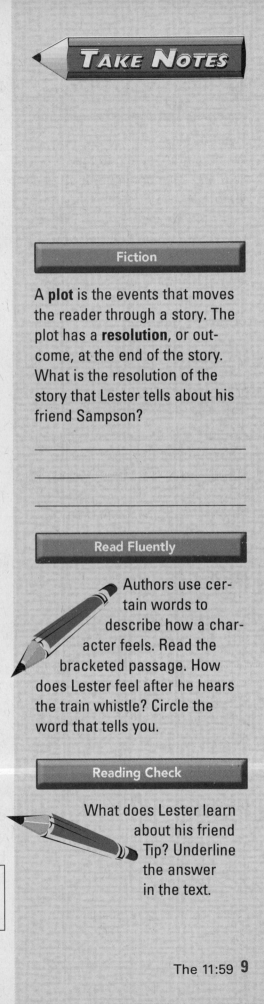

Fiction

A **plot** is the events that moves the reader through a story. The plot has a **resolution**, or outcome, at the end of the story. What is the resolution of the story that Lester tells about his friend Sampson?

_____

_____

_____

Read Fluently

Authors use certain words to describe how a character feels. Read the bracketed passage. How does Lester feel after he hears the train whistle? Circle the word that tells you.

Reading Check

What does Lester learn about his friend Tip? Underline the answer in the text.

TAKE NOTES

Fiction

Point of view is the view from which a story is told to the reader. **First-person point of view** is used when the story is told from the view of a character. **Third-person point of view** is used when the story is told from the view of a person outside the story. From which point of view is this story told?

_____

_____

Read Fluently

Authors use exclamation points (!) to add punch to words or sentences. Read the underlined sentence. Why do you think the author used an exclamation point here? How would the sentence sound if it ended with a period?

_____

_____

_____

Reading Check

What is supposed to happen at 11:59? Circle the answer in the text.

Fear quickened his step. Reaching his small apartment, he hurried up the steps. His heart pounded in his ear, and his left arm tingled. He had an idea, and there wasn't a moment to waste. But his own words haunted him. _Ain't no way to escape the final ride on the 11:59._

"But I'm gon' try!" Lester spent the rest of the night plotting his escape from fate.

♦   ♦   ♦

Lester decides not to eat or drink anything the next day so that he will not choke or die of food poisoning. He shuts off his space heater, nails all the doors and windows shut, and unplugs all of his appliances to avoid any dangers. He plans to escape Death and live to tell the story to the young porters.

Lester spends the next day in his chair, too scared to move. He checks his watch every few minutes and listens to its constant ticking. He thinks about his thirty years of working on the railroad. He wonders what his life would have been like if he had decided to settle down in one place and get married. Finally, he decides that he has lived a good life and has no regrets.

When night comes, Lester starts praying. His arm starts tingling, and his legs get stiff. He wonders whether he will be the first porter to avoid the 11:59 and cheat Death. Then he hears a train whistle, lights a match, and sees that the time is now 11:57. He hears the whistle again, but he is unable to move. The pain in his chest gets worse, and it is hard for him to breathe.

♦   ♦   ♦

Time had run out! Lester's mind reached for an explanation that made sense. But reason failed when a glowing phantom dressed in the porters' blue uniform stepped out of the grayness of Lester's confusion.

"It's *your* time, good brother." The specter spoke in a thousand familiar voices.

Freed of any restraint now, Lester stood, bathed in a peaceful calm that had its own glow. "Is that you, Tip?" he asked, squinting to focus on his old friend standing in the strange light.

"It's me, ol' partner. Come to remind you that none of us can escape the last ride on the 11:59."

"I know. I know," Lester said, chuckling. "But man, I had to try."

Tip smiled. "I can dig it. So did I."

"That'll just leave Willie, won't it?"

"Not for long."

"I'm ready."

◆　◆　◆

Lester dies. Two days later, his friends find him dead on the floor, with his eyes still staring at his gold watch. The watch stopped at exactly 11:59.

TAKE NOTES

Fiction

What is the **resolution** to Lester's story?

_____

_____

Fiction

A **theme** is a message about life that a story attempts to tell. What do you think is the theme of Lester's story?

_____

_____

_____

Reading Check

What is Tip's reason for coming to see Lester? Underline the answer in the text.

Nonfiction and Fiction

1. **Interpret:** What causes Lester's death in "The 11:59"?

   _____

   _____

2. **Classify:** Use the chart below to record information about the railroad figures discussed in "The Baker Heater League." List the heroes. Write the facts and legends that are given about each one.

Railroad Heroes	Fact	Legend/Fiction
Casey Jones	His real name was John Luther Jones. He was an engineer on Cannonball No. 382.	Jones chose to stay on the the train to protect the lives of others.

3. **Fiction:** What details in the **setting** make "The 11:59" seem to have actually happened?

   _____

   _____

4. **Nonfiction:** Authors of nonfiction often use fictional parts in their writing. Why does the author include tales about famous railroad figures in "The Baker Heater League"?

   _____

   _____

   _____

RESEARCH THE AUTHOR

Talk Show

Present a **talk show**. The following tips will help you create your show.

- Read some of the authors' works. Patricia and Fredrick McKissack's books include *Christmas in the Big House, Christmas in the Quarters; Bugs!; Martin Luther King, Jr.: Man of Peace; Rebels Against Slavery: American Slave Revolts;* and *Let My People Go.*

  What I learned from the McKissacks' writing:

  _____

  _____

  _____

  _____

- Search the Internet: Use words and phrases such as "Patricia McKissack article."

  What I learned about Patricia and Fredrick McKissack:

  _____

  _____

  _____

  _____

- Watch the video interview with Patricia McKissack. Add what you learn from the video to what you have already learned about the author and her husband.

  Additional information learned about the authors:

  _____

  _____

  _____

  _____

Use your notes to write your talk show.

A Retrieved Reformation • Raymond's Run

READING SKILL

Good readers **make predictions** as they read. A prediction is a guess about what will happen in a story. Look for facts and events that hint at what will happen next. Use them as clues to **support your predictions**. Also use your own experiences to help you make predictions. You might predict that rain is coming if you hear the rumble of thunder.

Look for clues to help you make predictions as you read. Use the chart to record your predictions.

LITERARY ANALYSIS

The events of a story make up the **plot**. Plots have six main parts:

- **Exposition:** introduction to the characters and the problem

- **Conflict:** struggle between two characters or between two forces

- **Rising Action:** part of a story that builds excitement or interest

- **Climax:** high point in the story

- **Falling Action:** events that follow the climax

- **Resolution:** end of the story

Look for each of the plot parts as you read.

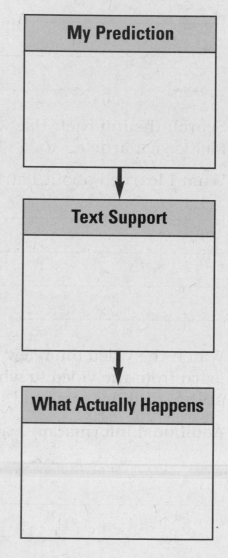

My Prediction

Text Support

What Actually Happens

A Retrieved Reformation

O. Henry

Summary Jimmy Valentine leaves prison and plans to go back to robbing safes. But he falls in love and decides to become honest. He changes his name and opens a store. A detective shows up to arrest Jimmy for recent robberies. However, Jimmy's actions show that he has changed.

Reading/Writing Connection

List three reasons that a person might have for changing his or her ways, or "turning over a new leaf."

1. One reason for turning over a new leaf is to alter _____.

2. Another reason could be to establish _____.

3. A third reason might be to impress _____.

Note-taking Guide

Use this character web to describe Jimmy Valentine's character.

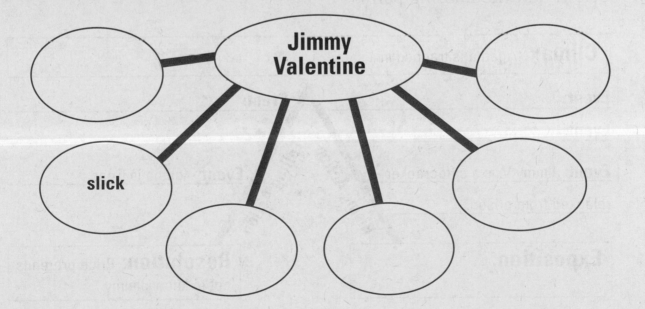

A Retrieved Reformation

1. **Deduce:** One of the first people Jimmy sees in Elmore is Annabel Adams. How does seeing her make him change?

   _____

   _____

2. **Make a Judgment:** Jimmy has been breaking the law for a long time. He now plans to stop. Do you think people like Jimmy can change their ways? Explain.

   _____

   _____

3. **Reading Skill:** A **prediction** is a guess about what will happen later. You might predict that Ben Price will arrest Jimmy. What clues can you find to support that prediction?

   _____

   _____

4. **Literary Analysis:** A **plot** chart shows the parts of a story. In the chart below, add the missing parts.

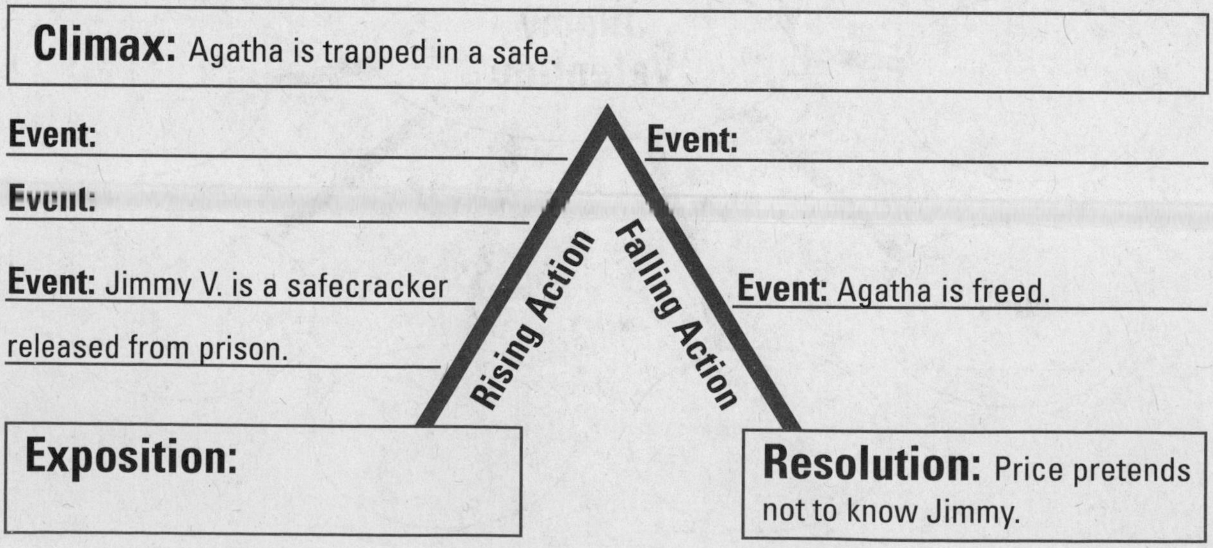

Climax: Agatha is trapped in a safe.

Event: _____

Event: _____

Event: Jimmy V. is a safecracker released from prison.

Rising Action

Falling Action

Event: _____

Event: Agatha is freed.

Exposition:

Resolution: Price pretends not to know Jimmy.

SUPPORT FOR WRITING AND EXTEND YOUR LEARNING

Writing: New Ending

Write a **new ending** to the story. How would the story be different if Ben Price had arrested Jimmy? Use this chart to show how Jimmy's arrest would have changed these people's lives:

Jimmy	Annabel Adams	Ben Price

Use your notes to write your new ending for the story

Listening and Speaking: Radio Broadcast

Write and perform a **radio broadcast** of Jimmy's rescue of Agatha. What would each of the following people say and do?

- Jimmy _____

  _____

- Annabel _____

  _____

- Agatha _____

- Agatha's mother _____

  _____

- Mr. Adams _____

  _____

Use your notes to write your radio broadcast.

Raymond's Run

Toni Cade Bambara

Summary Squeaky is the fastest runner in her class. She cares for her "not quite right" brother Raymond. She protects him from teasing and from getting hurt. During the annual May Day races, Squeaky learns lessons about herself, a runner named Gretchen, and Raymond.

Reading/Writing Connection

Complete each sentence to describe a way that you can earn or show respect.

1. I <u>demonstrate</u> my respect for an adult by _____.

2. I <u>signify</u> I have respect for someone else's home by _____.

3. I know that I could <u>acquire</u> the coach's respect if I _____.

Note-taking Guide

Use this chart to record the order of the four most important events in the story.

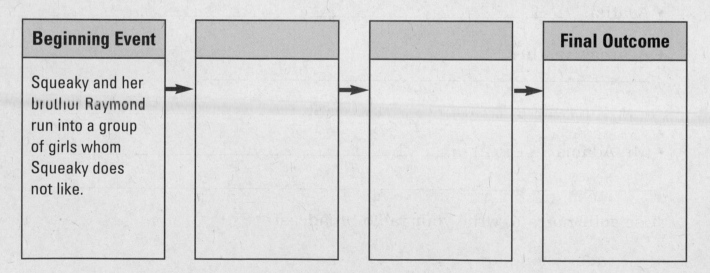

Beginning Event			Final Outcome
Squeaky and her brother Raymond run into a group of girls whom Squeaky does not like.			

Raymond's Run
Toni Cade Bambara

Squeaky is a confident, sassy young girl who lives in Harlem in New York City. Squeaky has to take care of her brother Raymond, who is "not quite right." She boldly protects Raymond from kids who try to tease him. Squeaky loves to run races, and she is the fastest runner in her neighborhood.

◆　◆　◆

There is no track meet that I don't win the first place medal. I used to win the twenty-yard dash when I was a little kid in kindergarten. Nowadays, it's the fifty-yard dash. And tomorrow I'm subject to run the quarter-meter relay all by myself and come in first, second, and third.

◆　◆　◆

This year, for the first time, Squeaky has some serious competition in the race, a new girl named Gretchen.

◆　◆　◆

So as far as everyone's concerned, I'm the fastest and that goes for Gretchen, too, who has put out the tale that she is going to win the first-place medal this year. Ridiculous. In the second place, she's got short legs. In the third place, she's got freckles. In the first place, no one can beat me and that's all there is to it.

◆　◆　◆

Squeaky takes a walk down Broadway with Raymond. She is practicing her breathing exercises to get in shape for the race. Raymond is pretending to drive a stage coach.

Squeaky works hard to be a good runner. She dislikes people who pretend that they do not need to work hard to be good at something.

Then, Squeaky sees Gretchen and two of her friends coming toward her and Raymond.

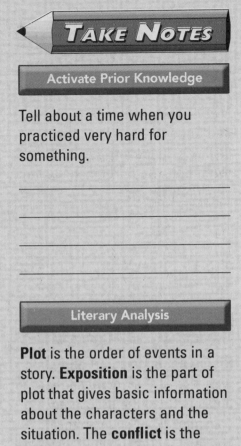

TAKE NOTES

Activate Prior Knowledge

Tell about a time when you practiced very hard for something.

_____

_____

_____

_____

Literary Analysis

Plot is the order of events in a story. **Exposition** is the part of plot that gives basic information about the characters and the situation. The **conflict** is the struggle between two forces in the story. Read the bracketed passage. Is this passage part of the exposition or part of the conflict? Explain your answer.

_____

_____

_____

_____

Reading Check

What is Squeaky's special talent? Circle the text that tells you.

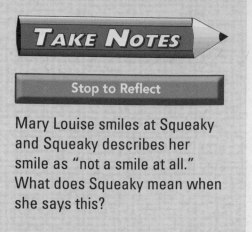

Stop to Reflect

Mary Louise smiles at Squeaky and Squeaky describes her smile as "not a smile at all." What does Squeaky mean when she says this?

_____

_____

_____

Literary Analysis

Rising action is a part of **plot** with events that increase the tension. Read the bracketed passage. What event in this passage increases the tension of the story?

_____

_____

_____

Reading Check

Squeaky feels that she is talking to only one of the girls. Which girl is it? Underline the text that tells you.

One of the girls, Mary Louise, used to be Squeaky's friend. Now she hangs out with Gretchen and does not like Squeaky anymore. Rosie, the other girl, always teases Raymond. Squeaky considers going into a store to avoid the girls, but she decides to face them.

◆　◆　◆

"You signing up for the May Day races?" smiles Mary Louise, only it's not a smile at all.

A dumb question like that doesn't deserve an answer. Besides, there's just me and Gretchen standing there really, so no use wasting my breath talking to shadows.

"I don't think you're going to win this time," says Rosie, trying to <u>signify</u> with her hands on her hips all salty, completely forgetting that I have whupped her many times for less salt than that.

"I always win cause I'm the best," I say straight at Gretchen who is, as far as I'm concerned, the only one talking in this ventriloquist-dummy routine.

Gretchen smiles, but it's not a smile, and I'm thinking that girls never really smile at each other because they don't know how and don't want to know how and there's probably no one to teach us how cause grown-up girls don't know either. Then they all look at Raymond who has just brought his mule team to a standstill. And they're about to see what trouble they can get into through him.

◆　◆　◆

Mary Louise starts to tease Raymond, but Squeaky defends him. Gretchen and her friends leave, and Squeaky smiles at her brother.

The next day, Squeaky arrives late at the May Day program because she does not want

---

Vocabulary Development

signify (SIG nuh fy) *v.*　represent something

to see the May Pole dancing. She thinks it is silly. She arrives just as the races are starting. She puts Raymond on the swings and finds Mr. Pearson, a tall man who gives the racers their numbers.

♦ ♦ ♦

"Well, Squeaky," he says, checking my name off the list and handing me number seven and two pins. And I'm thinking he's got no right to call me Squeaky, if I can't call him Beanstalk.

"Hazel Elizabeth Deborah Parker," I correct him and tell him to write it down on his board.

"Well, Hazel Elizabeth Deborah Parker, going to give someone else a break this year?" I squint at him real hard to see if he is seriously thinking I should lose the race on purpose just to give someone else a break.

♦ ♦ ♦

Mr. Pearson suggests that Squeaky let Gretchen, the new girl, win the race. Squeaky gets mad and walks away.

When it is time for the 50-yard dash, Squeaky and Gretchen line up with the other runners at the starting line. Squeaky sees that Raymond has left the swings and is getting ready to run on the other side of the fence.

Squeaky mentally prepares herself to win and takes off like a shot, zipping past the other runners.

♦ ♦ ♦

I glance to my left and there is no one. To the right a blurred Gretchen, who's got her chin jutting out as if it would win the race all by itself. And on the other side of the fence is Raymond with his arms down to his side and the palms

---

Vocabulary Development

squint (skwint) *v.* narrow your eyes so that you can see better

jutting (JUT ing) *adj.* sticking out

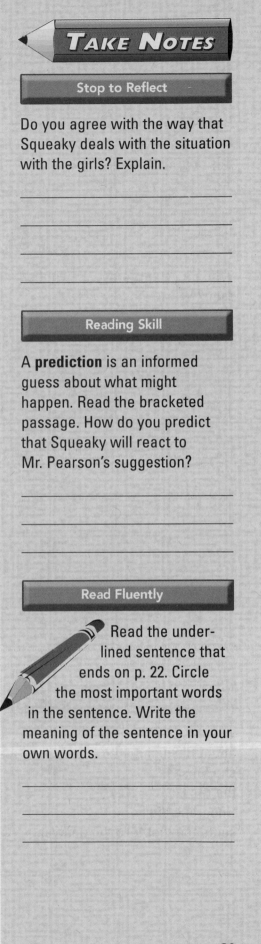

Stop to Reflect

Do you agree with the way that Squeaky deals with the situation with the girls? Explain.

_____

_____

_____

_____

Reading Skill

A **prediction** is an informed guess about what might happen. Read the bracketed passage. How do you predict that Squeaky will react to Mr. Pearson's suggestion?

_____

_____

_____

Read Fluently

Read the under-lined sentence that ends on p. 22. Circle the most important words in the sentence. Write the meaning of the sentence in your own words.

_____

_____

_____

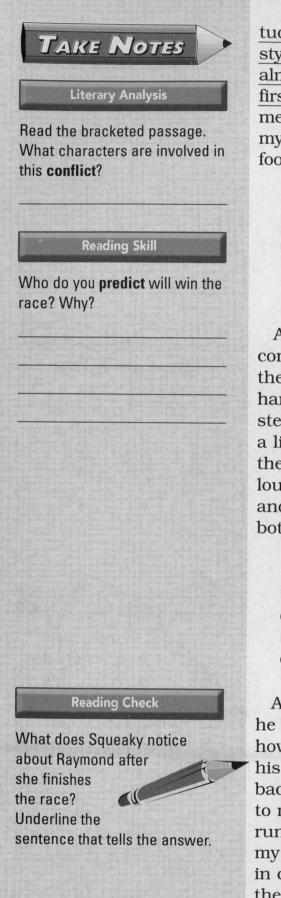

TAKE NOTES

Literary Analysis

Read the bracketed passage. What characters are involved in this **conflict**?

_____

_____

Reading Skill

Who do you **predict** will win the race? Why?

_____

_____

_____

_____

Reading Check

What does Squeaky notice about Raymond after she finishes the race? Underline the sentence that tells the answer.

tucked up behind him, running in his very own style, and it's the first time I ever saw that and I almost stop to watch my brother Raymond on his first run. But the white ribbon is bouncing toward me and I tear past it, racing into the distance till my feet with a mind of their own start digging up footfuls of dirt and brake me short.

◆ ◆ ◆

Squeaky believes that she has won the race, but it turns out that she and Gretchen crossed the finish line at almost the same time. The judges are not sure which girl is the winner.

◆ ◆ ◆

And I lean down to catch my breath and here comes Gretchen walking back, for she's overshot the finish line too, huffing and puffing with her hands on her hips taking it slow, breathing in steady time like a real pro and I sort of like her a little for the first time. "In first place . . ." and then three or four voices get all mixed up on the loudspeaker and I dig my sneaker into the grass and stare at Gretchen who's staring back, we both wondering just who did win.

◆ ◆ ◆

As Squeaky waits to find out whether she has won, Raymond calls out to her. He starts climbing up the fence. Suddenly, Squeaky remembers that Raymond ran the race too, on the other side of the fence.

◆ ◆ ◆

And it occurs to me, watching how smoothly he climbs hand over hand and remembering how he looked running with his arms down to his side and with the wind pulling his mouth back and his teeth showing and all, it occurred to me that Raymond would make a very fine runner. Doesn't he always keep up with me on my trots? And he surely knows how to breathe in counts of seven cause he's always doing it at the dinner table, which drives my brother George up the wall. And I'm smiling to beat the band cause if I've lost this race, or if me and Gretchen tied, or even if I've won, I can always retire as a runner and begin a whole new career as a coach with Raymond as my champion.

◆ ◆ ◆

Squeaky gets very excited about the idea of teaching Raymond to be a champion runner. She wants him to have something to be proud of. Raymond runs over to her, and she jumps up and down with happiness because of her plans to help him.

◆ ◆ ◆

<u>But of course everyone thinks I'm jumping up and down because the men on the loudspeaker have finally gotten themselves together and compared notes and are announcing "In first place—Miss Hazel Elizabeth Deborah Parker."</u> (Dig that.) "In second place—Miss Gretchen P. Lewis." And I look over at Gretchen wondering what the "P" stands for. And I smile. Cause she's good, no doubt about it. Maybe she'd like to help me coach Raymond; she obviously is serious about running, as any fool can see. And she nods to congratulate me and then she smiles. And I smile. We stand there with this big smile of respect between us.

© Pearson Education, Inc., publishing as Pearson Prentice Hall.

TAKE NOTES

Read Fluently

It helps to break down a long sentence into shorter sentences. Read the underlined sentence. How could you break this sentence into shorter sentences? Circle each part of the sentence that could be made into a shorter sentence.

Literary Analysis

Squeaky thinks more about her brother than about the race after she is done. How does Raymond affect the story's **conflict**?

_____

_____

_____

_____

Raymond's Run

1. **Respond:** Which parts of Squeaky's personality would make you want to be her friend?

   _____

2. **Analyze:** Squeaky is very protective of her brother, Raymond. How does Squeaky feel about taking care of him?

   _____

3. **Reading Skill:** When you **make predictions** about a story, you make informed guesses about what will happen next. List two predictions you made as you read "Raymond's Run."

   _____

   _____

4. **Literary Analysis:** The **rising action** contains events that increase the tension of the story. The **falling action** contains events that follow the climax. Complete the **plot** chart below. Write in two events from the **rising action** and one event from the **falling action**.

   Climax: Squeaky crosses the finish line.

   Event: _____   Event: _____
   Event: _____

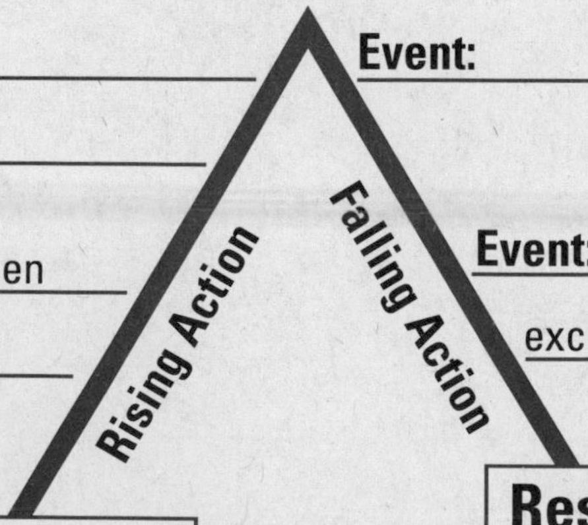

   Rising Action   Falling Action

   Event: Squeaky and Gretchen   Event: Squeaky and Gretchen
   will race.   exchange smiles.

   Exposition: **Resolution:**

SUPPORT FOR WRITING AND EXTEND YOUR LEARNING

Writing: New Ending

Imagine the ending of the story if Gretchen had won the race. Write a **new ending** to show how Squeaky might react to losing. Use your notes as you write your new ending.

Does Squeaky go through a change at the end of the story? If so, how would this change affect the way she would feel about losing? Explain.

_____

_____

Squeaky is proud, bold, and loyal. What other adjectives describe her?

_____

_____

Research and Technology: Oral Report

Use the Internet to research the Special Olympics, and then give an **oral report** on the games. In your report, describe the history of the Special Olympics and explain why this event is important.

Use the chart below to take notes about what you find.

Name and Address of Web Site	Information About the Special Olympics

Use your notes to help create your oral report.

Gentleman of Río en Medio • Cub Pilot on the Mississippi

READING SKILL

You can **make predictions** about a story. Use details in the story to guess what will happen later. **Reading ahead to confirm or correct predictions** helps you understand how events in the story are connected. Follow these steps:

- Read and look for details that suggest what might happen.

- Make your prediction.

- Use the chart below to write your prediction. Read ahead to see whether your prediction is right. You might read something that makes your prediction wrong. If this happens, change your prediction.

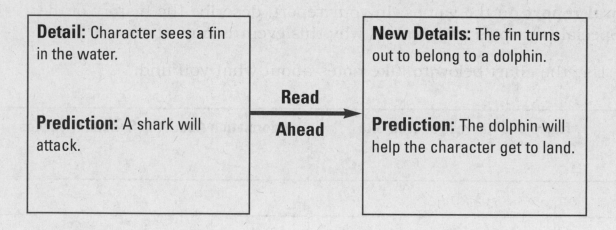

Detail: Character sees a fin in the water.		**New Details:** The fin turns out to belong to a dolphin.
	Read Ahead →	
Prediction: A shark will attack.		**Prediction:** The dolphin will help the character get to land.

LITERARY ANALYSIS

Conflict is a struggle in a story. There are two main kinds of conflict:

- A character can struggle against another character, nature, or society. This is called **external conflict**.

- A character can also struggle with two different feelings, beliefs, needs, or desires. This is called **internal conflict**.

The conflict in the story ends in the **resolution**. All problems are worked out.

Gentleman of Río en Medio

Juan A. A. Sedillo

Summary Don Anselmo is honest and proud. He sells his land to new American owners. They later have trouble with the village children. The new owners work with Don Anselmo to solve the problem with the children.

Reading/Writing Connection

Complete each sentence to explain why people sometimes keep old ways instead of changing.

1. It is a <u>challenge</u> to _____.

2. It is hard to <u>adapt</u> to _____.

3. The native language can <u>survive</u> by _____.

Note-taking Guide

Use this chart to record details about the traits of Don Anselmo.

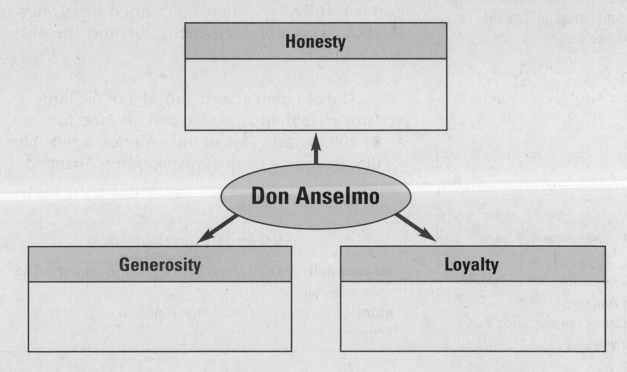

Honesty

Don Anselmo

Generosity

Loyalty

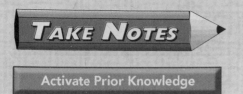

Gentleman of Río en Medio

Juan A. A. Sedillo

The title of this selection tells a good deal about the story. The main character is an old man, Don Anselmo, who dresses and acts in old-fashioned ways. But he is a man of great gentleness, honesty, and character.

Some American buyers are trying to work out a deal to buy Don Anselmo's land. It is land that his family has been farming for hundreds of years. After several months of bargaining, the two sides get together to make the deal.

◆ ◆ ◆

A buyer and a seller agree to certain things. Someone is selling a bicycle. List the things to which the buyer and seller might agree.

_____

_____

_____

_____

_____

_____

The day of the sale [Don Anselmo] came into the office. His coat was old, green and faded. . . . He also wore gloves. They were old and torn and his fingertips showed through them. He carried a cane, but it was only the skeleton of a worn-out umbrella. Behind him walked one of his <u>innumerable</u> kin—a dark young man with eyes like a <u>gazelle</u>.

The old man bowed to all of us in the room. Then he removed his hat and gloves, slowly and carefully. . . . Then he handed his things to the boy, who stood obediently behind the old man's chair.

◆ ◆ ◆

The old man speaks proudly of his large family. He then agrees to sell his land for $1,200 in cash. One of the Americans tells him that there has been a mistake. Don Anselmo

One way to follow the events of a story is to **predict**, or guess, what is going to happen. Use details from the story to **make predictions**. What do you predict will happen when Don Anselmo and the Americans get together to make the deal?

_____

_____

_____

_____

_____

Who comes to the meeting with Don Anselmo? Underline the sentence that tells you.

Vocabulary Development

innumerable (i NOO muhr uh buhl) *adj.*   too numerous to be counted

gazelle (guh ZEL) *n.*   an animal that looks like a small deer

---

actually owns twice as much land as they had thought. So they offer to pay him almost twice as much money.

◆ ◆ ◆

The old man hung his head for a moment in thought. Then he stood up and stared at me. "Friend," he said, "I do not like to have you speak to me in that manner." I kept still and let him have his say. "I know these Americans are good people, and that is why I have agreed to sell to them. But I do not care to be insulted. I have agreed to sell my house and land for twelve hundred dollars, and that is the price."

I argued with him but it was useless. Finally he signed the deed and took the money but refused to take more than the amount agreed upon. Then he shook hands all around, put on his ragged gloves, took his stick and walked out with the boy behind him.

◆ ◆ ◆

A month later the Americans have moved onto the property and fixed up the old house. But there is a problem. The village children are playing under the trees on the property. The new owners complain, but the children don't understand. So another meeting is arranged with Don Anselmo to settle the problem. One of the Americans explains the problem. He asks Don Anselmo to tell the children not to play in the orchard.

Don Anselmo explains that they all have learned to love the new American owners. But he sold them only the ground around the trees, not the trees themselves. The American protests that people usually sell everything that grows on the land they sell.

◆ ◆ ◆

"Yes, I admit that," [Don Anselmo] said. "You know," he added, "I am the oldest man in the village. Almost everyone there is my relative and

Literary Analysis

A **conflict** is a struggle between two forces. A conflict in a story usually leads to a situation called a **resolution**. Read the bracketed passage. What is the conflict? What is the resolution?

_____

_____

_____

_____

_____

_____

Reading Check

Why does Don Anselmo believe the trees do not belong to the new owners? Underline the sentence that tells you.

Reading Skill

What do you **predict** Don Anselmo will say when the owners ask him to keep the children out of the orchard? Explain.

_____

_____

_____

_____

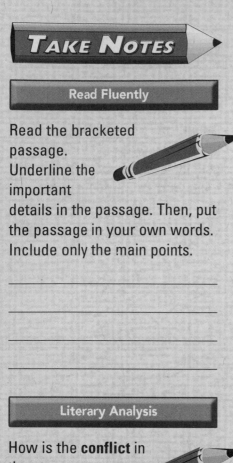

TAKE NOTES

Read Fluently

Read the bracketed passage. Underline the important details in the passage. Then, put the passage in your own words. Include only the main points.

_____

_____

_____

_____

Literary Analysis

How is the **conflict** in the story **resolved**? Underline the sentence that tells you.

all the children of Río en Medio are my *sobrinos* and *nietos*,[1] my <u>descendants</u>. Every time a child has been born in Río en Medio since I took possession of that house from my mother I have planted a tree for that child. The trees in that orchard are not mine, *Señor*, they belong to the children of the village. Every person in Río en Medio born since the railroad came to Santa Fe owns a tree in that orchard. I did not sell the trees because I could not. They are not mine."

There was nothing we could do. Legally we owned the trees but the old man had been so generous, refusing what amounted to a fortune for him. It took most of the following winter to buy the trees, individually, from the descendants of Don Anselmo in the valley of Río en Medio.

Vocabulary Development

descendants (di SEN duhnts) *n.*   people whose family roots can be traced back to a particular person or group

---

1. **sobrinos** (soh BREE nohs) and **nietos** (NYAY tohs) Spanish for "nieces and nephews."

Gentleman of Río en Medio

1. **Respond:** Were you surprised by what Don Anselmo says to the narrator in their first meeting about his land? Explain your answer.

   _____

   _____

2. **Analyze:** Think about how the narrator behaves toward Don Anselmo. Explain how the narrator's behavior helps solve the conflict of the story.

   _____

   _____

3. **Reading Skill:** What did you **predict** would be the outcome of the story? Explain.

   _____

   _____

4. **Literary Analysis:** What is the **conflict** after Don Anselmo sells his land? Complete this graphic organizer to describe the conflict.

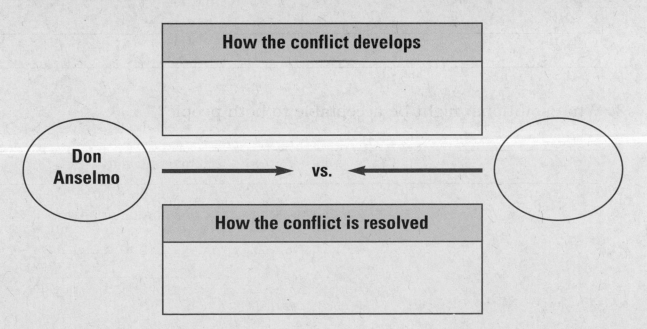

How the conflict develops

Don Anselmo ⟶ vs. ⟵

How the conflict is resolved

SUPPORT FOR WRITING AND EXTEND YOUR LEARNING

Writing: Letter

Write a **letter** to Don Anselmo. Thank him for trying to protect the right of the children to play in the orchard. Use the sentence starters to help you write your letter.

Dear Don Anselmo,

Thank you for _____.

I know that you care most about _____.

You have given the children of our village _____.

You have benefited the children by _____.

Listening and Speaking: Role Play

Role play the story's conflict. One person will play Don Anselmo. Another person will play the narrator. Answer these questions to help you create your role play.

1. How does Don Anselmo feel about the children playing in the orchard?

_____

_____

2. How does the narrator feel about the children playing in the orchard?

_____

_____

3. What solutions might be acceptable to both people?

_____

_____

Cub Pilot on the Mississippi

Mark Twain

Summary Mark Twain describes his experience as a cub pilot working on a Mississippi steamboat. He tries to please his boss, but nothing works. The conflict between them grows. Twain cannot control his anger.

Reading/Writing Connection

Complete these sentences to explain how a person might react to being bullied or unfairly criticized.

1. One way to deal with a bully is to <u>eliminate</u> _____.

2. Teasing a bully could <u>provoke</u> _____.

3. To <u>confront</u> a bully requires _____.

Note-taking Guide

Use this chart to note the differences between the two pilots in the story.

	Pilot Brown	Pilot Ealer
With which cub pilot does he work?	Mark Twain	
How does he treat cub pilots during work hours?		
How does each cub pilot react to his treatment?		

Cub Pilot on the Mississippi

1. **Infer:** Why were cub pilots assigned to work with experienced pilots like Brown?

   _____

2. **Draw Conclusions:** The captain is pleased that Twain has beaten Pilot Brown. What are the captain's feelings about Brown? How do you know?

   _____

   _____

3. **Reading Skill:** When you make **predictions**, you guess what will happen later in a story. What prediction did you make about the outcome of the conflict between Twain and Brown?

   _____

   _____

4. **Literary Analysis:** Use this chart to trace the **conflict** between Twain and Brown.

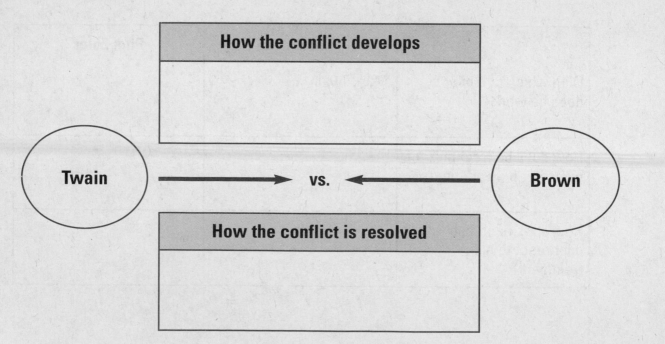

SUPPORT FOR WRITING AND EXTEND YOUR LEARNING

Writing: Letter

Imagine that you are Twain. Write a **letter** to your best friend, describing your first days as a cub pilot. Use the following sentence starters to think through some of your feelings.

1. When I first went on the boat, I felt _____

_____

2. When I see Pilot Brown, I feel _____

_____

3. When I see Pilot Ealer and George Ritchie together, I feel _____

_____

4. When I am alone in bed at night, I feel _____

_____

Research and Technology: Group Oral Presentation

Gather information about the Mississippi River. Use the information to prepare for a **group oral presentation**. Answer the following questions to help you begin.

1. Where does the Mississippi River begin and end? _____

_____

2. How did people use the Mississippi River in the 1800s? _____

_____

3. How do people use the Mississippi River today? _____

_____

Consumer Documents: Maps and Schedules

ABOUT MAPS AND SCHEDULES

Maps and schedules help people get where they want to go.

• Maps show how places are laid out.

• Schedules list arrival and departure times.

Maps and schedules are **consumer documents**.

• Consumer documents help you buy or use a product or service.

• Other consumer documents include brochures, labels, loan applications, assembly instructions, and warranties.

READING SKILL

Reading maps and schedules is different from reading other materials. You will **use text aids and features**. These tools will help you find information you need. Look at this chart for maps and schedules. It shows some common text aids and features.

Text Aids and Features of a Map	
Legend	Explains the map's symbols
Compass rose	Shows directions (north, south, east, west)
Text Aids and Features of a Schedule	
Headings	Show where to find departure and arrival times
Rows and columns	Allow easy scanning of arrival and departure times across and down the page
Special type and asterisks	Indicate exceptions, such as ferries that do not run on Sundays

FERRY SYSTEM SCHEDULE

1 CURRITUCK : KNOTTS ISLAND

Currituck	Knotts Island
YEAR-ROUND DEPARTURES	
6.00 a.m.	7.00 a.m.
9.00	10.00
11.00	Noon
1.00 p.m.	2.00 p.m.
3.30	4.30
5.30	6.30

Fare: Free
Crossing: 45 minutes

Ferry Information
(252) 232-2683

Tourism Information
Currituck County
www.currituckchamber.org
1-877-CURRITUCK
(252) 453-9497

CURRITUCK : COROLLA
Passenger ONLY Ferry 2

Currituck	Corolla
JULY 1 – AUG 16, 2004 DEPARTURES	
8.00 a.m.	9.00 a.m.
10.00	11.00
12.00 p.m.	1.00 p.m.
2.00	3.00
4.00	5.00
6.00	7.00

Currituck	Corolla
AUG 17, 2004 – JUNE 4, 2005 DEPARTURES	
6.20* a.m.	7.00 a.m.
8.00	9.00
10.00	11.00
12.00 p.m.	1.00 p.m.
1.45	2.30*
3.15	5.00

Fare One Way: $2
Crossing: 35 minutes
School children receive priority

Ferry Information
1-877-DOT-4YOU (368-4968)
(252) 232-2683

Tourism Information
Currituck County
www.currituckchamber.org
1-877-CURRITUCK
(252) 453-9497

Outer Banks Visitors Bureau
www.outerbanks.org
1-877-OBX-4FUN
(629-4386)

• Currituck Beach Lighthouse

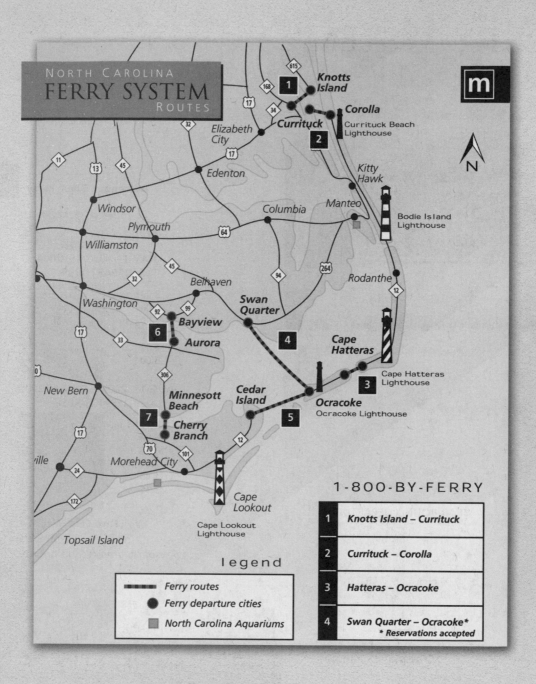

NORTH CAROLINA
FERRY SYSTEM
ROUTES

m

N

615
1 Knotts Island
168
17
34
32
Corolla
Currituck Beach Lighthouse
Currituck
Elizabeth City
2

11
13
45
Edenton
Kitty Hawk
Bodie Island Lighthouse
Manteo

Windsor
Columbia
Plymouth
64
Williamston
45
32
Belhaven
94
264
Rodanthe
12
Washington
92
99
Swan Quarter
6 Bayview
Aurora
4
Cape Hatteras
Cape Hatteras Lighthouse
17
33
306
3
Minnesott Beach
Cedar Island
Ocracoke
Ocracoke Lighthouse
New Bern
7 Cherry Branch
5
17
70
101
Morehead City
24
ville
Cape Lookout
172
Cape Lookout Lighthouse
Topsail Island

1-800-BY-FERRY

legend
- ▪▪▪▪▪ Ferry routes
- ● Ferry departure cities
- ▪ North Carolina Aquariums

1	**Knotts Island – Currituck**
2	**Currituck – Corolla**
3	**Hatteras – Ocracoke**
4	**Swan Quarter – Ocracoke*** * Reservations accepted

THINKING ABOUT THE MAP AND THE SCHEDULE

1. In what situation would this schedule and map be useful?

   _____

   _____

2. Explain how you can figure out what time a ferry will arrive.

   _____

   _____

READING SKILL

3. What time does the first ferry arrive at Knotts Island?

   _____

4. What symbol on the map does not appear in the map's legend?

   _____

TIMED WRITING: ITINERARY (20 minutes)

An **itinerary** is a written document that includes dates, times, and locations for a trip. Plan a round-trip itinerary. Use the North Carolina ferry schedule and map. Use this chart to help you make plans.

Place you will go	In which direction you will be heading	Departure time	Arrival time

The Adventure of the Speckled Band •
from An American Childhood

READING SKILL

An **author's purpose** is his or her reason for writing. Learn to **recognize details that indicate the author's purpose**; that is, look for clues that tell you why an author writes something. Three main reasons that authors write are these:

- To *inform*, an author might use facts or special language.

- To *persuade* or convince, an author might include reasons that readers should agree with an opinion.

- To *entertain*, an author might use facts that are funny.

The author often has two purposes in mind. One is a general, or overall, purpose, such as those above. The other is a specific purpose. It might be to show a feeling or to teach a lesson. As you read, use this chart to note both types of purposes.

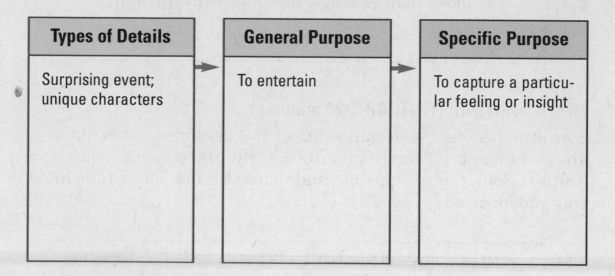

Types of Details	General Purpose	Specific Purpose
Surprising event; unique characters	To entertain	To capture a particular feeling or insight

LITERARY ANALYSIS

Mood is the overall feeling that a reader gets from a story. The mood can be serious, funny, or sad.

Different things help to set the mood. These include words, such as *grumpy* or *gleeful*; images, such as *a starlit night*; setting, such as *a dark room*; and events, such as *a storm*.

The Adventure of the Speckled Band

Sir Arthur Conan Doyle

Summary Sherlock Holmes, a great detective, meets Miss Helen Stoner. She needs his help. Miss Stoner wants to know who killed her sister. She also fears for her own life. Holmes follows the clues to find the murderer.

Reading/Writing Connection

Write three sentences explaining how detectives gather information.

1. A detective must <u>concentrate</u> to come up with _____.

2. A detective will often <u>consult</u> experts in order to _____.

3. A detective always tries to <u>deduce</u> _____.

Note-taking Guide

Use this graphic organizer to note details about Dr. Grimesby Roylott's actions.

How are Dr. Roylott and Miss Stoner related?	Why doesn't Dr. Roylott work as a doctor?	How does Dr. Roylott support himself?	How will Dr. Roylott's life change if the sisters marry?

The Adventure of the Speckled Band

1. **Compare:** Helen's sister, Julia, has died under strange circumstances. Helen's life is similar in some ways to Julia's just before Julia's death. In what ways is Helen's situation similar to Julia's?

   _____

   _____

2. **Speculate:** Suppose that Helen had not decided to ask Dr. Holmes for help. What do you think would have happened to her?

   _____

   _____

3. **Reading Skill:** Dr. Watson reports that Holmes has had many strange cases through the years. What does this detail tell you is the author's **general purpose**?

   _____

   _____

4. **Literary Analysis:** Reread Helen Stoner's description of the night her sister died. The mood is frightening and mysterious. Use this chart to list words, phrases, and images that create this mood.

Words	Phrases	Images
howling	wild night	the door moves slowly on its hinges

SUPPORT FOR WRITING AND EXTEND YOUR LEARNING

Writing: Personal Narrative

Write a **personal narrative** about a time that you used logic, or reasoning, to solve a problem. Record various problems and solutions. Decide which you will write about. Use your notes to write your personal narrative.

Problem	Solution
1.	1.
2.	2.
3.	3.

Listening and Speaking: Oral Description

Present a short **oral description** of the most exciting or interesting scene from "The Adventure of the Speckled Band." Use the following prompts to take notes for your oral description.

- What do you think is the most exciting scene in the story? Explain your answer.

_____

_____

- Describe the scene.

_____

_____

_____

_____

- What effect does the scene have on you as a reader?

_____

_____

_____

from An American Childhood

Annie Dillard

Summary The author shares an experience that scared her as a young child. She thinks there is a "presence" that will harm her if it reaches her. She figures out what it is. She realizes that her inside world is connected to the outside world.

Reading/Writing Connection

Complete this paragraph. Write about a fear you had as a small child that you now think is silly.

Most people would <u>define</u> their greatest childhood fear as

_____. When they are young, they do not <u>perceive</u> _____.

Most adults <u>comprehend</u> why _____.

Note-taking Guide

Use this chart to help you summarize the story.

Event
The author is frightened by mysterious, moving lights that she sees in her bedroom at night.
Cause
Main Idea

from An American Childhood
Annie Dillard

Annie Dillard describes something that scared her when she was young. She's only five years old and she is scared to go to bed. She's afraid to talk about the thing.

◆　◆　◆

Who could breathe as this thing searched for me over the very corners of the room? Who could ever breathe freely again?

◆　◆　◆

Dillard lies in the dark. Her younger sister, Amy, sleeps peacefully—she doesn't wake when the mysterious event takes place. Dillard is almost asleep when the thing slides into the room. First, it flattens itself against the door that is open.

◆　◆　◆

It was a <u>transparent</u>, <u>luminous</u> <u>oblong</u>. I could see the door whiten at its touch; I could see the blue wall turn pale where it raced over it, and see the maple headboard of Amy's bed glow. It was a swift spirit; it was an awareness. It made noise. It had two joined parts, a head and a tail, like a Chinese dragon. It found the door, wall, and headboard, and it swiped them, charging them with its luminous glance. After its fleet, searching passage, things looked the same, but weren't.

Vocabulary Development

transparent (trans PER uhnt) *adj.* clear; easily seen through

luminous (LOO muh nuhs) *adj.* giving off light; shining; bright

oblong (AHB lawng) *n.* a rectangular shape

TAKE NOTES

Activate Prior Knowledge

Tell about a time in childhood when you learned something on your own or about how the world works. For example, perhaps you learned that you could float more easily in salt water than you can in fresh water.

_____

_____

_____

Reading Skill

The **author's purpose** is his or her reason for writing. Learn to **look for details that show the author's purpose**. Sometimes authors use details to entertain the reader. Read the bracketed passage. Underline two words or phrases Dillard uses that make the "thing" seem alive.

Reading Check

What did Dillard see in her room each night when she was five? Underline the sentence Dillard uses to describe what comes into the room.

Literary Analysis

Mood is the overall feeling created for the reader. The **mood** may be serious, funny, or sad. One way the author sets the mood is by using certain kinds of words. Read the bracketed passages. Which details create a **mood** of suspense and fear?

_____

_____

_____

Reading Skill

The **author's purpose** can be to inform the reader. What fact does Dillard discover that explains what the "thing" really is?

_____

_____

_____

Stop to Reflect

How do Dillard's senses help her figure out what the "thing" really is?

_____

_____

_____

I dared not blink or breathe; I tried to hush my whooping blood. If it found another awareness, it would destroy it.

◆ ◆ ◆

But the thing never gets her. When it reaches the corner, it can't go any further. She tries to shrink down so it won't notice her. Then, she hears a roar when it dies or leaves. Worst of all is knowing that it may come back. Sometimes it does—usually it does. Dillard thinks the thing is restless.

◆ ◆ ◆

The light stripe slipped in the door, ran searching over Amy's wall, stopped, stretched lunatic at the first corner, raced wailing toward my wall, and vanished into the second corner with a cry.

◆ ◆ ◆

Dillard figures out that the thing is caused by a streetlight reflecting off the windshield of a passing car. She is thrilled to use reason to solve the mystery. She compares this mental process of problem solving to a diver who comes from the depths of the sea and breaks the surface of the water to reach the sunlight.

Dillard knows the sound the thing makes when it leaves. It sounds like a car coming down the street. She puts that together with the daytime sight and sound of a car passing. There is a stop sign at the corner of the street she lives on. The cars pass her house and then come to a stop. Then they shift gears as they go on.

◆ ◆ ◆

Vocabulary Development

whooping (WOOP ing) *v.*   shouting
lunatic (LOO nuh tik) *adv.*   wildly; crazily
vanished (VAN isht) *v.*   disappeared

What, precisely, came into the bedroom? A reflection from the car's oblong windshield. Why did it travel in two parts? The window sash split the light and cast a shadow.

◆ ◆ ◆

Dillard realizes that the world outside is connected to the world inside her home. She recalls once watching construction workers use jackhammers. Later, she had connected a new noise in her bedroom to the men she saw working outside. She thinks about the connection between outside and inside— going downstairs and then outside.

◆ ◆ ◆

"Outside," then, was <u>conceivably</u> just beyond my windows. It was the same world I reached by going out the front or the back door.

◆ ◆ ◆

Dillard realizes that she can choose to be connected to the outer world either by reason or by imagination. She pretends that the light coming into her room is after her. Then, she replaces her imagination with reason and identifies the real source of the light: a passing car.

Vocabulary Development

conceivably (kuhn SEE vuh blee) *adv.*   possibly

Reading Skill

Read the bracketed passage. What is the **author's purpose** in telling about the jackhammers?

_____

_____

_____

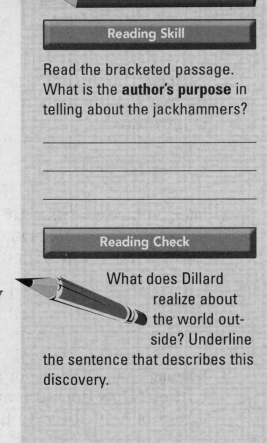

Reading Check

What does Dillard realize about the world outside? Underline the sentence that describes this discovery.

from An American Childhood

1. **Contrast:** The author's sister is in the room when the mysterious event happens. Why does her sister fail to react in the same way that Dillard does?

_____

2. **Infer:** Dillard learns that the light is from a passing car. After she solves the mystery, Dillard sometimes pretends that she does not know what is causing the light. Why does she do this?

_____

_____

3. **Reading Skill:** The author's general purpose is his or her reason for writing. How does the author's description of the object that she is afraid of contribute to her general **purpose**?

_____

_____

4. Before Dillard realizes what the light really is, her **mood** is one of fear. Use this chart to list one word, one phrase, and one image that contribute to this mood.

Words	Phrases	Images
scared	my whooping blood	its luminous glance

SUPPORT FOR WRITING AND EXTEND YOUR LEARNING

Writing: Personal Narrative

Write a **personal narrative** about an important childhood insight. Fill in the chart with clues that eventually led to the new understanding. Then, write what each clue turned out to mean.

Clue	What the Clue Meant

Use your notes to help you write your personal narrative.

Research and Technology

Write a brief **report** about an important scientific puzzle. Use the questions to help you write your report.

- Why is the puzzle important?

  _____

- What new knowledge was gained from the solution?

  _____

  _____

- What has been the impact of the new knowledge?

  _____

  _____

Magazine Articles

ABOUT MAGAZINE ARTICLES

A **magazine article** is a piece of nonfiction. A magazine article is usually short. Magazine articles can tell you about subjects such as these:

- Interesting things about people
- Animal behavior
- New technology

Magazine articles often have these parts:

- Drawings or photos that go with the text
- Captions, or words that explain the drawings or photos (refer to *captions*, as in box below)
- Sidebars with extra information

READING SKILL

You will see articles when you look through a magazine. You can **preview to determine your purpose for reading**. This means that you look over an article to decide whether you want to read it and why. When you preview an article, look at

- the title.
- the pictures or photographs.
- one paragraph.

These steps will give you an idea of the author's purpose for writing the article. Then, you can decide what purpose you have for reading it. You may decide that you have no reason to read the article. Use the questions below to help you look at parts of an article.

Questions to Help You Preview an Article
☐ What is the tone, or attitude, of the author?
☐ Are the pictures and captions designed to provide information or to entertain?
☐ As I skim the text, do I see statistics, quotations from experts, and facts?
☐ Do the first sentences of paragraphs introduce facts, opinions, or anecdotes?

Sun Suckers and Moon Cursers
Richard and Joyce Wolkomir

Night is falling. It is getting dark. You can barely see. But now . . . lights come on. Car headlights sweep the road. Windows light up. Neon signs glow red and green. Street lamps shine, bright as noon. So who cares if it is night?

But what if you are camping in a forest? Or a storm blows down power lines? Then the night would be inky. To see, you would have only star twinkle, or the moon's pale shine. Until about 1900, when electric power networks began spreading, that is how nights were: dark.

Roger Ekirch, an historian at Virginia Tech, studies those long-ago dark nights. For light, our ancestors had only candles, hearth fires, torches, walnut-oil lamps. And that made their nights different than ours.

"It used to be, when it got dark, people felt edgy," Ekirch says. He studies the years from about 1500 to 1830, when mostly only the wealthy could afford even candles. "People talked about being 'shut in' by the night," he says. Our ancestors imagined werewolves roaming at night, and demons. In their minds, they populated the darkness with witches, fairies and elves, and malignant spirits. Night had real dangers, too—robbers and murderers, but also ditches and ponds you could fall into.

TAKE NOTES

Reading Magazine Articles

Magazine articles often have these parts:

- Drawings or photos that go with the text
- Words that tell about the drawings or photos
- Sidebars with extra facts

Does this article have any of these parts? Explain.

_____

_____

Reading Skill

Look at this article.

Preview to determine your purpose for reading. Look at the pictures. Do they add information, or are they just for fun? Explain.

_____

_____

Reading Check

Who is Roger Ekirch? Circle the text that tells you.

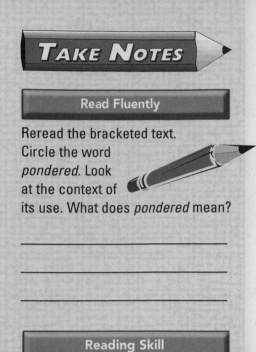

Reread the bracketed text. Circle the word *pondered*. Look at the context of its use. What does *pondered* mean?

_____

_____

_____

One way to **preview to determine your purpose for reading** a magazine article is to look at the first sentences in paragraphs. Look at the first sentence in each paragraph on this page. Do these sentences begin with facts, opinions, or events? Explain.

_____

_____

_____

_____

Who were the "moon cursers"? Underline the answer.

What was it like, when nights were so dark?

To find out, Roger Ekirch has combed through old newspapers, diaries, letters, everything from court records to sermons. He has pondered modern scientific research, too. He has found that, before the invention of electric lights, our ancestors considered night a different "season." At night, they were nearly blind. And so, to them, day and night seemed as different as summer and winter.

They even had special words for night. Some people called the last rays of the setting sun "sun suckers." Nighttime travelers, who relied on the moon called it the "parish lantern." But robbers, who liked to lurk in darkness, hated the moon. They called it "the tattler." And those darkness-loving criminals? They were "moon cursers."

Cities were so dark that people needing to find their way at night hired boys to carry torches, or "links." Such torchbearers were called "linkboys."

Country people tried to stay indoors at night, unless the moon was out. On moonless nights, people groping in the darkness frequently fell into ponds and ravines.[1] Horses, also blinded by darkness, often threw riders.

If you were traveling at night, you would wear light-colored clothing, so your friends could see you. You might ride a white horse. You might mark your route in advance by stripping away tree bark, exposing the white inner wood. In southern England, where the soil is chalky white, people planning night trips mounded up white chalk along their route during the day, to guide them later, in the moonlight.

It was dark inside houses, too. To dress in the darkness, people learned to fold their clothes just so. Swedish homeowners, Roger Ekirch says, pushed parlor furniture against walls at night, so they could walk through the room without tripping.

---

1. **ravines** (ruh VEENZ) *n.* long, deep hollows in Earth's surface.

People began as children to memorize their local terrain—ditches, fences, cisterns, bogs.[2] They learned the magical terrain, too, spots where ghosts and other imaginary nighttime frights lurked. "In some places, you never whistled at night, because that invited the devil," says Ekirch.

One reason people feared nightfall was they thought night actually did "fall." At night, they believed, malignant air descended. To ward off that sickly air, sleepers wore nightcaps. They also pulled curtains around their beds. In the 1600s, one London man tied his hands inside his bed at night so they would not flop outside the curtains and expose him to night air. . . .

At night, evildoers came out. Virtually every major European city had criminal gangs. Sometimes those gangs included wealthy young aristocrats who assaulted people just for the thrill. . . .

If you were law-abiding, you might clang your sword on the pavement while walking down a dark nighttime street to warn robbers you were armed. Or you might hold your sword upright in the moonlight. You tried to walk in groups. You walked down the street's middle, to prevent robbers from lunging at you from doorways or alleys. Robbers depended so much on darkness that a British criminal who attacked his victim in broad daylight was acquitted—jurors decided he must be insane.

Many whose days were blighted by poverty or ill treatment sought escape at night. Slaves in the American South, for instance, sneaked out at night to dances and parties. Or they stumbled through the darkness to other plantations, to visit their wives or children. After the Civil War, says Roger Ekirch, former slaveholders worried that their freed slaves might attack them. And so they rode out at night disguised as ghosts, to frighten onetime slaves into staying indoors.

2. **cisterns** (SIS ternz), **bogs** Cisterns are large underground areas for storing water; bogs are small marshes or swamps in which footing is treacherous.

Reading Skill

Skim the text. Underline any facts or quotations from experts. How does this help you **preview** the article? Does it change **your purpose for reading**?

_____

_____

_____

Stop to Reflect

Reread the bracketed text. What is one idea about being out in the dark that is still a good idea today?

_____

_____

_____

_____

Reading Check

Why did people clang a sword on the pavement when walking at night? Circle the answer.

Reading Magazine Articles

How does the picture support the information in the **magazine article**? Explain your answer.

_____

_____

_____

Reading Skill

Circle the last two sentences in the article. Articles often end with an interesting or funny thought or quote. Does this article end with a thought or a quotation?

_____

_____

Is it interesting, or is it funny? Explain.

_____

_____

_____

Reading Informational Materials

How has electricity changed the way people deal with darkness?

_____

_____

_____

_____

"At night, many servants felt beyond supervision, and they would often leave directly after their employers fell asleep," Ekirch adds. When they did sleep, it was fitfully, because of rumbling carts and watchmen's cries. And so Ekirch believes many workers got much too little sleep. "That explains why so many slaveowners and employers complained about their workers falling asleep during the day," he said.

Our ancestors had one overriding—and entirely real—nighttime fear: fire. Blazes were common because houses, often with thatched roofs,[3] ignited easily. At night, open flames flickered everywhere. Passersby carrying torches might set your roof ablaze. Also, householders commonly complained about servants forgetting to bank fires or snuff out candles. Roger Ekirch believes one reason night watchmen bellowed out each hour, to the irritation of sleepers, was precisely to keep everyone half awake, to be ready when fires erupted. . . .

Electricity changed the night. One electric bulb, Ekirch calculates, provided 100 times more light than a gas lamp. Night was becoming what it is today—an artificially illuminated extension of the day. Night has lost its spookiness.

Still, says Roger Ekirch, even in the electric age, his children sometimes fear the dark: "I tell them, 'Your daddy is an expert on night, and he knows a lot about the history of the night, and he can tell you there is nothing to be afraid of!' "

He shrugs. "It doesn't work well," he says.

---

3. **thatched** (thatchd) **roofs** roofs made of materials such as straw or rushes.

THINKING ABOUT THE MAGAZINE ARTICLE

1. Name three reasons why people were afraid of the night.

_____

2. People were more afraid of fire at night than in the day. Why?

_____

READING SKILL

3. What is the author's main purpose in writing this article?

_____

4. What item on the first page gives you the best clue to the subject of the article?

_____

TIMED WRITING: DESCRIPTION (20 minutes)

Suppose that you live in seventeenth-century Europe. Write a letter explaining why people should travel in the daytime. Record your ideas in the chart below.

Being safe from criminals	
Being safe from fire	
Being able to see where you are going	

from Travels With Charley •
The American Dream

READING SKILL

An author's **purpose** is his or her reason for writing. The author's reason for writing may be one of the following:

- to persuade

- to inform

- to entertain

Sometimes an author has more than one purpose or combines purposes. The purpose determines the kinds of details that the author uses. As you read, use this chart to **evaluate whether the author achieves his or her purpose**.

Author's Purpose	What details does the author use to support the purpose?	Evaluation

LITERARY ANALYSIS

An **author's style** is his or her way of using language. Important elements of an author's style are these:

- Word choice: the types of words the author uses

- Sentence length: how long or short the sentences are

- Tone: the author's attitude toward the subject of the writing

As you read, notice how word choice, sentence length, and tone produce the author's style.

from Travels With Charley

John Steinbeck

Summary John Steinbeck sets out across the United States to see the country and meet people. His dog, Charley, travels with him. This episode in his journey tells about his experiences in the Badlands of North Dakota.

Reading/Writing Connection

Think of three places you would like to visit in the United States. Complete these sentences to explain why you would like to visit each place.

1. A <u>highlight</u> of visiting _____.

2. A visit might help someone <u>appreciate</u> _____.

3. A visit would <u>enrich</u> _____.

Note-taking Guide

Use this chart to recall the highlights of Steinbeck's essay.

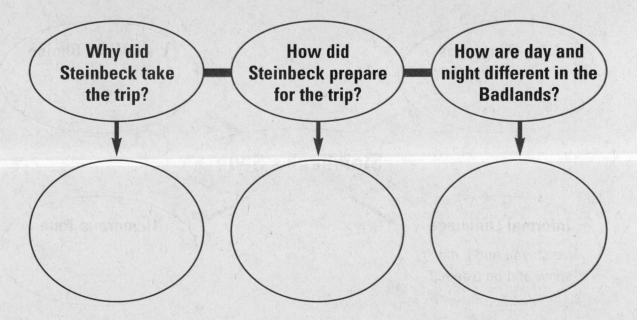

Why did Steinbeck take the trip?

How did Steinbeck prepare for the trip?

How are day and night different in the Badlands?

from Travels With Charley

1. **Infer:** Steinbeck has lived and worked in New York City for many years. What does he hope to gain or learn from making this trip across America?

   _____

   _____

2. **Contrast:** When Steinbeck enters the Badlands, he feels uneasy. How do Steinbeck's feelings about the Badlands change as night falls?

   _____

   _____

3. **Reading Skill:** Explain Steinbeck's **purpose** in writing this essay.

   _____

   _____

4. **Literary Analysis:** Fill in the chart below with examples of the **author's style**.

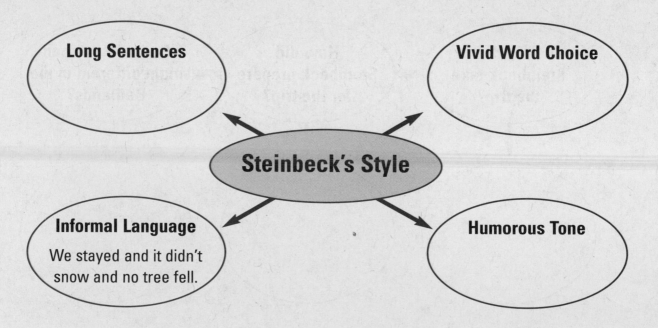

Long Sentences

Vivid Word Choice

Steinbeck's Style

Informal Language
We stayed and it didn't snow and no tree fell.

Humorous Tone

SUPPORT FOR WRITING AND EXTEND YOUR LEARNING

Writing: Observations Journal

Write an entry for an **observations journal** about a favorite place you have visited. Choose a place about which to write by identifying places you have visited in the chart below.

Favorite Places	
Near Home	**On Trips**

Listening and Speaking: Oral Presentation

Use library and Internet resources to research the life and work of John Steinbeck. Then, using your findings, prepare and deliver an **oral presentation** on Steinbeck.

- List three resources you checked for information. _____

_____

- Take notes on each of these topics:

  Steinbeck's life _____

  _____

  _____

  Steinbeck's writings _____

  _____

  _____

  Why Steinbeck is remembered as an author _____

  _____

The American Dream

Martin Luther King, Jr.

Summary In this speech, Martin Luther King, Jr. describes his dream for America. He says that America does not make it possible for everyone to share in the dream. He discusses ways that Americans can help make his dream a reality.

Reading/Writing Connection

Complete the paragraph below to explain how you can use persuasion effectively.

Some people would <u>emphasize</u> _____.

We can use speech to <u>communicate</u> _____.

If we work together, we can <u>accomplish</u> _____.

Note-taking Guide

Use this web to record King's ideas about the American dream.

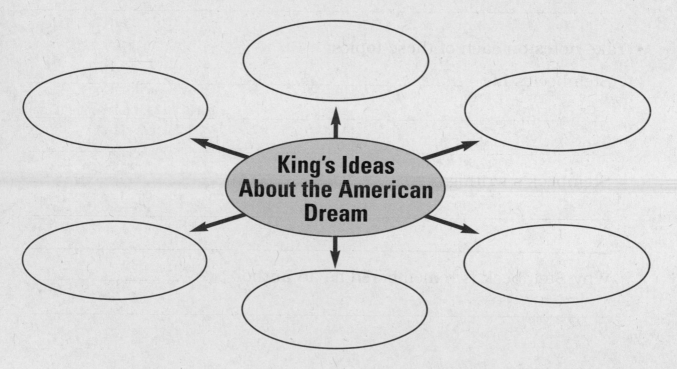

King's Ideas About the American Dream

The American Dream
Martin Luther King, Jr.

In this speech, King says that the American dream is based on the words of the Declaration of Independence: "all men are created equal." He says that the dream is supposed to apply to all Americans.

◆ ◆ ◆

It does not say some men, but it says all men. It does not say all white men, but it says all men, which includes black men. It does not say all Gentiles,[1] but it says all men, which includes Jews. It does not say all Protestants,[2] but it says all men, which includes Catholics.[3]

◆ ◆ ◆

King explains another important point in the Declaration: It says that all individuals have basic rights that come from God, not from governments.

Then King explains that America has never totally lived up to the dream of democracy. Slavery and the segregation of African Americans violated the idea that all people have equal rights. King says that America will destroy itself if it continues to deny equal rights to some Americans.

◆ ◆ ◆

The hour is late; the clock of destiny is ticking out. It is trite, but urgently true, that if America is to remain a first-class nation she can no longer have second-class citizens.

◆ ◆ ◆

1. **Gentiles** (JEN tylz) *n.* people who are not Jewish.
2. **Protestants** (PRAHT uhs tuhnts) *n.* members of a part of the Christian church that separated from the Roman Catholic Church in the 1500s.
3. **Catholics** (KATH liks) *n.* members of the part of the Christian church led by the Pope.

TAKE NOTES

Activate Prior Knowledge

Think about the way your family lives. At one time, not everyone had the same rights. On the lines below, finish the statement: "I am thankful that in America I can . . ."

_____

_____

_____

Read Fluently

To what does "It" in the bracketed passage refer?

_____

King is trying to make a point about what "it" means for Americans. His sentences tend to be long. Each sentence contrasts what "it" does not say in the first part of the sentence with what "it" does say in the second part. Draw lines breaking up the parts of each sentence to make the meaning clearer.

Literary Analysis

An **author's style** is his or her way of writing. Is King's style formal or informal?

_____

TAKE NOTES

Reading Skill

An **author's purpose** is his or her reason for writing. What is the **author's purpose** in the bracketed paragraph?
a) to persuade
b) to inform
c) to entertain
Explain your answer.

_____

_____

Stop to Reflect

What does King think will happen to America if its people cannot make the changes he suggests?

_____

_____

_____

Reading Check

How does King think Americans should learn to live? Underline the sentence in which he explains this.

King then claims that Americans must also consider the needs of the other countries in the world.

◆ ◆ ◆

The American dream will not become a reality <u>devoid</u> of the larger dream of a world of brotherhood and peace and good will.

◆ ◆ ◆

He points out that modern transportation has made contact between people of different nations much easier. He tells two jokes that focus on the speed of traveling by jet. He uses humor to stress that the world has now become one big neighborhood. Everyone is now connected, and we all depend on one another.

◆ ◆ ◆

Through our scientific genius we have made of this world a neighborhood; now through our <u>moral</u> and spiritual development we must make of it a brotherhood. In a real sense, we must all learn to live together as brothers, or we will all <u>perish</u> together as fools.

Vocabulary Development

devoid (di VOYD) *adj.*   completely lacking in something; empty
moral (MAWR uhl) *adj.*   relating to what is right behavior
perish (PER ish) *v.*   die

The American Dream

1. **Infer:** Why does King quote lines from the Declaration of Independence in his speech?

   _____

   _____

2. **Generalize:** According to King, what steps must Americans take to make the American dream a reality?

   _____

   _____

3. **Reading Skill:** An **author's purpose** is his or her reason for writing. What is King's purpose in writing this speech? Give reasons to support your answer.

   _____

   _____

4. **Literary Analysis:** Use the chart to help you think about the **author's style**. In each oval, write a word or phrase from the text that gives an example of that element.

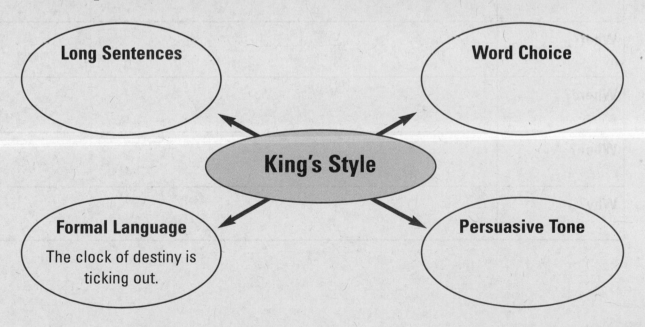

Long Sentences

Word Choice

King's Style

Formal Language
The clock of destiny is ticking out.

Persuasive Tone

SUPPORT FOR WRITING AND EXTEND YOUR LEARNING

Writing: Observations Journal

Write an entry for an **observations journal**. Record your thoughts about an aspect of today's society that could be improved.

• What could be improved in your school or community?

_____

_____

• What could be improved in your country?

_____

_____

• What could be improved in the world?

_____

_____

Listening and Speaking: Oral Presentation

Prepare and deliver an **oral presentation** on the 1963 March on Washington and King's role in that event. Use this chart to summarize the people, places, and ideas involved in the march.

Who?	
What?	
Where?	
When?	
Why?	

An Hour With Abuelo

Adventures, mysteries, and animal fables are a few types of short stories. Short stories share certain elements.

Conflict is a struggle between different forces. There are two types of conflict:

- **Internal conflict:** takes place in the mind of a character. A character struggles with his or her own feelings and thoughts.

- **External conflict:** takes place when a character struggles with another person or an outside force, such as a tornado.

Plot is the sequence of events in a story. It usually has five parts:

- **Exposition:** introduces the **setting**—the time and place of the story—the characters, and the situation.

- **Rising action** introduces the **conflict**, or problem.

- **Climax** is the turning point of a story.

- **Falling action** is the part of the story when the conflict begins to lessen.

- **Resolution** is the story's conclusion, or ending.

- A **subplot** is a secondary story that adds depth to the story.

Setting is the time and place of the action in a story. Sometimes it may act as a backdrop for the story's action. Setting can also be the source of the story's conflict. It can create the **mood**, or feeling, of the story.

Characters are the people or animals that take part in the action.

- **Character traits:** the qualities and attitudes that a character possesses. Examples are loyalty and intelligence.

- **Character's motives:** the reasons for a character's actions. A motive can come from an internal cause, such as loneliness. A motive can also come from an external cause, such as danger.

Theme is the main message in a story. It may be directly stated or implied.

- **Stated theme:** The author directly tells you what the theme is.

- **Implied theme:** The author does not tell you the theme. It is suggested by what happens to the characters.

- **Universal theme:** The author uses a repeating message about life that is found across time and cultures

Literary devices are tools that writers use to make their writing better. Examples of literary devices are in the chart below.

Literary Device	Description
Point of View	• the perspective from which a story is told • **First-person point of view:** presents the story from the perspective of a character in the story • **Third-person point of view:** tells the story from the perspective of a narrator outside the story. An **omniscient** third-person narrator is someone who knows everything that happens. He or she can tell the reader what each character thinks and feels. A **limited** third-person narrator is someone who can reveal the thoughts and feelings of only one character.
Foreshadowing	• the use of clues to hint at events yet to come in a story
Flashback	• the use of scenes that interrupt the time order of a story to reveal past events
Irony	• the contrast between an actual outcome and what a reader or a character expects to happen

An Hour With Abuelo

Judith Ortiz Cofer

Summary Arturo is sent to a nursing home to spend an hour with his grandfather. Arturo is not excited about the visit. Arturo finds his grandfather writing his life story. Arturo listens to his grandfather's story. He loses all track of time.

Note-taking Guide

Use the character wheel below to record what Arturo says, thinks, and does.

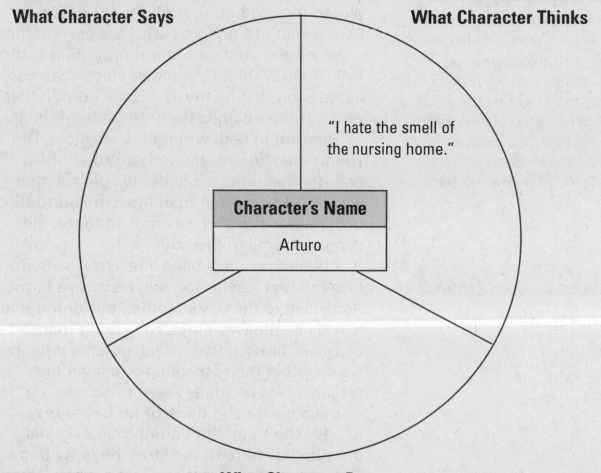

What Character Says

What Character Thinks

"I hate the smell of the nursing home."

Character's Name

Arturo

What Character Does

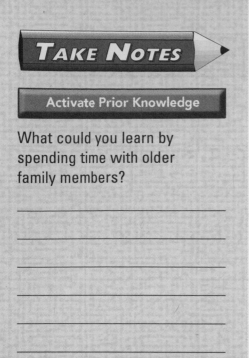
What could you learn by spending time with older family members?

_____

_____

_____

_____

_____

Short Story

Point of view is the perspective from which a story is told to the reader. **First-person point of view** tells the story from the perspective of a character. **Third-person point of view** tells the story from the view of a narrator outside of the story. From which point of view is this story told?

_____

Reading Check

Where does the narrator's grandfather live? Circle the text that tells you the answer.

An Hour With Abuelo
Judith Ortiz Cofer

"Just one hour, una hora, is all I'm asking of you, son." My grandfather is in a nursing home in Brooklyn, and my mother wants me to spend some time with him, since the doctors say that he doesn't have too long to go now. I don't have much time left of my summer vacation, and there's a stack of books next to my bed I've got to read if I'm going to get into the AP English class I want.

◆ ◆ ◆

Not only does the young man have better ways to spend his time than in visiting his grandfather, he hates the old people's home. Ordinarily he visits only at Christmastime along with many other relatives and spends most of his time in the recreation area. To please his mother, though, he agrees to an hour's visit at the home with his grandfather.

When the young man arrives, he finds the halls lined with old people in wheelchairs so depressing that he hurries to his grandfather's room. There he finds his grandfather (*abuelo* in Spanish) in bed, writing his life story. The young man, who is named Arturo after his grandfather, does not know his grandfather well because the old man lived in Puerto Rico until he got sick and was moved to the old people's home in Brooklyn.

Abuelo had once been a teacher in Puerto Rico but had lost his job and became a farmer. According to the boy's mother, this unfortunate fate is just the way life is. The young man promises himself that he will go after what he wants rather than accepting whatever life presents him as adults seem to do.

Because he can think of no better way to pass the time, the young man asks his grandfather to read the story he is writing. The young man is embarrassed when Abuelo catches him looking at his watch. Abuelo reassures his grandson that the short story of his life will not take up much time.

◆ ◆ ◆

Abuelo reads: " 'I loved words from the beginning of my life. In the campo[1] where I was born one of seven sons, there were few books. My mother read them to us over and over: the Bible, the stories of Spanish conquistadors and of pirates that she had read as a child and brought with her from the city of Mayaguez; that was before she married my father, a coffee bean farmer; and she taught us words from the newspaper that a boy on a horse brought every week to her. She taught each of us how to write on a slate with chalks that she ordered by mail every year. We used those chalks until they were so small that you lost them between your fingers.

◆ ◆ ◆

Abuelo continues his story. With great difficulty and against his father's wishes, he leaves home to attend high school, graduating first in his class. Then he returns to his mountain village to teach. Although he is poorly paid, he loves being surrounded by books and teaching his students to read and write poetry and plays.

Abuelo's happy life ends with the coming of World War II when he is drafted into the U.S. Army. Now the students in his village will have no teacher. He offers to teach in the army, but for being so pushy, he is instead assigned to clean latrines.

When Abuelo returns to Puerto Rico after the war, everything has changed. Teachers are required to have college degrees, and Abuelo must support his sick parents. So he gives up teaching for farming. Eventually, he marries and uses his skills to teach his

---

1. **campo** (KAHM poh) Spanish for "open country."

TAKE NOTES

Short Story

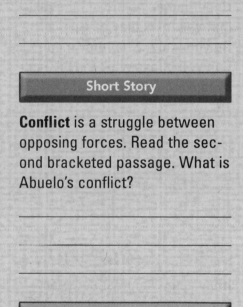

The **exposition** introduces the time and place, characters, and situation within a story. Read the first bracketed passage. Abuelo's own writings have an exposition that tells the reader about his life. What are some things you learn about Abuelo? Circle the details in the text. Then, write them in your own words.

_____

_____

_____

_____

Short Story

Conflict is a struggle between opposing forces. Read the second bracketed passage. What is Abuelo's conflict?

_____

_____

_____

Stop to Reflect

Why do you think that Abuelo is writing his life story?

_____

_____

_____

Short Story

Character traits are a character's main qualities. Read the underlined passage. What character traits do you think Arturo has?

_____

_____

Read Fluently

Abuelo speaks Spanish and English. The author has included some Spanish words in the story. Underline any words in the text that you think may be Spanish. Do you know what they mean? Can you guess what they mean by looking at them?

_____

_____

_____

_____

Short Story

Irony is the contrast between the outcome and what the reader or characters think will happen. Read the bracketed passage. How is this an example of irony?

_____

_____

_____

own children to read and write before they start school.

◆ ◆ ◆

Abuelo then puts the notebook down on his lap and closes his eyes.

"Así es la vida is the title of my book," he says in a whisper, almost to himself. Maybe he's forgotten that I'm there.

For a long time he doesn't say anything else. I think that he's sleeping, but then I see that he's watching me through half-closed lids, maybe waiting for my opinion of his writing. I'm trying to think of something nice to say. I liked it and all, but not the title. And I think that he could've been a teacher if he had wanted to bad enough. Nobody is going to stop me from doing what I want with my life. I'm not going to let la vida get in my way. I want to discuss this with him, but the words are not coming into my head in Spanish just yet.

◆ ◆ ◆

An old woman in a pink jogging outfit enters the room and reminds Abuelo that today is poetry-reading day in the rec room and he has promised to read his new poem. The old man perks up immediately. The grandson puts Abuelo's wheelchair together, helps seat his grandfather in it, and, at the old man's request, hands Abuelo a notebook titled _Poemas De Arturo_.

When the young man begins pushing the wheelchair toward the rec room, Abuelo smiles and reminds him that the time allotted for the visit is over. As the old woman wheels his grandfather away, the young man glances at his watch and is amused that his grandfather has made sure the visit lasted exactly an hour. He walks slowly toward the exit so that his mother won't think he was eager to end his visit with Abuelo.

Short Stories

1. **Respond:** Would you enjoy visiting Arturo's grandfather? Explain.

   _____

   _____

   _____

2. **Interpret:** Think about what happens at the end of the story. Do you think that Abuelo has found a new purpose in life? Explain your answer.

   _____

   _____

   _____

3. **Short Story: Conflict** is the struggle between different forces. What is the main conflict in this story?

   _____

   _____

4. **Short Story:** Use the diagram below to compare and contrast the **characters** in the story. Write one example under each category.

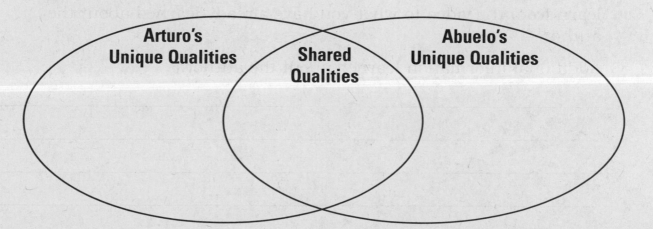

RESEARCH THE AUTHOR

Audio-cassette

Prepare an **audio-cassette** about Judith Ortiz Cofer. The following tips will help prepare you to create the cassette.

- Read some of the author's works. Judith Ortiz Cofer's books include *The Line of the Sun, The Meaning of Consuelo,* and *Call Me Maria.* Her short stories include "Catch the Moon," "Grandmother's Room," and "Lessons of Love."

  What I learned from Cofer's writing:

  _____

  _____

  _____

  _____

- Search the Internet: Use words and phrases such as "Judith Ortiz Cofer article."

  What I learned about Judith Ortiz Cofer:

  _____

  _____

  _____

  _____

- Watch the video interview with Judith Ortiz Cofer. Add what you learn from the video to what you have already learned about the author.

  Additional information learned about the author:

  _____

  _____

  _____

  _____

Use your notes to write and record your audio-cassette.

Who Can Replace a Man? • Tears of Autumn

READING SKILL

A **comparison** tells how two or more things are alike. A **contrast** tells how two or more things are different. You can see how things are alike and different by **asking questions to compare and contrast**. You can compare and contrast characters, settings, moods, and ideas. Comparing and contrasting details gives you a better understanding of what you read. Ask questions like those in this chart. Fill in the answers as you read.

LITERARY ANALYSIS

The **setting** is the time and place of a story. The setting shows where and when events happen. A setting can create a *mood.* It can make the story seem scary or sad. A setting can also make readers feel as if they are actually there. As you read, look for these details about the setting:

- the customs and beliefs of the characters

- the way the land looks (hilly, dry, many plants, and so on)

- the weather or the season (sunny or rainy, spring or winter)

- the time during which the story takes place (recent years or a long time ago)

> How is one character different from another?
> _____
> _____
> _____

?

> How is this story similar to another that I have read?
> _____
> _____
> _____

?

> How is this character's experience different from my own experience?
> _____
> _____
> _____

Who Can Replace a Man?

Brian Aldiss

Summary A group of machines does not receive orders as usual. The machines are programmed with different levels of intelligence. The smarter machines find out that all men have died. They try to figure out what to do.

Reading/Writing Connection

Complete these sentences to describe how machines and robots might behave toward one another or toward humans.

1. A robot might <u>respond</u> to another robot's question with _____

   _____.

2. A more intelligent machine will <u>dominate</u> _____.

3. Machines and robots must <u>rely</u> on _____.

Note-taking Guide

Use this diagram to describe the problem the machines face, their solution, and its result.

Problem	Solution	Result
The machines do not know what to do when all men die.		

Who Can Replace a Man?
Brian W. Aldiss

Morning filtered into the sky, lending it the grey tone of the ground below.

The field-minder finished turning the topsoil of a three-thousand-acre field. When it had turned the last furrow it climbed onto the highway and looked back at its work. The work was good. Only the land was bad. Like the ground all over Earth, it was vitiated by over-cropping. By rights, it ought now to lie fallow[1] for a while, but the field-minder had other orders.

It went slowly down the road, taking its time. It was intelligent enough to appreciate the neatness all about it. Nothing worried it, beyond a loose inspection plate above its nuclear pile which ought to be attended to. Thirty feet tall, it yielded no highlights to the dull air.

No other machines passed on its way back to the Agricultural Station. The field-minder noted the fact without comment. In the station yard it saw several other machines that it recognised; most of them should have been out about their tasks now. Instead, some were inactive and some careered round the yard in a strange fashion, shouting or hooting.

◆ ◆ ◆

The field-minder's simple request to the seed-distributor for seed potatoes could not be fulfilled because the storehouse had not been unlocked.

With its Class Three brain, the field-minder's thought processes were superior to those of most of the other machines, and it was able to decide to investigate. It entered the station.

◆ ◆ ◆

---

1. **vitiated** (VISH ee ayt id) **by over-cropping . . . lie fallow** (FAL oh) The soil has been spoiled by repeated plantings that have drawn out its nutrients. Letting the field lie fallow by not planting it would help renourish the soil.

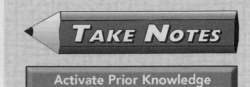

TAKE NOTES

Activate Prior Knowledge

In this story, machines do much of the work. What are some machines that help people do work today?

_____

_____

_____

_____

Literary Analysis

The **setting** is the time and place of a story's action. What details in the bracketed text show that the story is set in the future?

_____

_____

_____

_____

Reading Skill

A **contrast** tells how two or more things are different. How is the field-minder in the story different from machines today?

_____

_____

TAKE NOTES

Read Fluently

Notice the placement of commas and semicolons in the first bracketed passage. The commas separate phrases from the rest of the sentence. What punctuation mark could take the place of the semicolon in the last sentence? Rewrite the sentence below.

_____

_____

Literary Analysis

Read the second bracketed passage. How are the machines ranked in this **setting**?

_____

_____

_____

_____

Reading Skill

A **comparison** tells how two or more things are alike. How are the field-minder and the penner alike?

_____

_____

_____

_____

Most of the machines here were clerical, and consequently small. They stood about in little groups, eyeing each other, not conversing. Among so many <u>non-differentiated</u> types, the unlocker was easy to find. It had fifty arms, most of them with more than one finger, each finger tipped by a key; it looked like a pincushion full of variegated[2] hat pins.

◆　◆　◆

The unlocker had not received orders, so the warehouse remained locked. The pen-propeller explained that the radio station in the city had received no orders, so it could not pass any along.

◆　◆　◆

And there you had the <u>distinction</u> between a Class Six and a Class Three brain, which was what the unlocker and the pen-propeller possessed respectively. All machine brains worked with nothing but logic, but the lower the class of brain—Class Ten being the lowest—the more literal and less informative the answers to questions tended to be.

"You have a Class Three brain; I have a Class Three brain," the field-minder said to the penner. "We will speak to each other."

◆　◆　◆

The field-minder and pen-propeller figured out that the men who ran everything had broken down and that the machines had replaced them.

The pen-propeller headed to the top of the tower to find out whether the radio operator

Vocabulary Development

non-differentiated (nahn dif uh REN shee ayt id) *adj.* not different; the same

distinction (di STINGK shuhn) *n.* a clear difference between things

---

2. **variegated** (VER ee uh gayt id) *adj.* varied in color or form.

had any more news. The penner relayed what it learned to the field-minder out of the hearing of the lower-brained machines, which were going mad from the disruption in their routines.

◆ ◆ ◆

The seed-distributor to which the field-minder had recently been talking lay face downwards in the dust, not stirring; it had <u>evidently</u> been knocked down by the rotavator, which now hooted its way wildly across a planted field. Several other machines plowed after it, trying to keep up with it. All were shouting and hooting without restraint.

◆ ◆ ◆

According to what the penner learned from the radio operator, all of the men had starved to death because the overworked land could no longer feed them. Machines were fighting all over the city. The radio operator, with its Class Two brain, had a plan.

The quarrier, following orders, knocked down the station and freed the radio operator. Demonstrating good dexterity, it ripped off the wall and lowered the radio operator onto its back. The penner climbed onto the quarrier's tailboard. Along with the field-minder, a servicer, two tractors, and a bulldozer, the party left the field station after crushing an unfortunate locker machine that tried to follow along.

◆ ◆ ◆

As they proceeded, the radio operator addressed them.

"Because I have the best brain here," it said, "I am your leader. This is what we will do: we will go to a city and rule it. Since man no longer

---

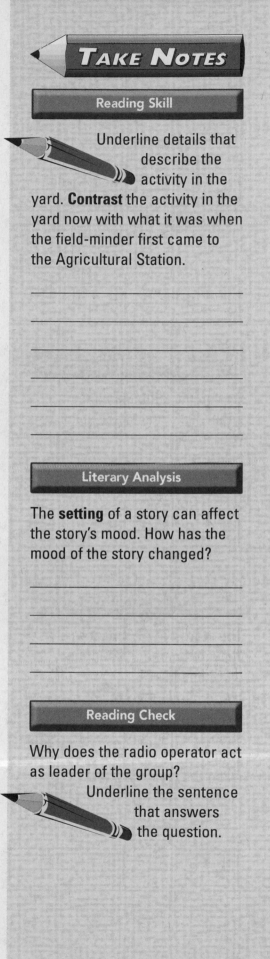

TAKE NOTES

Reading Skill

Underline details that describe the activity in the yard. **Contrast** the activity in the yard now with what it was when the field-minder first came to the Agricultural Station.

_____
_____
_____
_____
_____
_____

Literary Analysis

The **setting** of a story can affect the story's mood. How has the mood of the story changed?

_____
_____
_____
_____

Reading Check

Why does the radio operator act as leader of the group? Underline the sentence that answers the question.

Vocabulary Development

evidently (EV uh duhnt lee) *adv.* obviously; clearly

Literary Analysis

The landscape can be part of the **setting**. How has the landscape changed from the beginning of the machines' journey?

_____

_____

_____

_____

Stop to Reflect

Do you think the machines behave like humans? Explain your answer.

_____

_____

_____

_____

Read Fluently

The word *coupled* means "linked together." Read the underlined sentence. Circle the two things in the sentence that the author is trying to link by using the word *coupled*.

rules us, we will rule ourselves. To rule ourselves will be better than being ruled by man. On our way to the city, we will collect machines with good brains. They will help us to fight if we need to fight. We must fight to rule."

◆　◆　◆

As they traveled, the quarrier kept repeating again and again that it had a supply of fissionable materials, and a passing vehicle transmitted the information that men were extinct. The field-minder explained the meaning of *extinct* to the machines that did not understand the meaning of the word. The machines concluded that if the men were gone forever, they would have to take care of themselves. The penner said it was better that the men were gone.

The group continued traveling into the night, switching on their infra-red so that they could see to navigate. Near morning they learned that the city they were approaching was engulfed in warfare between Class Two machines and the Class One brain that had taken command. After intense discussion, they concluded that because they were country machines, they should stay in the country. They decided on the advice of the bulldozer who had been there to travel to the Badlands in the South.

◆　◆　◆

To reach the Badlands took them three days, during which time they skirted a burning city and destroyed two machines which approached and tried to question them. The Badlands were extensive. Ancient bomb craters and soil erosion joined hands here; man's talent for war, coupled with his inability to manage forested land, had produced thousands of square miles of temperate purgatory, where nothing moved but dust.

◆　◆　◆

On the third day, the servicer got stuck in a crevice and was left behind. The next day, the group saw mountains in the distance, where they believed they would be safe. They planned to start a city and destroy any machines that opposed their rule.

They learned from a flying machine, which subsequently crashed, that a few men were alive in the mountains. Reminding the group once again of its fissionable materials, the quarrier remarked that men were more dangerous than machines. But the mountains were vast and the number of men too few to concern the machines.

On the fifth day, the machines reached the mountains. The penner, which had fallen from the quarrier and been damaged, was left behind because it was no longer useful. When the group of machines reached a plateau just before daylight, they stopped and gathered together. Turning a corner, they entered a dell with a stream.

◆　◆　◆

By early light, the dell looked desolate and cold. From the caves on the far slope, only one man had so far emerged. He was an abject[3] figure. Except for a sack slung round his shoulders, he was naked. He was small and wizened, with ribs sticking out like a skeleton's and a nasty sore on one leg. He shivered continuously. As the big machines bore down on him, the man was standing with his back to them.

When he swung suddenly to face them as they loomed over him, they saw that his countenance[4] was ravaged by starvation.

"Get me food," he croaked.

"Yes, Master," said the machines. "Immediately!"

TAKE NOTES

Literary Analysis

What about the **setting** tells you that humans would have trouble living there?

_____

_____

_____

_____

_____

Stop to Reflect

Why do you think the quarrier says that men are more dangerous than machines?

_____

_____

_____

_____

_____

Reading Check

How does the man at the end of the story look? Circle the sentence that answers the question.

---

3. **abject** (AB jekt) *adj.* miserable.
4. **countenance** (KOWNT uh nuhns) *n.* face or facial expression.

Who Can Replace a Man?

1. **Infer:** The quarrier keeps repeating himself. What does this repetition say about the quarrier's personality? What does it say about the personalities of other machines in its class?

_____

_____

_____

2. **Evaluate:** Are the machines' rankings and special tasks similar to the way our own society is organized? Explain.

_____

_____

3. **Reading Skill: Contrast** the machines in the story. How are the machines in the story different from one another?

_____

_____

4. **Literary Analysis:** The **setting** is the time and place of the action of a story. Use the diagram shown to compare and contrast the setting of the story with today's world. List differences in the outer circles. List similarities in the center.

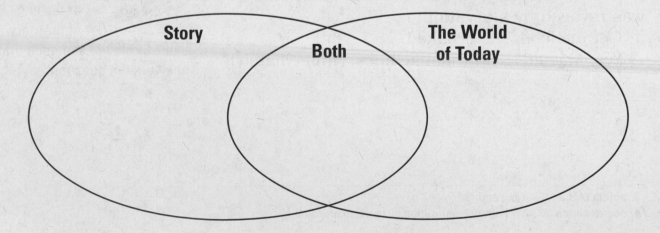

Story   Both   The World of Today

SUPPORT FOR WRITING AND EXTEND YOUR LEARNING

Writing: Description

Write a brief **description** of a futuristic setting. Use colorful adjectives to create vivid descriptions. The following questions will prepare you to revise your description.

- What are two descriptions of the land in the future?

  _____

  _____

- What adjectives could you use to make these descriptions more vivid?

  _____

- What are two descriptions of the people in the future?

  _____

  _____

- What adjectives could you use to make these descriptions more vivid?

  _____

Research and Technology: Oral Report

Gather information for an **oral report** about what one writer, artist, filmmaker, or scientist thinks the future will be. Use the chart below to list possible subjects in each category. Brainstorm ways in which each one would be interesting.

	Name	Why an interesting choice
Writer		
Artist		
Filmmaker		
Scientist		

Tears of Autumn

Yoshiko Uchida

Summary Hana Omiya is from a traditional Japanese family. Her uncle is looking for a wife for a Japanese man in California. Hana has few chances for a better life. She goes to America to marry the man. When she arrives, she is nervous and disappointed. Then, she remembers why she came. She looks forward to her new life.

Reading/Writing Connection

Complete this paragraph to describe three important qualities a person would look for in someone he or she was about to marry.

A person would want a partner to <u>communicate</u> openly about

_____. A person would look for a partner whose choices

in life <u>emphasize</u> _____. Before marrying someone, a

person would <u>verify</u> that _____.

Note-taking Guide

Complete this chart as you read to record Hana's changing emotions.

What was happening?	How did Hana feel?
Taro wanted a wife.	
Hana received Taro's letters.	
Hana finally met Taro.	

Tears of Autumn

1. **Draw Conclusions:** Think about Hana's life in Japan. How do the details about her life explain why Hana wants to marry Taro?

   _____

   _____

2. **Interpret:** Taro takes care of everything and laughs warmly when Hana and Taro meet. He does not say anything about the marriage. What does this tell the reader about Taro's personality?

   _____

   _____

3. **Reading Skill: Compare and contrast** Hana and her sisters.

   _____

   _____

   _____

4. **Literary Analysis:** The **setting** is the time and place of a story. The setting can include the way people think and live. Fill in the Venn diagram below. Write ideas about marriage where you live in the circle on the right. Write ideas about marriage that are the same in the story and where you live in the center.

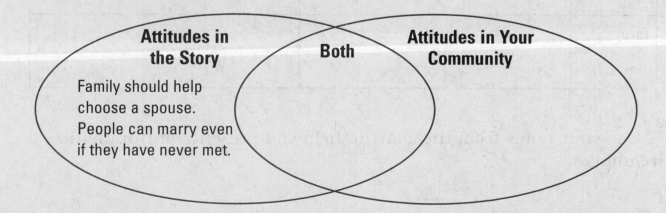

Attitudes in the Story

Family should help choose a spouse. People can marry even if they have never met.

Both

Attitudes in Your Community

SUPPORT FOR WRITING AND EXTEND YOUR LEARNING

Writing: Description

Write a brief **description** of the life Hana might have in America. Think about how she might use her time each day. Use this chart to help you think through a possible day.

Time of Day	Activities
Morning	
Afternoon	
Evening	

Use your notes from the chart above to write your description.

Listening and Speaking: Dramatic Reading

Present the final scene in the story as a **dramatic reading**. When you read the dialogue in the scene, say the words as you think the character would say them. Perform the actions you imagine the character would make in the scene. Use the chart below to help you play the roles of the characters.

Character	Tone of Voice	Actions
Hana		
Taro		

Use your notes from the chart to help you present your dramatic reading.

Hamadi • The Tell-Tale Heart

READING SKILL

Look for similarities and differences among the people in a story to **compare and contrast characters**. One way to compare is to **identify each character's perspective**. Perspective means viewpoint. This is the way a person understands the world.

- Find details about the main character.

- Decide whether the main character's actions, emotions, and ideas are similar to or different from those of the other characters.

- Decide whether you trust what the character says.

Use the chart to fill in details about the main character.

LITERARY ANALYSIS

Character traits are the things that make a character special. One character may be lazy and untrustworthy. Another character may be hardworking and loyal.

- **Round characters** are complex. They show many different character traits.

- **Flat characters** are one-sided. They show just a single trait.

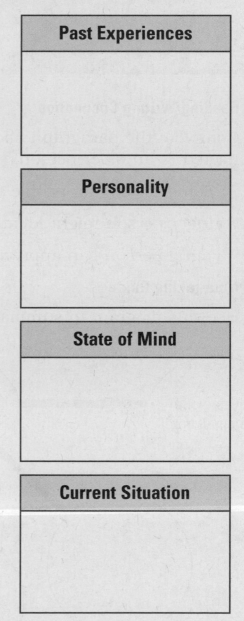

Past Experiences

Personality

State of Mind

Current Situation

Hamadi

Naomi Shihab Nye

Summary Susan is a Palestinian American high school student living in Texas. She enjoys spending time with Hamadi. He is like a grandparent to her. She likes the wisdom and kindness he shares.

Reading/Writing Connection

Complete the paragraph about why a young person may feel connected to an older person.

    Sometimes older people <u>assume</u> _____. A

younger person might <u>identify</u> with _____.

A young person can <u>appreciate</u> _____.

Note-taking Guide

Use this diagram to summarize information about Hamadi.

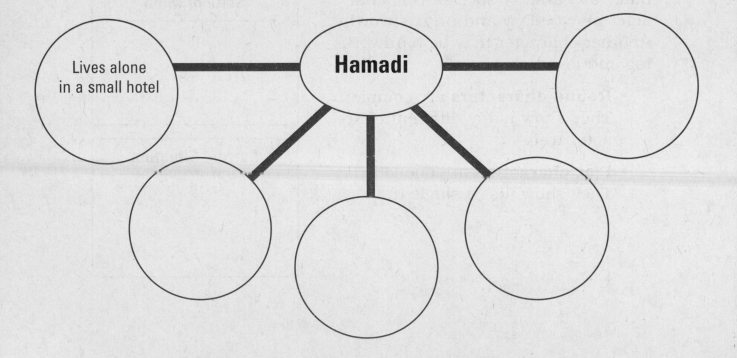

Lives alone in a small hotel — **Hamadi**

Hamadi
Naomi Shihab Nye

Susan was born in Palestine, but her family now lives in Texas. She is fourteen, and she thinks a lot about the very different life she knew in Palestine. Saleh Hamadi, a wise older man and a family friend, helps her to work out her sense of who she is.

♦ ♦ ♦

Maybe she thought of [Hamadi] as escape, the way she used to think about the Sphinx at Giza[1] when she was younger. She would picture the golden Sphinx sitting quietly in the desert with sand blowing around its face, never changing its expression. She would think of its <u>wry</u>, slightly crooked mouth and how her grandmother looked a little like that as she waited for her bread to bake in the old village north of Jerusalem. Susan's family had lived in Jerusalem for three years before she was ten and drove out to see her grandmother every weekend. . . .

Now that she was fourteen, she took long walks in America with her father down by the drainage ditch at the end of their street. Pecan trees shaded the path. She tried to get him to tell stories about his childhood in Palestine. She didn't want him to forget anything. . . .

♦ ♦ ♦

Susan is always eager to find reasons to visit Hamadi. She tells her mother that he would like to have some of her cheese pie. They wrap some up and drive downtown to see Hamadi, who lives simply in a sixth-floor

Vocabulary Development

wry (ry) *adj.*   dryly humorous

---

1. **Sphinx** (sfingks) **at Giza** (GEE zah) huge statue, located in Egypt.

Look for ways the people in a story are alike and different to **compare and contrast characters**. What does Susan's father think about where Hamadi lives? What does Hamadi think about where he lives?

_____

_____

_____

_____

Hamadi is a **round character**. He has many different qualities. Underline three details that tell about Hamadi's character. What do these details tell about his character?

_____

_____

_____

_____

Why does speaking Arabic make Hamadi feel sad? Underline the sentence that tells you.

hotel room. When Susan's father suggests he should move, Hamadi answers . . .

◆   ◆   ◆

"A white handkerchief spread across a tabletop, my two extra shoes lined by the wall, this spells 'home' to me, this says '*mi casa*.' What more do I need?"

Hamadi liked to use Spanish words. They made him feel <u>expansive</u>, worldly. . . . Occasionally he would speak Arabic, his own first language, with Susan's father and uncles, but he said it made him feel too sad, as if his mother might step in to the room at any minute, her arms <u>laden</u> with fresh mint leaves. He had come to the United States on a boat when he was eighteen years old, and he had never been married. "I married books," he said. "I married the wide horizon."

◆   ◆   ◆

Hamadi is not a relative of Susan's. Her father cannot even remember exactly how the family met him. But it might have been through a Maronite priest who claimed to know the Lebanese poet Kahlil Gibran. Gibran is a hero to Hamadi, and Susan learns to love his work from Hamadi. Susan asks him if he really met Gibran.

◆   ◆   ◆

"Yes, I met brother Gibran. And I meet him in my heart every day. When I was a young man— shocked by all the visions of the new world—the tall buildings—the wild traffic—the young people without shame—the proud mailboxes in their blue uniforms—I met him. And he has stayed with me every day of my life."

Vocabulary Development

expansive (ek SPAN siv) *adj.*   capable of expanding; grand in scale

laden (LAYD n) *adj.*   weighed down with a load

"But did you really meet him, like in person, or just in a book?"

He turned dramatically. "Make no such distinctions, my friend. Or your life will be a pod with only dried-up beans inside. Believe anything can happen."

Susan's father looked irritated, but Susan smiled. "I do," she said. "I believe that. I want fat beans. If I imagine something, it's true, too. Just a different kind of true."

◆ ◆ ◆

Susan asks Hamadi why he doesn't go back to visit his village in Lebanon. He says that he visits his family every day just by thinking about them. Susan's father doesn't understand the way Hamadi expresses himself. He says that the old man "talks in riddles."

Susan begins to carry around a book of Gibran's poetry, *The Prophet.* She and her friend Tracy read aloud from the book at lunch. Susan and Tracy are different from the other kids. They eat by themselves, outside, and they don't eat meat. Tracy admits to Susan that she hates a classmate named Debbie because Debbie likes the same boy that she does: Eddie. Susan tells Tracy that she is being selfish.

◆ ◆ ◆

"In fact, we *all* like Eddie," Susan said. "Remember, here in this book—wait and I'll find it—where Gibran says that loving teaches us the secrets of our hearts and that's the way we connect to all of Life's heart? You're not talking about liking or loving, you're talking about owning."

◆ ◆ ◆

Vocabulary Development

distinctions (di STINGK shuhns) *n.*   differences

TAKE NOTES

Literary Analysis

A **flat character** is one who shows just a single trait. Which character in the story is a flat character? Explain.

_____

_____

_____

_____

_____

_____

Reading Skill

Perspective is the way a person understands the world. How are Susan's and Tracy's perspectives about Eddie different?

_____

_____

_____

_____

Reading Check

What do Susan and Tracy have in common? Circle the text that tells you.

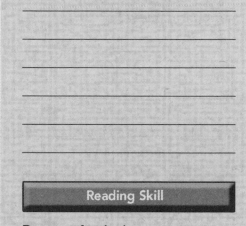

Underline the sentence that tells for whom Susan is decorating a coffee can. What does this say about her **character traits**?

_____

_____

_____

A strategy for comparing characters is to **identify each character's perspective**. This is the way a person understands the world. Underline the sentences that describe how Susan views Hamadi.

Read the bracketed text. Study the phrase "word that just drifted into my mouth." Hamadi means that he has just remembered a word from another language. Circle the name of that language. How does Hamadi describe this language?

_____

_____

Susan decides that it would be a wonderful idea to invite Hamadi to go Christmas caroling with the English club. Her father points out that Hamadi doesn't really know the songs. But Susan insists, and Hamadi says that he will be thrilled to join them.

Susan decorates a coffee can to take donations for a children's hospital in Bethlehem while they carol. Her father asks her why she doesn't show as much interest in her uncles as she shows in Hamadi.

◆ ◆ ◆

Susan laughed. Her uncles were dull. Her uncles shopped at the mall and watched TV. "Anyone who watches TV more than twelve minutes a week is uninteresting," she said.

Her father lifted an eyebrow.

"He's my surrogate grandmother," she said. "He says interesting things. He makes me think. Remember when I was little and he called me The Thinker? We have a connection." . . .

◆ ◆ ◆

When the day comes, Hamadi joins Susan and her friends and family for the caroling. They sing joyfully all over the neighborhood. Hamadi sings out, too, but often in a language that seems to be his own. When Susan looks at him, he says,

◆ ◆ ◆

"That was an Aramaic word that just drifted into my mouth—the true language of the Bible, you know, the language Jesus Christ himself spoke."

◆ ◆ ◆

As they reach their fourth block, Eddie comes running toward the group. He says hello to Tracy and starts to say something into her ear. Then Lisa moves to Eddie's other side and says,

◆ ◆ ◆

"I'm so *excited* about you and Debbie!" she said loudly. "Why didn't she come tonight?"

Eddie said, "She has a sore throat."

Tracy shrank up inside her coat.

◆ ◆ ◆

Knowing that Eddie is planning to take Debbie to the big Sweetheart Dance in February, Tracy breaks down in tears as the caroling goes on. Hamadi notices her weeping and asks,

◆ ◆ ◆

"Why? Is it pain? Is it gratitude? We are such mysterious creatures, human beings!"

Tracy turned to him, pressing her face against the old wool of his coat, and wailed. The song ended. All eyes on Tracy, and this tall, courteous stranger who would never in a thousand years have felt comfortable stroking her hair. But he let her stand there, crying as Susan stepped up to stand firmly on the other side of Tracy, putting her arms around her friend. Hamadi said something Susan would remember years later, whenever she was sad herself, even after college, a creaky anthem sneaking back into her ear, "We go on. On and on. We don't stop where it hurts. We turn a corner. It is the reason why we are living. To turn a corner. Come, let's move."

Above them, in the heavens, stars lived out their lonely lives. People whispered, "What happened? What's wrong?" Half of them were already walking down the street.

TAKE NOTES

Reading Skill

Compare and contrast Susan's and Hamadi's reactions to Tracy with the reactions of the others.

_____

_____

_____

_____

Literary Analysis

Think about how Hamadi and Susan respond to Tracy. What **character traits** do Hamadi and Susan share?

_____

_____

Stop to Reflect

Why do you think that Susan never forgets the words of wisdom that Hamadi speaks to Tracy?

_____

_____

Reading Check

What makes Tracy break into tears? Underline the answer.

Hamadi

1. **Interpret:** Hamadi never married. What does he mean when he says "I married the wide horizon"?

_____

_____

2. **Speculate:** Many people were caroling with Tracy. Why does she turn to Hamadi for comfort?

_____

_____

3. **Reading Skill:** Look for ways that characters are alike and different to **compare and contrast** them. Compare and contrast Hamadi and Susan's father.

_____

_____

_____

4. **Literary Analysis: Character traits** are the personal qualities and attitudes that make a character special. Use the chart shown to describe two character traits of Hamadi. Follow the example given to you.

Character	Trait	Example
Susan	sympathetic	She comforts her friend Tracy.
Hamadi		

SUPPORT FOR WRITING AND EXTEND YOUR LEARNING

Writing: Character Profile

Write a **character profile** of Saleh Hamadi. The questions below will help get you started. Use your notes to create your profile.

• What happens at the end of the story?

_____

_____

• Why does Hamadi act the way he does at the end?

_____

_____

• What character traits may have caused his action at the end?

_____

_____

_____

Research and Technology: Annotated Bibliography

Prepare an **annotated bibliography** of three books by Naomi Shihab Nye. Use the chart below to record information for your bibliography. Write the name of the book. Then, write the publication information. In the final column, write a short summary of the book.

Book Title	Publication Information	Summary

The Tell-Tale Heart

Edgar Allan Poe

Summary The narrator describes how he murders an old man. He murders the man after careful planning. He is confident in his hiding place for the man's body parts. The arrival of the police and the sound of a beating heart haunt the narrator.

Reading/Writing Connection

Complete this paragraph to describe what a fearful person might hear while lying awake in the dark.

Something <u>approaches</u>, and he thinks it might be _____.

He can <u>identify</u> the sound only because _____. One

thing that happens to <u>maximize</u> his fear is _____.

Note-taking Guide

Use this chart to recall the events of the story.

Exposition	A man is obsessed with an old man's cloudy eye. He wants to kill the old man.
Rising Action	
Climax	
Falling Action	
Resolution	

The Tell-Tale Heart

1. **Draw Conclusions:** At first, the narrator is calm while he talks to police. Why does he get nervous?

   _____

   _____

2. **Apply:** People who have done something wrong often confess. They confess even when they could get away with their wrongdoing. Why do you think these people confess?

   _____

   _____

   _____

3. **Reading Skill:** The story tells only the narrator's thoughts. Do you trust the narrator's details to be correct? Explain your answer.

   _____

   _____

4. **Literary Analysis: Character traits** are qualities, attitudes, and values. Use the chart to describe one character trait of the narrator. Give examples that show the trait. Use the examples as a guide.

Character	Trait	Example
The narrator	nervousness	He is afraid that the neighbors will hear the beating heart.
The narrator	patience	He waits an hour in silence after the old man cries out.
The narrator		

SUPPORT FOR WRITING AND EXTEND YOUR LEARNING

Writing: Character Profile

Write a **character profile** for the narrator in "The Tell-Tale Heart."
The questions below will help get you started. Use your notes to create
the profile.

- What happens at the end of the story?

  _____

  _____

- Why does the narrator act as he does at the end of the story?

  _____

  _____

- Why might the narrator have acted in this way? What character traits
  may have caused his action?

  _____

  _____

  _____

Listening and Speaking: Panel Discussion

Plan a **panel discussion**. Think about your responses to the main
character in "The Tell-Tale Heart." Use the chart below to prepare notes
for a panel discussion.

Question	Possible Answer	Why I Feel This Way

Summaries

ABOUT SUMMARIES

A **summary** tells the main ideas and important details of a work. You can find summaries in many places.

- Newspapers and magazines have summaries of movies.
- An encyclopedia of literature has summaries of important books and other kinds of writing.
- Science research reports often begin with summaries of the researchers' findings.

Reading a summary is a quick way to preview before you read. Writing a summary is a good way to help you remember what you read.

READING SKILL

A good way to understand a summary is to **compare an original text with its summary**. You will see that a summary has some details, but not others.

This diagram shows how an original work and its summary are the same and different.

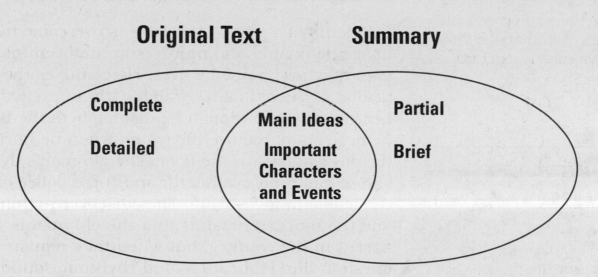

Original Text   **Summary**

Complete

Detailed

Main Ideas

Important Characters and Events

Partial

Brief

A good summary will include all of the main ideas. It will also include important details about both plot and characters. A good summary must tell the hidden meaning of a story. A summary should be shorter than the original work.

Reading Summaries

This **summary** starts by giving information about the author. It also gives information about when the book was published. Why might this information be important?

_____

_____

_____

_____

Read Fluently

Some sentences are confusing. One way to make sense of them is to look for the most important words. Look at the last sentence of the summary. A comma divides the sentence into two parts. Underline the four most important words in each part.

Reading Check

Who are the main characters in "The Tell-Tale Heart?" Circle the characters in the summary text.

Summary of
The Tell-Tale Heart

From Short Story Criticism
Anna Sheets Nesbitt, Editor

Tell-Tale Heart, The, *story by Poe.• published in The Pioneer (1843). It has been considered the most influential of Poe's stories in the later development of stream-of-consciousness fiction.*

A victim of a nervous disease is overcome by homicidal mania and murders an innocent old man in whose home he lives. He confuses the ticking of the old man's watch with an excited heartbeat, and although he dismembers the body he neglects to remove the watch when he buries the pieces beneath the floor. The old man's dying shriek has been overheard, and three police officers come to investigate. They discover nothing, and the murderer claims that the old man is absent in the country, but when they remain to question him he hears a loud rhythmic sound that he believes to be the beating of the buried heart. This so distracts his diseased mind that he suspects the officers know the truth and are merely trying his patience, and in an insane fit he confesses his crime.

Summary of The Tell-Tale Heart

From The Oxford Companion to American Literature

James D. Hart, Editor

Plot and Major Characters

The tale opens with the narrator insisting that he is not mad, avowing that his calm telling of the story that follows is confirmation of his sanity. He explains that he decided to take the life of an old man whom he loved and whose house he shared. The only reason he had for doing so was that the man's pale blue eye, which was veiled by a thin white film and "resembled that of a vulture," tormented him, and he had to rid himself of the "Evil Eye" forever.

After again declaring his sanity, the narrator proceeds to recount the details of the crime. Every night for seven nights, he says, he had stolen into the old man's room at midnight holding a closed lantern. Each night he would very slowly unlatch the lantern slightly and shine a single ray of light onto the man's closed eye. As he enters the room on the eighth night, however, the old man stirs, then calls out, thinking he has heard a sound. The narrator shines the light on the old man's eye as usual, but this time finds it wide open. He begins to hear the beating of a heart and, fearing the sound might be heard by a neighbor, kills the old man by dragging him to the floor and pulling the heavy bed over him. He dismembers the corpse and hides it beneath the floorboards of the old man's room.

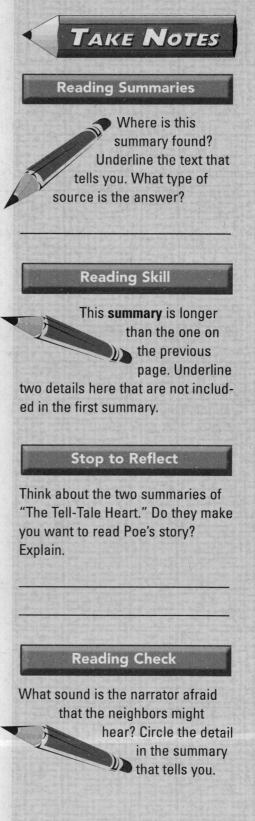

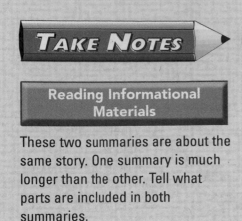

Reading Informational Materials

These two summaries are about the same story. One summary is much longer than the other. Tell what parts are included in both summaries.

_____

_____

Reading Check

Why do the policemen ask to search the house? Underline the sentence that tells you.

At four o'clock in the morning, the narrator continues, three policemen come asking to search the premises because a neighbor has reported a shriek coming from the house. The narrator invites the officers in, explaining that the noise came from himself as he dreamt. The old man, he tells them, is in the country. He brings chairs into the old man's room, placing his own seat on the very planks under which the victim lies buried. The officers are convinced there is no foul play, and sit around chatting amiably, but the narrator becomes increasingly agitated. He soon begins to hear a heart beating, much as he had just before he killed the old man. It grows louder and louder until he becomes convinced the policemen hear it too. They know of his crime, he thinks, and mock him. Unable to bear their derision and the sound of the beating heart, he springs up and, screaming, confesses his crime.

THINKING ABOUT THE SUMMARY

1. Find four details that are in both summaries.

_____

_____

2. How is reading a summary a different experience from reading the full text? Support your answer with examples from the summaries.

_____

_____

READING SKILL

3. According to both summaries, why does the narrator kill the old man?

_____

4. A story is made up of different parts: plot, setting, characters, and theme. Which part do the summaries focus on most?

_____

TIMED WRITING: COMPARISON (20 minutes)

Write a comparison of the two summaries of "The Tell-Tale Heart." Write about how correct and complete each is. Discuss their styles. Tell how effective each summary is in serving its purpose. Answer the following questions to help you get started.

• Which summary is more helpful in understanding the story?

_____

• Which summary is easier to read?

_____

Flowers for Algernon • Charles

READING SKILL

As a reader, you will often **make inferences**. This means that you will look at the information that is given. You will see little clues. Then, you will think about the information that is not given. **Use details** that the author gives as clues to make inferences. Notice details such as what the characters say about one another and what the characters do.

This chart shows how to use details to uncover the information that is not given.

Detail	Possible Inference
• A waitress is careless and rude.	• She does not take pride in her job.
• A toddler breaks his toy.	• He is upset.

Fill in the chart as you read.

Story Detail	Possible Inference

LITERARY ANALYSIS

Point of view is the outlook from which the story is told. Most stories are told from one of these points of view:

- **First person:** The narrator, or person telling the story, is also in the story. The narrator knows only things that his or her character would know. The narrator calls himself or herself *I*.

- **Third person:** The narrator is not in the story. He or she tells the story from the "outside." The narrator uses *he*, *she*, and *they* to describe the characters.

Flowers for Algernon

Daniel Keyes

Summary Charlie is a factory worker who is chosen to be the subject of a new brain surgery. His skills are watched and compared with those of Algernon, a mouse. Charlie's skills grow. He becomes smarter than his doctors. However, Charlie's life is not perfect.

Reading/Writing Connection

Complete this paragraph to describe why a character might want to fit in or be accepted.

A character might need to <u>interact</u> with others so that _____

_____. Others might <u>isolate</u> the character

from _____. All people must

<u>participate</u> in society if _____.

Note-taking Guide

Use this chart to record the changes that take place in Charlie's life.

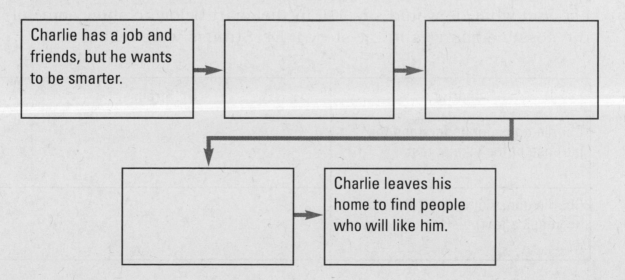

Charlie has a job and friends, but he wants to be smarter. → ☐ → ☐

☐ → Charlie leaves his home to find people who will like him.

Flowers for Algernon

1. **Compare:** Like Charlie, Algernon is part of the experiment. Explain how changes in Charlie are similar to changes in Algernon.

_____

_____

2. **Take a Position:** Do you think Charlie should have had the operation? Explain your answer.

_____

_____

3. **Reading Skill:** Remember Miss Kinnian's attitude toward Charlie's co-workers, her relationship with Charlie, and her reaction to Charlie's changes. What **inference** can you make about her from the way she treats Charlie?

_____

_____

4. **Literary Analysis:** Charlie is telling this story, so the story is told from his **point of view**. Think about how the story would be different if Dr. Strauss told it. Think about the kinds of words Dr. Strauss would use and what he would say. Fill in the chart below to show some of the possible changes in the story if Dr. Strauss were telling it.

Charlie	Dr. Strauss
Charlie does not understand the purpose of the inkblot test.	
Charlie does not understand why he keeps a journal. He does anyway.	

SUPPORT FOR WRITING AND EXTEND YOUR LEARNING

Writing: Dialogue

Write **dialogue** for a movie scene from "Flowers for Algernon." First, write a description of each character. Then, complete the chart below. Use your notes to write your dialogue.

Character	What would be unique about the way this person talks?	Who would this person treat as a friend?	How would this person treat other characters?
Charlie			
Dr. Strauss			
Dr. Nemur			
Miss Kinnian			

Research and Technology: Summary

Write a **summary** on two articles about human intelligence and the development of the brain. Use the questions below to help you choose which articles to summarize.

• Who is the author? Is he or she an expert on the subject?

_____

• What information does the author use to support the main idea?

_____

_____

_____

Charles

Shirley Jackson

Summary Laurie is rude to his parents after his first day of kindergarten. He tells his parents about a boy named Charles. Each day, Laurie has a new story about Charles. Laurie's mother is surprised when she learns the truth about Charles.

Reading/Writing Connection

Complete the paragraph by writing three things you would tell a child starting kindergarten.

It is important to participate _____. Try

to focus attention on _____. People need

to cooperate _____.

Note-taking Guide

Use this diagram to write what happens in the story.

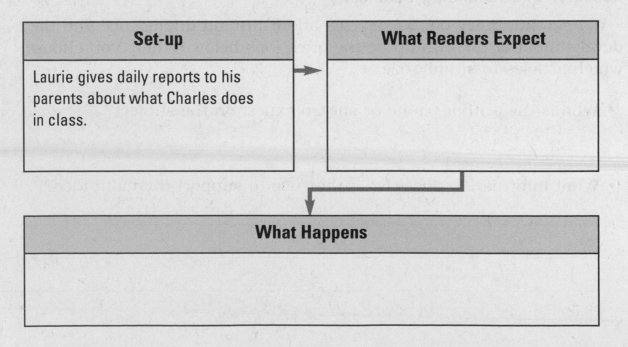

Set-up		What Readers Expect
Laurie gives daily reports to his parents about what Charles does in class.	→	

What Happens

Charles
Shirley Jackson

As children, we all go through a time when we want to grow up all at once. In Laurie's case, that time is his first day of kindergarten. According to Laurie's mother, who tells the story, Laurie bounds home on that first day with a bold new attitude.

◆ ◆ ◆

He came home the same way, the front door slamming open, his cap on the floor, and the voice suddenly becomes <u>raucous</u> shouting, "Isn't anybody *here*?"

◆ ◆ ◆

During lunch, Laurie is rude to his father. He also spills his sister's milk. Laurie tells the family that his teacher has told them they should not take the Lord's name in vain. Over the next few days, Laurie's rude behavior at home continues. Laurie's behavior seems just like the bad behavior of his classmate, Charles. Thanks to Laurie's admiring stories, Charles's daily pranks and punishments become the regular dinnertime subject of the household. Each day, Charles has been up to something that Laurie seems to admire or enjoy. One day, Laurie is very pleased to tell the family that Charles was bad again—he struck the teacher.

◆ ◆ ◆

"Good heavens," I said, mindful of the Lord's name. "I suppose he got spanked again?"
"He sure did," Laurie said. . . .

◆ ◆ ◆

All week long, Charles is bad. When he bounces a see-saw on the head of a little girl,

---

© Pearson Education, Inc., publishing as Pearson Prentice Hall.

TAKE NOTES

Activate Prior Knowledge

Describe how you felt or acted on your first day of kindergarten or elementary school.

_____

_____

_____

Reading Skill

Use the information the author gives to **make inferences**, or logical guesses, about what the author does not say. What **details** show that Laurie admires Charles's behavior?

_____

_____

_____

Literary Analysis

Point of view is the perspective from which a story is told. **First-person** point of view means that the narrator is part of the story. Read the bracketed passage. Circle the pronoun that tells you that this story is written from the first-person point of view.

Vocabulary Development

raucous (RAW kuhs) *adj.* unpleasantly or harshly noisy

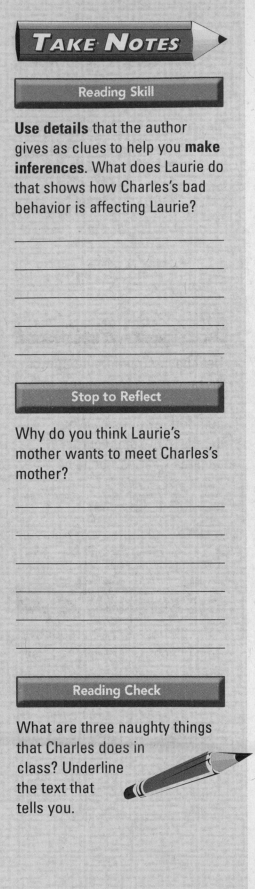

Reading Skill

Use details that the author gives as clues to help you **make inferences**. What does Laurie do that shows how Charles's bad behavior is affecting Laurie?

_____

_____

_____

_____

_____

Stop to Reflect

Why do you think Laurie's mother wants to meet Charles's mother?

_____

_____

_____

_____

_____

_____

_____

Reading Check

What are three naughty things that Charles does in class? Underline the text that tells you.

the teacher has him stay inside for recess. Then, Charles has to stand in the corner because he disrupts storytime for the class. When he throws chalk, Charles loses the privilege of drawing and writing on the chalkboard. Laurie still enjoys telling these stories about Charles when he comes home from school each day.

Meanwhile, Laurie is behaving more rudely at home. Laurie's mother begins to wonder whether Charles is having a bad influence on her son. She wants to go to the first Parent Teacher Association meeting to find out what Charles's parents are like. But Laurie's sister is sick with a cold, so their mother has to stay home and miss the opportunity to see or meet Charles's parents.

The day after that first PTA meeting, Laurie tells about Charles's latest victim, a friend of the teacher's who came to class to lead the students in exercises. Laurie demonstrates how the man had them touch their toes. Then he goes back to his story about Charles, who was fresh with the man. When the man told Charles to touch his toes, Charles kicked the man. Charles wasn't allowed to do any more exercises because of his bad behavior.

◆ ◆ ◆

"What are they going to do about Charles, do you suppose?" Laurie's father asked him.

Laurie shrugged <u>elaborately</u>. "Throw him out of school, I guess," he said.

◆ ◆ ◆

Charles is not thrown out of school, but after three weeks of these stories, his name becomes part of Laurie's family's vocabulary.

Vocabulary Development

elaborately (i LAB rit lee) *adv.*   carried out with many details

---

Each time something bad happens, the family calls the event a "Charles."

◆ ◆ ◆

. . . the baby was being a Charles when she cried all afternoon; Laurie did a Charles when he filled his wagon full of mud and pulled it through the kitchen; even my husband, when he caught his elbow in the telephone cord and pulled the telephone, ashtray, and a bowl of flowers off the table, said, after the first minute, "Looks like Charles."

◆ ◆ ◆

During the third and fourth weeks, Laurie tells of a new Charles who suddenly becomes kind and helpful. One day Charles helps pass out crayons and picks up books afterwards. He is so good that the teacher gives him an apple. This good behavior goes on for more than a week.

Then the old Charles returns with a new prank. He tells one of the girls in the class to say a bad word. The teacher washes her mouth out with soap—of course, Charles thinks this is funny.

◆ ◆ ◆

"What word?" his father asked unwisely, and Laurie said, "I'll have to whisper it to you, it's so bad." He got down off his chair and went around to his father. His father bent his head down and Laurie whispered joyfully. His father's eyes widened.

"Did Charles tell the little girl to say *that*?" he asked respectfully.

"She said it *twice*," Laurie said. "Charles told her to say it *twice*."

"What happened to Charles?" my husband asked.

"Nothing," Laurie said, "He was passing out the crayons."

◆ ◆ ◆

That evening Laurie's mother goes to the PTA meeting at the school. While there, she

Reading Skill

Make an **inference** about why Laurie fills his wagon with mud and pulls it through the kitchen.

_____

_____

Literary Analysis

Changing the story's **point of view** would give you more information about certain characters. What might you learn about Charles's good behavior if the story were told from his point of view?

_____

_____

Read Fluently

Identifying the speakers of dialogue can help you better understand the story. Read the bracketed passage. Underline everything Laurie says. Circle everything Laurie's father says.

Reading Check

What does Charles tell a little girl to do? Bracket the text that tells you.

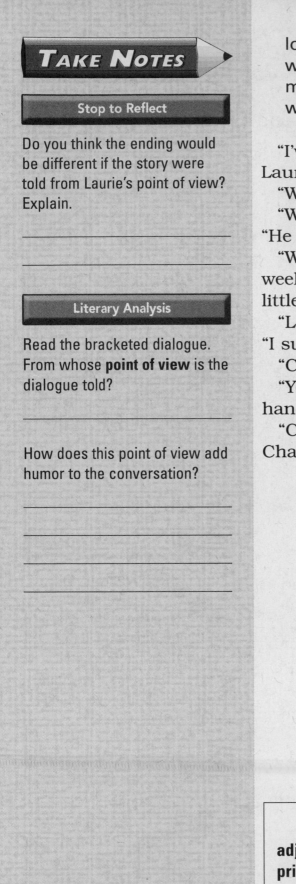

TAKE NOTES

Stop to Reflect

Do you think the ending would be different if the story were told from Laurie's point of view? Explain.

_____

_____

Literary Analysis

Read the bracketed dialogue. From whose **point of view** is the dialogue told?

_____

How does this point of view add humor to the conversation?

_____

_____

_____

looks around, trying to figure out which woman is Charles's mother. After the meeting is over, she finds Laurie's teacher while everyone is having refreshments.

◆   ◆   ◆

"I've been so anxious to meet you," I said, "I'm Laurie's mother."

"We're all so interested in Laurie," she said.

"Well, he certainly likes kindergarten," I said. "He talks about it all the time."

"We had a little trouble adjusting, the first week or so," she said primly, "but now he's a fine little helper. With occasional lapses, of course."

"Laurie usually adjusts very quickly," I said. "I suppose this time it's Charles's influence."

"Charles?"

"Yes," I said, laughing, "you must have your hands full in that kindergarten, with Charles."

"Charles?" she said. "We don't have any Charles in the kindergarten."

Vocabulary Development

adjusting (uh JUST ing) *v.*   getting used to new conditions

primly (PRIM lee) *adv.*   in a manner that is stiffly formal and proper

lapses (LAP siz) *n.*   slight errors or failures

Charles

1. **Draw Conclusions:** On the first day of kindergarten, Laurie stops wearing overalls. He starts wearing jeans with a belt. How does this signal a change in Laurie's behavior?

   _____

   _____

2. **Compare and Contrast:** How is Charles's behavior at school like Laurie's behavior at home? How is it different?

   _____

   _____

   _____

3. **Reading Skill:** Laurie's teacher speaks very carefully to Laurie's mother. She does not talk about his bad behavior. What **inferences** can you make about the teacher by the way she speaks to Laurie's mother?

   _____

   _____

4. **Literary Analysis:** The story is told from the **first-person point of view** of Laurie's mother. Use the chart below to write one way the story would be different if it were told from Laurie's point of view.

Mother	Laurie
Mother thinks Laurie has a classmate named Charles.	
Mother worries that Charles is a bad influence on Laurie.	Laurie knows that he is a bad influence in the classroom.

SUPPORT FOR WRITING AND EXTEND YOUR LEARNING

Writing: Dialogue

Write **dialogue** for a movie scene that you adapt from "Charles." Select a scene from the story. Use the following questions to help you write the dialogue.

- What details do you think the author left out of the conversation in the chosen scene?

  _____

  _____

  _____

- What do you think the characters will say in your adapted scene?

  _____

  _____

  _____

Listening and Speaking: Interview

Plan an **interview** between Laurie (as "Charles") and one of his classmates. Use the following questions to brainstorm ideas for your interview.

- What did Laurie do in class?

  _____

  _____

- What do you think the teacher said to him?

  _____

  _____

- How do you think the other students reacted to his behavior?

  _____

  _____

  _____

Thank You, M'am • The Story-Teller

READING SKILL

An **inference** is a logical guess. It is based on details the writer hints at or suggests. Making an inference is a way to find meaning behind the actions and events in a story. As you read, **identify connections to make inferences about the author's meaning**.

Ask yourself what the author is suggesting by making these connections. This strategy is illustrated in the example shown. Fill in the chart below with examples as you read the story.

Event		Event		Inference
A boy spends all of his money on candy and does not share.	+	He gets sick from eating too much candy.	=	People should not be selfish.

LITERARY ANALYSIS

The **theme** is the main idea or message in a story. It can also be an insight. It is often a general statement about life or people. Themes can come from the characters' experiences. They can also come from events in the story.

- The author tells a **stated theme** directly in a story.

- A theme can also be **unstated**, or **implied**. You use the characters' actions and the story's events to infer the theme.

One story can have more than one theme. A theme is correct if it can be supported with details from the story.

Thank You, M'am

Langston Hughes

Summary A teenage boy tries to steal a woman's purse. The woman catches the boy and brings him to her home. She teaches him a lesson about kindness and trust.

Reading/Writing Connection

Complete this paragraph to describe what someone would need to do to win your trust.

To <u>earn</u> a person's trust it is important to be _____.

A person can <u>acquire</u> many _____ by treating people

fairly. A person should _____ to <u>obtain</u> trust.

Note-taking Guide

Use this diagram to summarize the major events of the story.

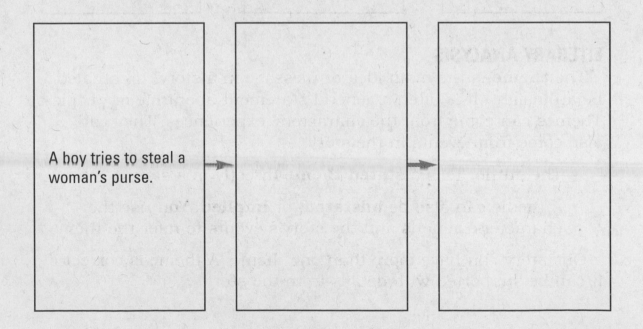

A boy tries to steal a woman's purse.

Thank You, M'am

Langston Hughes

This story tells how a woman's kindness surprises and changes a young man who has tried to rob her. She is a large woman, and she is walking home alone at night. She carries a very large purse with a long strap. A boy comes from behind her and tries to snatch her purse.

◆　◆　◆

The strap broke with the sudden single tug the boy gave it from behind. But the boy's weight and the weight of the purse combined caused him to lose his balance. Instead of taking off full blast as he had hoped, the boy fell on his back on the sidewalk and his legs flew up. The large woman simply turned around and kicked him right square in his blue-jeaned sitter.

◆　◆　◆

Next, the woman grabs the boy's shirt and picks him up in the air. She shakes him hard but doesn't let go of him. Then—still holding him—she asks whether he is ashamed of himself. The boy says that he is ashamed. Next, the woman asks the boy whether he will run away if she lets him go. He says that he will. She says that she will continue to hold on to him. The woman says that she is going to take the boy to her home to wash his dirty face. The boy is fourteen or fifteen years old. He looks frail and is dressed in tennis shoes and blue jeans. The woman starts dragging the boy toward her home. She announces that he ought to be her son—she would make sure to teach him "right from wrong." She decides that she may not be able to teach him that, but she can make sure he has a clean face that night. As she's dragging him along the street, she asks whether he's hungry.

◆　◆　◆

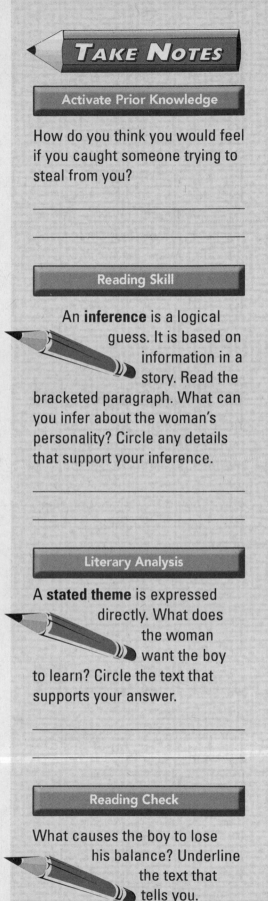

TAKE NOTES

Activate Prior Knowledge

How do you think you would feel if you caught someone trying to steal from you?

_____

_____

Reading Skill

An **inference** is a logical guess. It is based on information in a story. Read the bracketed paragraph. What can you infer about the woman's personality? Circle any details that support your inference.

_____

_____

Literary Analysis

A **stated theme** is expressed directly. What does the woman want the boy to learn? Circle the text that supports your answer.

_____

_____

Reading Check

What causes the boy to lose his balance? Underline the text that tells you.

Literary Analysis

The **theme** is the main idea, or message, in a story. Some themes are **unstated,** or **implied**. This means the author does not directly tell you the theme. What is the woman's attitude toward the boy?

_____

_____

_____

Reading Skill

You can **identify connections to make inferences about the author's meaning**. You should look for what characters do and why they do it. Why do you think Roger goes to the sink instead of the door?

_____

_____

_____

Read Fluently

A contraction combines two words and makes them into one word. A writer uses an apostrophe (') to make a contraction. Read the bracketed passage. Circle the contraction. What two words were combined to make this word?

_____

"No'm," said the being-dragged boy. "I just want you to turn me loose."

"Was I bothering _you_ when I turned that corner?" asked the woman.

"No'm."

"But you put yourself in <u>contact</u> with _me_," said the woman. . . . "When I get through with you, sir, you are going to remember Mrs. Luella Bates Washington Jones."

◆ ◆ ◆

The boy struggles to get away, but Mrs. Jones drags him up the street and into her rooming house. He hears other people who rent rooms in the house. Mrs. Jones asks the boy his name, and he says that it is Roger.

◆ ◆ ◆

"Then, Roger, you go to that sink and wash your face," said the woman, whereupon she turned him loose—at last, Roger looked at the door—looked at the woman—looked at the door—_and went to the sink._

◆ ◆ ◆

Roger asks Mrs. Jones whether she's going to send him to jail. She says not as long as he has such a dirty face. The boy tells her that he has not had supper because there's nobody at home at his house. So Mrs. Jones tells Roger that they'll eat. She thinks he must be hungry because he tried to take her purse.

◆ ◆ ◆

"I wanted a pair of blue suede shoes,"[1] said the boy.

"Well, you didn't have to snatch my pocket-book to get some suede shoes, . . . you could of asked me."

◆ ◆ ◆

Vocabulary Development

contact (KAHN takt) _n._   touch; communication

1. **blue suede** (swayd) **shoes** style of shoes worn by "hipsters" in the 1940s and 1950s; made famous in a song sung by Elvis Presley.

This answer surprises Roger. He is not used to generous people. When Mrs. Jones steps behind a screen and he has a chance to run away, he doesn't. Later, Mrs. Jones tells Roger that she was once young and did some bad things, too—things she does not want to talk about. Roger now wants the woman to trust him. He asks her whether she needs some milk at the store. She says she does not, and she offers to make him some cocoa; he accepts. She then heats up some ham and beans and feeds him dinner.

During dinner, Mrs. Jones tells Roger all about her life and her job at a hotel beauty shop. She describes all of the beautiful women who come in and out of the store.

◆ ◆ ◆

When they were finished eating, she got up and said, "Now here take this ten dollars and buy yourself some blue suede shoes. And next time, do not make the mistake of latching onto *my* pocketbook *nor nobody else's.* . . . "Goodnight! Behave yourself, boy!" she said, looking into the street as he went down the steps.

The boy wanted to say something other than, "Thank you, m'am," to Mrs. Luella Bates Washington Jones, but although his lips moved, he couldn't even say that as he turned at the foot of the barren stoop and looked up at the large woman in the door. Then she shut the door.

Literary Analysis

What do you think is the story's **theme**, or main point?

_____

_____

_____

_____

Reading Skill

Why does Mrs. Jones give Roger ten dollars to buy himself shoes? Make an **inference** that is based on details in the text.

_____

_____

_____

Stop to Reflect

Would you have been speechless at the end of the story, as Roger is? If not, what do you think you would have said to Mrs. Jones?

_____

_____

_____

Reading Check

Where does Mrs. Jones work? Circle the text that tells you.

Vocabulary Development

latching (LACH ing) *v.*   grasping or attaching oneself to
barren (BER uhn) *adj.*   empty

Thank You, M'am

1. **Interpret:** Why is Roger unable to say what he wants to say as he leaves the apartment?

   _____

   _____

   _____

2. **Predict:** Mrs. Jones feeds Roger and gives him money. How might Mrs. Jones's behavior affect Roger's future actions?

   _____

   _____

3. **Reading Skill:** An **inference** is a logical guess that is based on information in a story. What inference can you make about the author's message about stealing?

   _____

   _____

   _____

4. **Literary Analysis:** The **theme** is the main message in a story. A theme for the story has been written below. Tell whether it is **stated** or **implied**. Write details in the second column to support the interpretation.

Theme (stated or implied)	Details
Trust and kindness can change someone's life.	

SUPPORT FOR WRITING AND EXTEND YOUR LEARNING

Writing: Personal Essay

Write a **personal essay** showing how a theme of "Thank You, M'am" applies to everyday life. Use the outline to organize your essay.

A. Introduction of Your Essay

    1. State your theme: _____

    _____

    2. Summarize your experiences: _____

    _____

    _____

B. Conclusion of Your Essay

    1. Restate your theme: _____

    _____

    _____

    2. Explain how your theme applies to everyday life: _____

    _____

Use your notes to help you write your personal essay.

Research and Technology: Multimedia Exhibit

Gather information for a **multimedia exhibit** about Langston Hughes and the Harlem Renaissance. Use the chart below to help organize your information.

Type of Media	Description of Information

The Story-Teller

Saki (H.H. Munro)

Summary A stranger on a train tells a story that entertains three children. The story's ending makes the children's aunt very angry. It goes against all of her lectures about proper behavior.

Reading/Writing Connection

Complete these sentences to describe the types of plot elements and characters that you enjoy in a story.

1. Characters <u>enhance</u> a story by _____.

2. A plot can <u>enrich</u> a story by _____.

3. Good characters <u>expand</u> _____.

Note-taking Guide

Use the chart to recall the events of the story.

Problem	The children will not be quiet on the trip.
Event	
Event	
Event	
Outcome	

The Story-Teller

1. **Analyze:** Do you think the bachelor feels sorry for the aunt or for the children? Think about his actions in the story. Explain your answer.

_____

_____

2. **Evaluate:** The aunt says that the bachelor's story is not appropriate for children. Do you agree? Why or why not?

_____

_____

3. **Reading Skill:** An **inference** is a logical guess that is based on details in a story. The author comments on what children like and how children should be raised. What inference can you make about what the author thinks?

_____

_____

_____

4. **Literary Analysis:** The **theme** is the main idea of a story. It can be **stated** or **implied**. The theme of the story is written in the first column. Decide whether the theme is **stated** or **implied**. In the second column, write details from the story that support the theme.

Theme (stated or implied)	Details
Stories should entertain, not preach.	

SUPPORT FOR WRITING AND EXTEND YOUR LEARNING

Writing: Personal Essay

Write a **personal essay** showing how a theme of "The Story-Teller" applies to everyday life. Use the outline to help organize your essay.

A. Introduction of Your Essay

   1. State your theme: _____

   _____

   2. Summarize your experiences: _____

   _____

   _____

B. Conclusion of Your Essay

   1. Restate your theme: _____

   _____

   2. Explain how your theme applies to everyday life: _____

   _____

Listening and Speaking: Panel Discussion

Have a **panel discussion**. Discuss whether the bachelor should have told the children such a gruesome story. Use the questions below to prepare your thoughts before the discussion.

1. Do you think there are some things that should always be included in a children's story? Give one example.

   _____

2. Do you think there are some things that should never be included in a children's story? Give one example.

   _____

Advertisements

ABOUT ADVERTISEMENTS

Advertisements are paid messages. Companies use advertising to persuade customers to buy products or services. Advertisers use appeals to do this. An appeal is a technique used to make a product attractive or interesting. Advertisers use two kinds of appeals:

- **Rational appeals** are based on facts. These ads may show how different products compare. They may show product features. Sometimes these appeals talk about price.
- **Emotional appeals** are based on feelings. Such appeals suggest that customers will be happier, more respected, or more popular if they buy a certain product.

READING SKILL

It is important to know the difference between a rational appeal and an emotional appeal. This knowledge can help you understand how an advertisement works. Recognize and ignore **appeals to emotion**. These appeals are not based on facts. Use facts to help you make up your mind.

Study this chart. It shows some common ways that advertisers and writers appeal to emotion. Question whether you believe these arguments.

Device	Example	Explanation
Bandwagon appeal	Everyone loves Muncheez!	Words like *everyone* appeal to people's desire to belong.
Loaded language	Muncheez is incredibly delicious.	*Incredibly* and *delicious* are claims that cannot be proved.
Testimonials	Tina Idol says Muncheez gives her energy.	Just because a celebrity or "expert" says it, it does not mean the claim is true.
Generalization	Muncheez is not only the best, it's the healthiest.	Claims that are too broad or vague cannot be proved.

Meet <u>MRS</u>. Casey Jones

CASEY'S gone to war . . . so Mrs. Jones is "working on the railroad!"

She is putting in a big day's work oiling and swabbing down giant engines, cleaning and vacuuming cars, handling baggage, selling tickets, moving through the aisles as a trainman.

In fact, she is doing scores of different jobs on the Pennsylvania Railroad — and doing them well. So the men in the armed forces whom she has replaced can take comfort in the fact Mrs. Casey Jones is "carrying on" in fine style.

Since the war began, Pennsylvania Railroad has welcomed thousands of women into its ranks of loyal, busy and able workers. They are taking a real part in the railroad's big two-fold job of moving troops and supplies and serving essential civilian needs during the war emergency.

You will find these women, not merely in expected places, such as offices, telephone exchanges and ticket windows . . . you will find them out where "man-size" jobs have to be done: in the round house, in the shops, in the yards, in the terminals, in the cars.

We feel sure the American public will take pride in the way American womanhood has pitched in to keep the Victory trains rolling!

PENNSYLVANIA RAILROAD
Serving the Nation

★ 34,101 in the Armed Forces   ★ 38 have given their lives for their country

While the Storm rages...

THE TRAIN GOES THROUGH !

The sky darkens... lightning crackles—soon comes the deluge, blotting out all visibility!

No matter—your Pennsylvania Railroad train takes weather as it comes... the good with the bad.

And if you've temporarily lost one horizon *outside*—you've gained another, new and more beautiful, *inside!*

For now those two famed all-coach streamliners — *The Trail Blazer*, New York-Chicago and *The Jeffersonian*, New York-

Washington-St. Louis—and the *Liberty Limited*, Washington-Chicago, proudly welcome you to Pennsylvania Railroad's grand postwar coaches.

So roomy... only 44 seats to the car!

So magnificently lighted... fluorescent lights *four times* stronger, yet soft and... shadowless.

So much easier riding... credit that to the improved undercarriage and those new lightweight but sturdy steels.

Your window is a full 6 feet wide, the largest

we've ever made... and the washrooms likewise are extra spacious, each with two toilet annexes and three washstands.

Even your coach doors admit you with an ease never before known—they're electro-pneumatic and open at a finger's touch.

From the ground up, from door to door, these postwar coaches invite you to enjoy not only new comfort, new riding ease, new beauty—but an utterly new experience in dependable low-cost travel. So step aboard!... to a comfortable seat reserved for you at NO EXTRA COST!

PENNSYLVANIA RAILROAD
for *WEATHERPROOF* service

THINKING ABOUT THE ADVERTISEMENTS

1. The first ad is in support of women who work in railroad jobs. Study the ad. How can you tell that the ad supports this?

   _____

2. The most important purpose of the second advertisement is to sell train tickets. What is a secondary, or less important, purpose?

   _____

READING SKILL

3. To what emotion does the first advertisement appeal?

   _____

4. On what part of train travel does the second ad focus most?

   _____

TIMED WRITING: COMPARISON (20 minutes)

Compare and contrast these two advertisements. Be sure to answer the following questions in your comparison.

- How are the two ads the same?

   _____

- How are the two ads different?

   _____

- What kind of appeal does each ad make?

   _____

- What words or pictures does each ad use to persuade customers to use the product or service?

   _____

Making Tracks on Mars:
A Journal Based on a Blog

Essays and articles are types of nonfiction. These types of nonfiction discuss real people, events, places, and ideas. You can explore these pieces to:

- learn about the lives of others
- find important information
- reflect on new ideas
- look at arguments about important issues

Organization is the way a writer arranges information in a piece of nonfiction. The chart below contains different types of organization. Many pieces of nonfiction use a combination of these types of organization. It depends on the author's reasons for writing.

Types of Organization	
Organization	**Characteristics**
Chronological Organization	presents details in time order—from first to last— or sometimes from last to first
Comparison-and-Contrast Organization	shows the ways in which two or more subjects are similar and different
Cause-and-Effect Organization	shows the relationship among events
Problem-and-Solution Organization	identifies a problem and then proposes a solution

Author's tone is the writer's attitude toward his or her audience and subject. This tone can often be described by a single adjective, such as: *formal* or *informal*, *serious* or *playful*, *friendly* or *cold*.

Voice is a writer's way of "speaking" in his or her writing. One writer could write a piece in one voice. Then, he or she could write in a different voice in another work. Voice may also represent a characteristic literary personality. Voice can be based on

- word choice
- tone
- sound devices
- pace
- grammatical structure

Here are the most common types of nonfiction writing:

- **Letters:** written texts addressed to a certain person or organization

- **Memoirs and journals:** personal thoughts and reflections

- **Web logs** (also known as "blogs"): journals posted and often updated for an online audience

- **Biography:** a life story written by another person

- **Autobiography:** a writer's account of her or her own life

- **Media accounts:** nonfiction works written for newspapers, magazines, television, or radio

Essays and **articles** are short nonfiction works about a certain subject. They may follow the structure of these types of writing:

- **Persuasive writing:** convinces the reader that he or she should have a certain opinion or take a certain action

- **Expository writing:** presents facts or explains a process

- **Narrative writing:** tells the story of real-life experiences

- **Reflective writing:** looks at an experience and has the writer's thoughts about the event's importance

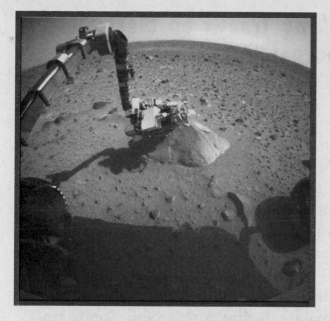

Making Tracks on Mars: A Journal Based on a Blog

Andrew Mishkin

Summary Andrew Mishkin talks about the landing of the rover, *Spirit*, on Mars. The rover explores the planet. It experiences some problems. Mishkin describes his excitement and worry. He also talks about another Mars rover, *Opportunity*. He describes the pictures it takes of Mars.

Note-taking Guide

Use the chart to recall the main events of Mishkin's journal.

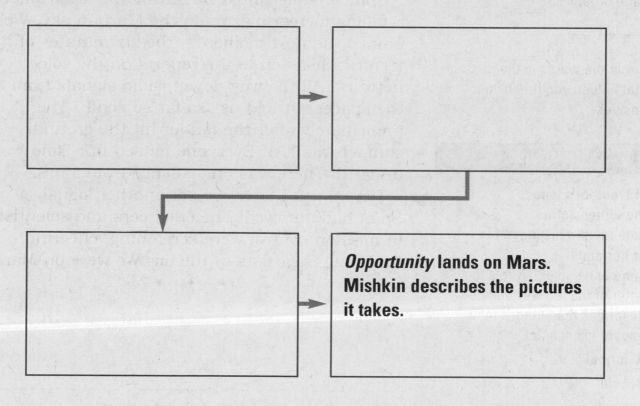

Opportunity lands on Mars. Mishkin describes the pictures it takes.

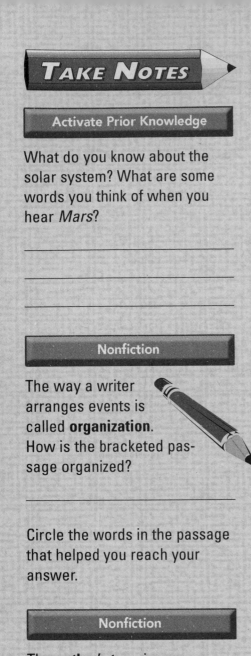

TAKE NOTES

Activate Prior Knowledge

What do you know about the solar system? What are some words you think of when you hear *Mars*?

_____

_____

_____

Nonfiction

The way a writer arranges events is called **organization**. How is the bracketed passage organized?

_____

Circle the words in the passage that helped you reach your answer.

Nonfiction

The **author's tone** is the writer's attitude toward his or her audience and subject. Circle the letter of the answer that best describes the author's tone toward his subject.

A. formal

B. cold

C. excited

Underline the words and phrases that support your choice.

Making Tracks on Mars: A Journal Based on a Blog
Andrew Mishkin

◆ ◆ ◆

The journal opens with the question of whether life ever existed on Mars. We know that water is needed for life as we know it. Mars appears to have no water, but what about in the past? Two robotic explorers are scheduled to land on the planet soon. In six days, *Spirit* will arrive there. Three weeks later, *Opportunity* will. The author talks about a British spacecraft that tried to land on Mars five days earlier but has sent back no signals. The author hopes that *Spirit* lands smoothly. Saturday, January 3, 2004, is landing day.

◆ ◆ ◆

Spirit's lander must be hitting the atmosphere, a falling meteor blazing in the Martian sky. We'd named the next moments "the six minutes of terror." I listened to the reports on the voice network. All the way down, radio signals from the spacecraft told us "so far so good." Then, immediately after the lander hit the ground, contact was lost. Everyone tensed up. Time dragged. There was only silence from Mars.

Ten minutes later, we got another signal. *Spirit* had survived! The engineers and scientists in mission control were screaming, cheering, thrusting their fists in the air. We were on Mars!

◆ ◆ ◆

Vocabulary Development

meteor (MEE tee er) *n.*   a small piece of rock or metal that produces a bright burning line in the sky

Pictures start arriving from *Spirit* within two hours. The pictures are clear. They show the view through *Spirit's* eyes from the landing site. The next entry is January 11, 2004. The engineers are working on Mars time. The next task is to send a signal commanding *Spirit* to drive around and take some pictures.

◆ ◆ ◆

The Mars day (called a "sol") is just a bit longer than an Earth day, at twenty-four hours and thirty-nine and a half minutes. Since the rover is solar powered, and wakes with the sun, its activities are tied to the Martian day. And so are the work shifts of our operations team on Earth. Part of the team works the Martian day, interacting with the spacecraft, sending commands, and analyzing the results. But those of us who build new commands for the rover work the Martian night, while the rover sleeps.

◆ ◆ ◆

It is difficult for the engineers to keep track of time. Because the rover wakes up about forty Earth minutes later each day, so do the engineers. By January 15, the author is getting Mars time and Earth time mixed up.

◆ ◆ ◆

My team delivered the commands for sol 12—drive off day—but nobody went home. This would be *Spirit's* most dangerous day since landing. There was a small chance the rover could tip over or get stuck as it rolled off the lander platform onto the dust of Mars. When the time came, the Flight Director played the theme from "Rawhide"—"rollin', rollin', rollin'…"[1]—and everyone crowded into mission control cheered and applauded. The command to drive shot through space.

◆ ◆ ◆

---

1. **"Rawhide"** popular 1960s television show about cattle drivers in the 1860s. Its theme song was also extremely popular.

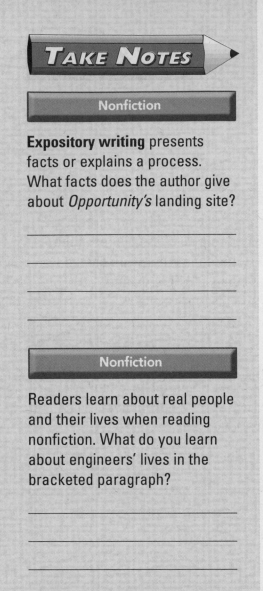
Expository writing presents facts or explains a process. What facts does the author give about *Opportunity's* landing site?

_____

_____

_____

_____

Readers learn about real people and their lives when reading nonfiction. What do you learn about engineers' lives in the bracketed paragraph?

_____

_____

_____

What happened to the rover *Opportunity*? Underline the sentences in the text that tell you.

Even though they have done their jobs, the engineers continue to worry about what might go wrong. On January 15, twelve days after the landing, they get a signal from *Spirit*. Images begin to appear. They see wheel tracks in the Martian soil. Knowing that *Spirit* has obeyed the command to move, the engineers go wild with applause and joy. By January 22, the rover stops responding. The engineers try for days to fix the problem. Finally, they start receiving data from Spirit. It is garbled, but now they have something to work with.

Meanwhile, *Opportunity*, the second rover, has been approaching Mars. It lands safely and begins to take photos.

♦ ♦ ♦

Opportunity's first photos were amazing, even for Mars. It looks like we rolled to a stop at the bottom of a bowl—actually a small <u>crater</u>. The soil is a grayish red, except where we've disturbed it with our airbags; there it looks like a deep pure red.

♦ ♦ ♦

Opportunity also sends back pictures of a rock outcropping. This is unlike anything ever seen on Mars before. One scientist in mission control says, "Jackpot!"

Vocabulary Development

crater (KRAY ter) *n.* a round hole in the ground

Types of Nonfiction

1. **Infer:** A British spacecraft tried to land on Mars. It failed. Why does Mishkin mention this failure?

   _____

   _____

2. **Speculate:** Mishkin sometimes talks about the robot as if it were a person. Why do you think he does this?

   _____

   _____

   _____

3. **Nonfiction: Reflective writing** includes the writer's insights about an event's importance. Use the chart to identify one personal **reflection** of Mishkin's. Write a related fact or event that created the reflection.

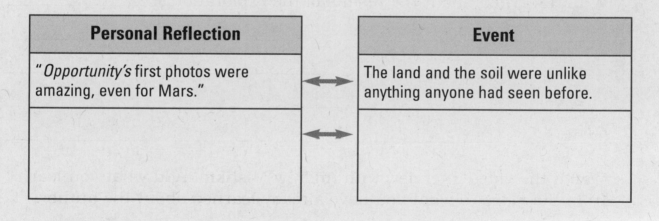

Personal Reflection	Event
"*Opportunity's* first photos were amazing, even for Mars."	The land and the soil were unlike anything anyone had seen before.

4. **Nonfiction: Voice** is a writer's way of "speaking" in his or her writing. Mishkin's voice is more casual than literary. Do you agree or disagree? Explain.

   _____

   _____

   _____

RESEARCH THE AUTHOR

Illustrated Report

Prepare an **illustrated report** about Andrew Mishkin and the Mars mission. Use the following tips to create your report.

- Search the Internet or the library for information on Andrew Mishkin.

  What I learned about Andrew Mishkin: _____

  _____

  _____

  _____

- Search the Internet or the library for information on the Mars mission.

  What I learned about the goals of the mission: _____

  _____

  _____

  _____

  What I learned about the results of the exploration: _____

  _____

  _____

  _____

  _____

- Watch the video interview with Andrew Mishkin. Add what you learn from the video to what you have already learned about the author.

  Additional information about the author: _____

  _____

  _____

  _____

Use your notes to write your illustrated report.

Harriet Tubman: Guide to Freedom • Baseball

READING SKILL

A nonfiction writing piece has a **main idea**. A main idea is the author's central message. Sometimes an author explains the main idea to the reader. Other times an author hints at, or implies, the main idea.

Look at how details are connected to **identify the implied main idea**. Try to see what the details have in common. You should then be able to figure out the main idea of a passage or work.

LITERARY ANALYSIS

A **narrative essay** tells the story of real events, people, and places. Narrative essays have some things in common with fictional stories. For example, both have these parts:

- People's traits are developed through things they say, do, and think.

- The setting of the action may be important.

Use this chart to track the elements of a narrative essay.

Narrative Essay		
Setting(s)	People	Event(s)

Harriet Tubman: Guide to Freedom

Ann Petry

Summary Harriet Tubman led a group of enslaved persons from Maryland to freedom in Canada. The trip was cold and difficult. Tubman worked hard to keep them going. She said that people would help them along the way.

Reading/Writing Connection

Think about leading a group of people who are trying to escape to safety. Write three sentences telling how you would keep the group going.

1. They should <u>rely</u> on _____.

2. They would have to <u>minimize</u> _____.

3. Friends would need to <u>assist</u> _____.

Note-taking Guide

Use this chart to help you recall the plans Harriet Tubman made.

How did Tubman let slaves know that she was in the area?	
How did Tubman let the slaves know when to leave?	
Whom did Tubman arrange to stay with along the journey?	
Where did Tubman plan for the people to stay when they got to Canada?	

Harriet Tubman: Guide to Freedom

1. **Analyze Causes and Effects:** One of the runaway slaves said that he was going back. Tubman points a gun at him. Explain why she believes that she must act this way.

_____

_____

2. **Assess:** Think about Tubman as a leader in today's world. Do you think she would be successful? Why or why not?

_____

_____

_____

3. **Reading Skill:** Use the chart to write a detail you learned about Tubman. Look at all of the details. The **main idea** of a work of nonfiction is the central point that the author makes. What is the main idea the author shows about Tubman? Write your answer in the chart.

Detail		Detail		Detail		Main Idea
If she were caught, she would be hanged.	+	She hid the fact that she did not know the new route.	+		=	

4. **Literary Analysis:** A **narrative essay** tells the story of real events, people, and places. List the two most important events in this narrative essay.

_____

_____

SUPPORT FOR WRITING AND EXTEND YOUR LEARNING

Writing: Biographical Sketch

Write a **biographical sketch** of a person who has taken risks to help others or to reach a goal. Use your notes from the questions below to create your sketch.

- What risks did this person take?

  _____

  _____

- What event or action happened that caused this person to take a risk?

  _____

  _____

- What was the result of the person's risk-taking?

  _____

  _____

Research and Technology: Annotated Timeline

Research the history of slavery from 1740 to 1865. Use your notes from the questions below to create an **annotated timeline**.

- What are three important events that happened between 1740 and 1865?

  _____

  _____

  _____

- What were the results of the events?

  _____

  _____

  _____

Baseball

Lionel G. García

Summary The author shares a memory from his childhood in this story. He describes the new rules of baseball that he and his childhood friends invented. García presents a snapshot into the world of a young Catholic boy through this story.

Reading/Writing Connection

Think about the way you play games. Do you like being part of a team? Would you rather play games with your friends? Complete each sentence.

1. Neighborhood games <u>involve</u> _____.

2. Some neighborhoods <u>maintain</u> _____.

3. Professional teams <u>select</u> _____.

Note-taking Guide

García explains how he used to play baseball in his neighborhood. Use this chart to describe the role of each player in the game.

Catcher	Batter	Pitcher	Bases	Outfielders

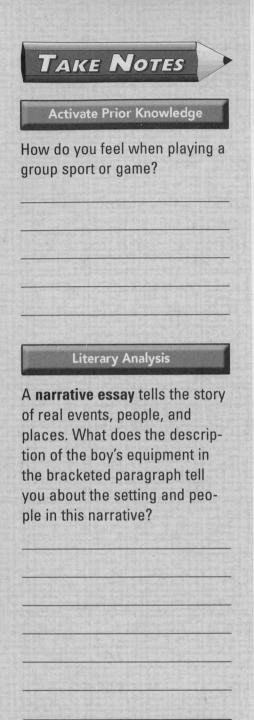

Baseball

Lionel G. García

We loved to play baseball. We would take the old mesquite[1] stick and the old ball across the street to the parochial[2] school grounds to play a game. Father Zavala enjoyed watching us. We could hear him laugh mightily from the screened porch at the rear of the rectory[3] where he sat.

The way we played baseball was to <u>rotate</u> positions after every out. First base, the only base we used, was located where one would normally find second base. This made the batter have to run past the pitcher and a long way to the first baseman, increasing the odds of getting thrown out. The pitcher stood in line with the batter, and with first base, and could stand as close or as far from the batter as he or she wanted. Aside from the pitcher, the batter and the first baseman, we had a catcher. All the rest of us would stand in the outfield. After an out, the catcher would come up to bat. The pitcher took the position of catcher, and the first baseman moved up to be the pitcher. Those in the outfield were left to their own <u>devices</u>. I don't remember ever getting to bat.

◆　◆　◆

Another rule of the children's game was that the player who caught a ball on the fly would become the next batter. Also, first base was wherever Matías, Juan, or Cota tossed a stone. The size of the stone was more important than how far it fell from

---

Take Notes

Activate Prior Knowledge

How do you feel when playing a group sport or game?

_____

_____

_____

_____

Literary Analysis

A **narrative essay** tells the story of real events, people, and places. What does the description of the boy's equipment in the bracketed paragraph tell you about the setting and people in this narrative?

_____

_____

_____

_____

_____

Reading Check

Who enjoyed watching the boys play baseball? Underline the sentence that tells you.

Vocabulary Development

rotate (ROH tayt) *v.*　change

devices (di VYS iz) *n.*　techniques or means for working things out

---

1. **mesquite** (me SKEET) *n.* thorny shrub of North America.
2. **parochial** (puh ROH kee uhl) *adj.* supported by a church.
3. **rectory** (REK tuhr ee) *n.* residence for priests.

home plate. First base was sometimes hard to find as it started to get dark.

◆   ◆   ◆

When the batter hit the ball in the air and it was caught that was an out. So far so good. But if the ball hit the ground, the fielder had two choices. One, in keeping with the standard rules of the game, the ball could be thrown to the first baseman and, if caught before the batter arrived at the base, that was an out. But the second, more interesting option allowed the fielder, ball in hand, to take off running after the batter. When close enough, the fielder would throw the ball at the batter. If the batter was hit before reaching first base, the batter was out. But if the batter evaded being hit with the ball, he or she could either run to first base or run back to home plate. All the while, everyone was chasing the batter, picking up the ball and throwing it at him or her. To complicate matters, on the way to home plate the batter had the choice of running anywhere possible to avoid getting hit.

◆   ◆   ◆

Sometimes the batters hid behind trees until they could reach home plate. Sometimes they ran several blocks toward town. In one game, the children ended up across town. They cornered the batter, held him down, and hit him with the ball. The tired players all fell down laughing in a pile. The men in town watched these unusual games, but they did not understand them.

◆   ◆   ◆

It was the only kind of baseball game Father Zavala had ever seen. What a wonderful game it must have been for him to see us hit the ball,

---

TAKE NOTES

Reading Skill

The **main idea** of a nonfiction work is the author's central message. Often, the author suggests the main idea. Read the bracketed passage. What main idea is implied? Circle the details that support this main idea.

_____

_____

Read Fluently

One way to organize a list of details in a paragraph is to use a number system. You could write *first, second,* and *third.* Another choice would be *one, two,* and *three.* The author uses a number system to tell about the fielder's choices in the bracketed paragraph. Underline the key words he uses to organize his list.

Stop to Reflect

Name one difference between this game and regular baseball.

_____

_____

_____

_____

Vocabulary Development

standard (STAN derd) *adj.*   typical, ordinary
option (AHP shuhn) *n.*   choice
evaded (i VAYD id) *v.*   avoided

Literary Analysis

In this **narrative essay**, the narrator discusses two people who watched the game. Compare Father Zavala's view of the neighborhood game with that of Uncle Adolfo. Who enjoys watching the boys more? Why do you think he enjoys watching them more?

_____

_____

_____

Reading Check

What did García's uncle say when he saw how the children were playing baseball? Underline the sentence that tells the answer.

run to a rock, then run for our lives down the street. He loved the game, shouting from the screened porch at us, pushing us on. And then all of a sudden we were gone, running after the batter. What a game! In what enormous stadium would it be played to allow such freedom over such an <u>expanse</u> of ground.

◆ ◆ ◆

García's Uncle Adolfo had been a major league pitcher. He had given the ball to the children. When he saw how the children played the sport, he said that they were wasting a good baseball.

Vocabulary Development

expanse (ik SPANS) *n.*   a large area

Baseball

1. **Analyze Cause and Effect:** Think about where first base was located in García's version of baseball. How did this location of the base affect the way he and his friends played the game?

_____

_____

2. **Take a Position:** García's Uncle Adolfo played baseball for the Yankees as a young man. When he sees the way García and his friends are playing the game, he says that they are wasting a good baseball. Do you agree with his statement? Explain.

_____

_____

3. **Reading Skill:** Read the details about the baseball game listed in the diagram below. Then, write a sentence that states the **main idea**.

Detail		Detail		Detail		Main Idea
The boys did not have good equipment.	+	The boys did not know official baseball rules.	+	The children's version involved everyone running after the batter.	=	

4. **Literary Analysis:** A setting describes the place and time of a story. Identify the setting in this **narrative essay**.

_____

_____

SUPPORT FOR WRITING AND EXTEND YOUR LEARNING

Writing: Biographical Sketch

Write a **biographical sketch** of a famous leader, athlete, or entertainer who ignored the old rules for success and found a new way to do something. Use this chart to organize details about the person you choose. Use your notes as you write your biographical sketch.

What is this person's name?	Name three things that describe this person.	What is this person known for doing?	How did this person find a different way of doing something?

Listening and Speaking: Skit

Write a **skit** about children playing official baseball or a variation of it. Answer the following questions to help prepare your skit. Use your notes as you write your final draft.

• Where is your favorite place to play baseball?

_____

_____

• What do you do if there are not enough or too many players?

_____

_____

_____

_____

• Name one baseball rule you dislike. How would you change it?

_____

_____

_____

_____

from I Know Why the Caged Bird Sings •
from Always to Remember:
The Vision of Maya Ying Lin

READING SKILL

Main ideas are the most important parts of a piece of writing. Writers often follow the main idea with supporting paragraphs. **Make connections** between supporting paragraphs and the main idea to follow the writer's path in an essay.

- Stop to look at the main ideas of paragraphs or sections.

- Write the main ideas and important details in notes.

Read the example in the chart below. Then, fill the empty boxes with main ideas and supporting details from the essays.

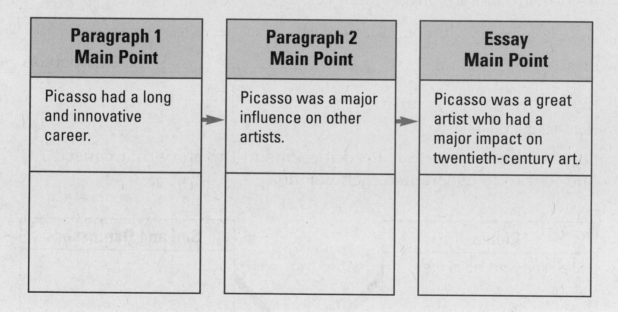

Paragraph 1 Main Point	Paragraph 2 Main Point	Essay Main Point
Picasso had a long and innovative career.	Picasso was a major influence on other artists.	Picasso was a great artist who had a major impact on twentieth-century art.

LITERARY ANALYSIS

- A **biographical essay** is a short piece of writing. The writer tells about an important event in the life of another person.

- An **autobiographical essay** is also a short piece of writing. The writer tells about an event in his or her own life. The writer shares his or her thoughts and feelings.

from I Know Why the Caged Bird Sings

Maya Angelou

Summary In this story, the writer describes growing up in her grandmother's house in Stamps, Arkansas. She describes her friendship with a woman named Mrs. Flowers. Mrs. Flowers introduces her to poetry.

Reading/Writing Connection

Complete this paragraph. Describe a relative, teacher, coach, or friend who has inspired you.

It is a <u>benefit</u> to spend time with _____. He or she can <u>challenge</u> _____. This person <u>devotes</u> _____.

Note-taking Guide

Look at the chart below. Record events in the story that caused Marguerite to experience each emotion.

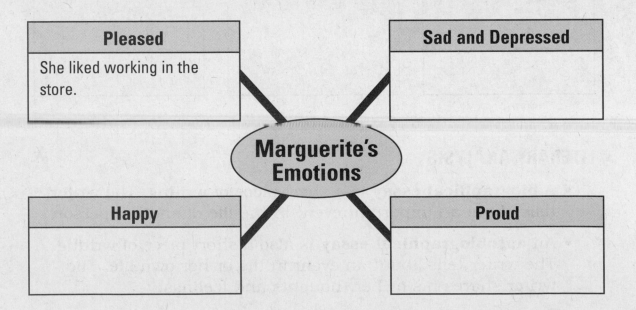

Pleased
She liked working in the store.

Sad and Depressed

Marguerite's Emotions

Happy

Proud

from I Know Why the Caged Bird Sings

1. **Infer:** Some customers tell Marguerite that she is cheating them. How does she feel when customers accuse her of cheating?

_____

2. **Interpret:** The author writes that Mrs. Flowers was "the lady who threw me my first lifeline." Lifelines are used to save people from drowning. What does the author mean by these words?

_____

_____

3. **Reading Skill: Main ideas** are the most important points in a story. Write three main ideas from the section about Mrs. Flowers.

_____

_____

_____

4. **Literary Analysis:** This story is an **autobiographical essay**. The writer tells a story about an important event in her own life. Complete this chart with details about her life.

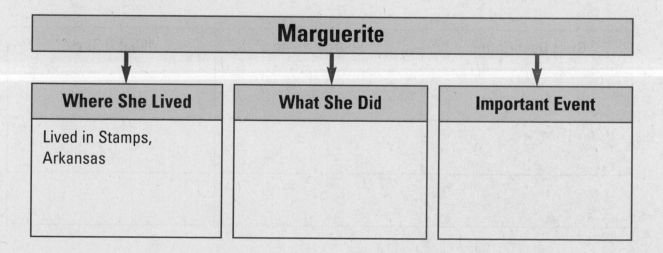

Marguerite		
Where She Lived	**What She Did**	**Important Event**
Lived in Stamps, Arkansas		

SUPPORT FOR WRITING AND EXTEND YOUR LEARNING

Writing: Reflective Composition

Write a **reflective composition** about a story, poem, play, or novel that made an impression on you. Answer the questions below. Use your notes to help you organize your reflective composition.

- What is the name of the work you have chosen? Why is it important to you?

  _____

  _____

  _____

- What will be the main points of your composition?

  _____

  _____

- What details will you use to support your main points?

  _____

  _____

Research and Technology: Proposal for a Multimedia Presentation

Write a **proposal for a multimedia presentation** about the Great Depression. In the first column, write a brief description of any quotations, photos, music, or artwork you found. In the second column, write the source the media came from. In the third column, write what your media says about the Depression.

Brief Description	Source Name	What It Says

from Always to Remember: The Vision of Maya Ying Lin

Brent Ashabranner

Summary In the early 1980s, more than 2,500 people entered a competition to design a memorial. The men and women who lost their lives in the Vietnam War would be honored by the memorial. This essay describes the competition. It also describes the college student who wins.

Reading/Writing Connection

What kinds of characteristics should a memorial have? Finish each sentence.

1. A memorial should <u>capture</u> _____.

2. It is important that a memorial <u>communicate</u> _____.

3. A monument should deeply <u>impress</u> _____.

Note-taking Guide

Use this chart to record details about the winning design for the Vietnam Veterans Memorial.

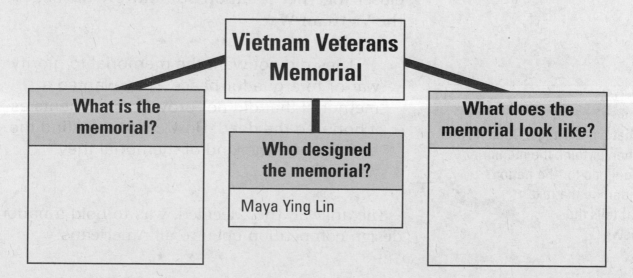

Vietnam Veterans Memorial

What is the memorial?

Who designed the memorial?

Maya Ying Lin

What does the memorial look like?

Think about a memorial or statue you have seen. What was it? Write two details you remember about it.

_____

_____

_____

_____

_____

Reading Skill

The **main ideas** are the most important points of the work. The author **makes connections** between a main idea and paragraphs that support it. Underline the **main idea** in the bracketed passage.

Reading Check

What did Scruggs, Doubek, and Wheeler think the memorial should do for the nation? Underline the text that tells the answer.

from Always To Remember: The Vision of Maya Ying Lin
Brent Ashabranner

This nonfiction selection tells the true story of how a young college student named Maya Lin came to design the Vietnam Veterans Memorial in Washington, D.C.

♦ ♦ ♦

In the 1960s and 1970s, the United States was involved in a war in Vietnam. Because many people opposed the war, Vietnam veterans were not honored as veterans of other wars had been. Jan Scruggs, a Vietnam veteran, thought that the 58,000 U.S. servicemen and women killed or reported missing in Vietnam should be honored with a memorial.

♦ ♦ ♦

Scruggs got two lawyers named Robert Doubek and John Wheeler to help him get support for building a memorial. In 1980, Congress agreed that a memorial should be built.

♦ ♦ ♦

What would the memorial be? What should it look like? Who would design it? Scruggs, Doubek, and Wheeler didn't know, but they were determined that the memorial should help bring closer together a nation still bitterly divided by the Vietnam War.

♦ ♦ ♦

They did not want the memorial to glorify war or to argue for peace. They wanted a memorial that did not provoke arguments as it honored the dead. How could they find the best idea for the kind of memorial they wanted?

♦ ♦ ♦

The answer, they decided, was to hold a national design competition open to all Americans.

♦ ♦ ♦

The winner of the competition would receive a $20,000 prize. More important, the winner would have the honor of being part of American history. The memorial would be built in Washington, D.C., between the Washington Monument and the Lincoln Memorial. This part of the city is called the Mall.

More than 5,000 Americans asked for the booklet that told the rules of the competition. Many of them were well-known architects and sculptors. The booklet told what kind of memorial would win the competition.

◆ ◆ ◆

The memorial could not make a political statement about the war; it must contain the names of all persons killed or missing in action in the war; it must be in <u>harmony</u> with its location on the Mall.

◆ ◆ ◆

More than one thousand designs were submitted for the competition. Eight judges had to decide which design best met the standards for winning: The memorial had to honor the memory of the soldiers who had died in the war. It had to blend in with the other monuments nearby. It had to be an important work of art. It also had to be practical to build and take care of.

The designs were displayed in an airplane hangar. They were labeled by number, instead of showing the designer's name, so that the judges could be objective. On May 1, 1981, the judges chose the winner and praised the winning design.

◆ ◆ ◆

TAKE NOTES

Reading Skill

Underline one detail that supports the **main idea** that the winner would be a part of American history.

Read Fluently

Read the bracketed passage. Semicolons show a break between clauses, or complete sentence parts. What is another way to separate clauses?

_____

Literary Analysis

A **biographical essay** describes an important event in the life of a person. What person do you think this essay is going to be about?

_____

_____

Reading Check

How many designs were submitted in the competition? Underline the sentence that tells you.

Vocabulary Development

harmony (HAR muh nee) *n.* a situation in which things or people are at peace or in agreement with one another

This memorial, with its wall of names, becomes a place of quiet reflection, and a <u>tribute</u> to those who served their nation in difficult times. All who come here can find it a place of healing. This will be a quiet memorial, one that achieves an excellent relationship with both the Lincoln Memorial and Washington Monument, and relates the visitor to them. It is uniquely horizontal, entering the earth rather than piercing the sky.

◆ ◆ ◆

Americans were amazed when they learned that the winner of the contest was not a famous architect or sculptor. She was a 21-year-old college student named Maya Lin.

◆ ◆ ◆

Maya Lin, reporters soon discovered, was a Chinese-American girl who had been born and raised in the small midwestern city of Athens, Ohio. Her father, Henry Huan Lin, was a ceramicist of <u>considerable</u> reputation and dean of fine arts at Ohio University in Athens. Her mother, Julia C. Lin, was a poet and professor of Oriental and English literature.

◆ ◆ ◆

Maya Lin's parents were immigrants from China. Maya had always been interested in art, especially sculpture. At Yale University, she decided to major in architecture. She became interested in cemetery architecture, especially when she visited cemeteries in Europe, which were also used as parks.

In her senior year at Yale, one of Maya Lin's professors asked his students to enter

Reading Skill

Read the bracketed passage. Underline the **main idea** of the passage.

Literary Analysis

Why did the author of this **biographical essay** include details about Maya Ying Lin's family and background?

_____

_____

_____

Stop to Reflect

What effect do you think Maya Ying Lin's interest in cemeteries had on her entry into the competition?

_____

_____

_____

Vocabulary Development

tribute (TRIB yoot) *n.* something that shows respect for someone or something

considerable (kuhn SI der uh buhl) *adj.* large enough to have a noticeable effect the Vietnam Veterans Memorial competition as a class assignment. Maya and two of her classmates traveled to Washington, D.C., to look at the site where the memorial would be built. While she was there, Maya was inspired. In her mind, she saw a vision of the memorial she wanted to design. Like the cemetery designs she had seen in Europe, her design fit in with the land around it and would maintain the site as a park.

◆ ◆ ◆

"When I looked at the site I just knew I wanted something horizontal that took you in, that made you feel safe within the park, yet at the same time reminding you of the dead. So I just imagined opening up the earth. . . ."

◆ ◆ ◆

Back at Yale, Maya made a clay model of her vision and then drew the design on paper. She mailed in her entry just in time to make the deadline. A month later, she got a call from Washington, D.C. She had won the competition. Her design would be used to build the Vietnam Veterans Memorial.

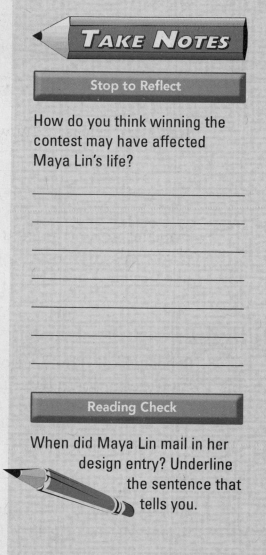

from Always to Remember: The Vision of Maya Ying Lin

1. **Draw Conclusions:** Why was Maya Ying Lin's win so surprising?

   _____

   _____

2. **Evaluate:** Reread pages 150 and 151. Explain whether you think Maya Ying Lin's memorial met the design criteria.

   _____

   _____

3. **Reading Skill:** The section about Maya Ying Lin on pages 152–153 includes information about her background. Reread these pages. Construct a sentence that states the **main idea** of the section.

   _____

   _____

4. **Literary Analysis:** This **biographical essay** gives information about the life of Maya Ying Lin. Complete this chart with details from the essay.

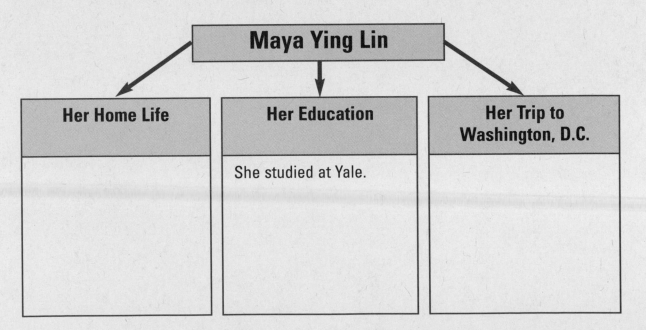

Maya Ying Lin		
Her Home Life	**Her Education**	**Her Trip to Washington, D.C.**
	She studied at Yale.	

SUPPORT FOR WRITING AND EXTEND YOUR LEARNING

Writing: Reflective Composition

Write a **reflective composition** in which you discuss a work of fine art or music that is inspiring. Answer the following questions. Use your notes to help you write your composition.

- What item or piece of art did you choose to write about? Why did you choose it?

  _____

- Describe the piece of art or music you chose.

  _____

  _____

- What could be the main points of your composition? How could you support these points?

  _____

  _____

Listening and Speaking: Memorial Speech

Write a **memorial speech** about a person, place, or event that you believe is significant. Use this chart to help you to organize ideas about possible topics for your speech. Also, write reasons why each would be a good topic for your speech.

Name an important person whom you admire.	
Name an event that you think is important.	
Name a place you have visited that is important to you.	

Textbooks

ABOUT TEXTBOOKS

A **textbook** is a nonfiction book that presents information about one subject such as math, history, or science. Different textbooks are alike in some ways.

- **Purpose:** Textbooks present information to students. The writer starts with a main idea and builds around it.
- **Structure:** Most textbooks have sections, chapters, or units. The table of contents lists the titles and page numbers of these parts.
- **Text Format:** Type size, color, and boldface type are used. They highlight key words or sections.

READING SKILL

Most textbooks have a great deal of information. Sometimes you need to find something quickly. You can **skim** and **scan** instead of reading every word.

- **Skimming** is glancing to get a general idea of the meaning.
- **Scanning** is looking for specific words or ideas.

Use the tips in this chart to find information in a textbook.

Tips for Skimming and Scanning	
Skim the table of contents to find the chapter you need.	**Scan** the index at the back of the book to find information on your topic.
Skim the first sentence of paragraphs that might include the information you need.	**Scan** the headings to find the main idea of each chapter.

The War in Vietnam

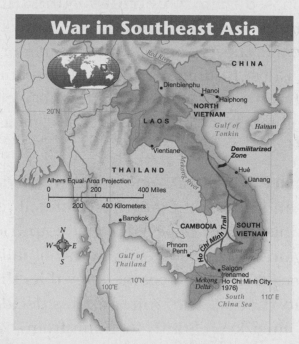

War in Southeast Asia

Early Involvement in Vietnam

Vietnam is a narrow country that stretches about 1,000 miles along the South China Sea. Since the late 1800s, it had been ruled by France as a colony.

The United States became involved in Vietnam slowly, step by step. During the 1940s, Ho Chi Minh (HO CHEE MIHN), a Vietnamese nationalist and a Communist, had led the fight for independence. Ho's army finally defeated the French in 1954.

An international peace conference divided Vietnam into two countries. Ho Chi Minh led communist North Vietnam. Ngo Dinh Diem (NOH DIN dee EHM) was the noncommunist leader of South Vietnam. In the Cold War world, the Soviet Union supported North Vietnam. The United States backed Diem in the south.

Discontent Diem lost popular support during the 1950s. Many South Vietnamese thought that he favored wealthy landlords and was corrupt. He failed to help the nation's peasant majority and ruled with a heavy hand. As discontent grew,

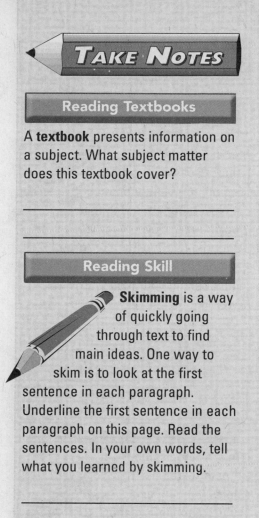

TAKE NOTES

Reading Textbooks

A **textbook** presents information on a subject. What subject matter does this textbook cover?

_____

_____

Reading Skill

Skimming is a way of quickly going through text to find main ideas. One way to skim is to look at the first sentence in each paragraph. Underline the first sentence in each paragraph on this page. Read the sentences. In your own words, tell what you learned by skimming.

_____

_____

Reading Textbooks

Graphics, such as the map on this page, provide additional information. Name a country that borders Vietnam.

_____

_____

Reading Check

Which did the United States support, North Vietnam or South Vietnam? Circle the text that tells you.

Scanning is looking for specific words or ideas. Scan this page to find out what happened in November 1963. Begin by looking for "November 1963." Underline it. Read two or three sentences around it to find what you need. In your own words, tell what happened.

_____

_____

_____

Reading Textbooks

Text format is important in textbooks. It helps you find and understand information. On this page, type size and boldface are both used. Circle an example of each. Then, explain how they help you understand the information on this page.

Type size:

_____

_____

Boldface:

_____

_____

many peasants joined the **Vietcong**— guerrillas who opposed Diem. **Guerrillas** (guh RIHL uhz) are fighters who make hit-and-run attacks on the enemy. They do not wear uniforms or fight in large battles. In time, the Vietcong became communist and were supported by North Vietnam. Vietcong influence quickly spread, especially in the villages.

American Aid Vietcong successes worried American leaders. If South Vietnam fell to communism, they believed, other countries in the region would follow—like a row of falling dominoes. This idea became known as the **domino theory**. The United States decided that it must keep South Vietnam from becoming the first domino.

During the 1950s and 1960s, Presidents Eisenhower and Kennedy sent financial aid and military advisers to South Vietnam. The advisers went to help train the South Vietnamese army, not to fight the Vietcong. Diem, however, continued to lose support. In November 1963, Diem was assassinated. A few weeks later, President John F. Kennedy was assassinated. Vice President Lyndon Baines Johnson became President.

The Fighting in Vietnam Expands

Lyndon Johnson was also determined to keep South Vietnam from falling to the communists. He increased aid to South Vietnam, sending more arms and advisers. Still, the Vietcong continued to make gains.

Gulf of Tonkin Resolution In August 1964, President Johnson announced that North Vietnamese torpedo boats had attacked an American ship patrolling the Gulf of Tonkin off the coast of North Vietnam. At Johnson's urging,

Congress passed the Gulf of Tonkin Resolution. It allowed the President "to take all necessary measures to repel any armed attack or to prevent further aggression." Johnson used the resolution to order the bombing of North Vietnam and Vietcong-held areas in the south.

With the Gulf of Tonkin Resolution, the role of Americans in Vietnam changed from military advisers to active fighters. The war in Vietnam escalated, or expanded. By 1968, President Johnson had sent more than 500,000 troops to fight in Vietnam.

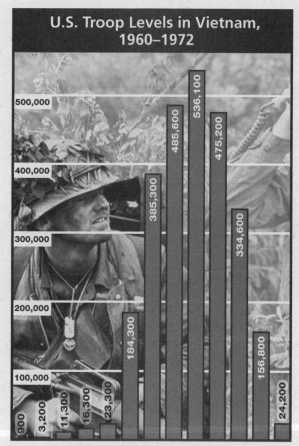

U.S. Troop Levels in Vietnam, 1960–1972

500,000
400,000
300,000
200,000
100,000

900 | 3,200 | 11,300 | 16,300 | 23,300 | 184,300 | 385,300 | 485,600 | 536,100 | 475,200 | 334,600 | 156,800 | 24,200

1960 1961 1962 1963 1964 1965 1966 1967 1968 1969 1970 1971 1972

Source: U.S. Department of Defense

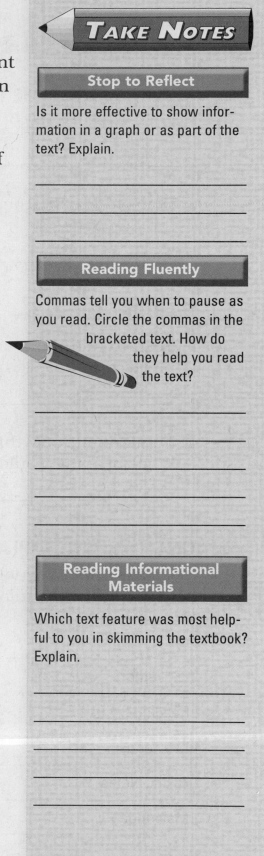

TAKE NOTES

Stop to Reflect

Is it more effective to show information in a graph or as part of the text? Explain.

_____

_____

_____

Reading Fluently

Commas tell you when to pause as you read. Circle the commas in the bracketed text. How do they help you read the text?

_____

_____

_____

_____

Reading Informational Materials

Which text feature was most helpful to you in skimming the textbook? Explain.

_____

_____

_____

_____

THINKING ABOUT THE TEXTBOOK

1. Explain the significance of the domino theory.

   _____

2. How did the Vietcong make fighting even more difficult for the Americans?

   _____

READING SKILL

3. Scan to find the year in which the United States became involved in the Vietnam War. What was the year?

   _____

4. Think about how this textbook's table of contents would look. What heading would you likely find?

   _____

TIMED WRITING: EXPLANATION (20 minutes)

Choose one of the following features. Explain how it could help you learn the information in this chapter. Use this chart to help you.

Feature	How It Could Help Me
Reading Focus	
Key Terms	
Taking Notes	
Main Idea	

On Woman's Right to Suffrage •
The Trouble With Television

READING SKILL

A **fact** is a statement that can be proved true. An **opinion** is a statement that cannot be proved true. A **generalization** is a conclusion that is supported by facts. An **overgeneralization** is a conclusion that overstates the facts. **Use clue words** to find the different kinds of statements.

- Writers use words such as *best* and *worst* to tell their feelings and beliefs. These words usually state an opinion.

- Words such as *therefore*, *so*, and *because* connect facts. These words may signal a generalization. Words such as *always*, *never*, and *only* may signal an overgeneralization.

LITERARY ANALYSIS

Persuasive techniques are tools that a writer uses to try to make people do something or think a certain way. Here are some common persuasive techniques:

- **Repetition:** An author says something more than once.

- **Rhetorical questions:** An author asks questions with obvious answers.

Other common persuasive techniques are in the chart.

Persuasive Techniques
Appeal to Authority
Example: Quotations from experts or reliable sources
Appeal to Emotions
Example: Words that appeal to emotions such as patriotism
Appeal to Reason
Example: Logical arguments based on evidence such as statistics

On Woman's Right to Suffrage

Susan B. Anthony

Summary Susan B. Anthony gives a speech to United States citizens in 1873. It is a time when women can not vote. She says that the U.S. Constitution protects all people. She says that women should have the same rights as men.

Reading/Writing Connection

Complete this paragraph to describe reasons that the right to vote is important to all citizens of the United States.

Citizens can <u>contribute</u> _____. Voting allows people to <u>participate</u> _____. Voters <u>select</u> the person _____.

Note-taking Guide

Use the graphic organizer to record details that support Susan B. Anthony's argument.

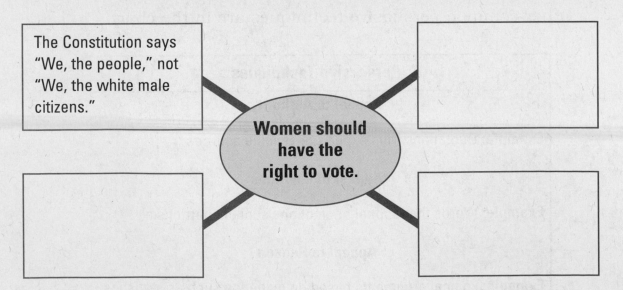

On Woman's Right to Suffrage

1. **Connect:** Anthony tries to vote. She says that she did not break the law. How does she connect this comment to the Constitution?

   _____

   _____

2. **Apply:** Anthony says that a democracy gives rights to all of its citizens. Does Anthony believe that she lives in a true democracy? Explain.

   _____

   _____

3. **Reading Skill:** Determine whether each statement in the chart is a **fact**, an **opinion**, a **generalization**, or an **overgeneralization**. Write your choice next to the statement. Then, explain your choice.

Statement	Type of Statement	Explanation
To [women] this government is...the most hateful aristocracy ever established.		
[I] voted at the last . . . election, without having a lawful right to vote.	Fact	She did try to vote. This was against the law.
Webster . . . define[s] a citizen to be a person entitled to vote.		

4. **Literary Analysis:** Anthony **repeats** "We, the people" throughout her speech. Why does she repeat these words?

   _____

   _____

SUPPORT FOR WRITING AND EXTEND YOUR LEARNING

Writing: Evaluation

Write an **evaluation** of the persuasive arguments in Anthony's speech. Use the questions below to gather ideas for your evaluation.

- What is Anthony's position?

  _____

  _____

- What are two of her arguments?

  _____

  _____

- What are two counterarguments for the arguments you just listed?

  _____

  _____

- How well does Anthony deal with these counterarguments?

  _____

  _____

Use your notes to write your evaluation.

Research and Technology: Statistical Snapshot

Create a **statistical snapshot** of women in the United States. Fill in the chart with the information you found in your research. Complete the chart with questions you could ask in your survey about the information you found.

Facts and Statistics	Questions You Could Ask

The Trouble With Television

Robert MacNeil

Summary Robert MacNeil has worked as a reporter for radio and television. He thinks that watching television keeps people from paying close attention to things. He thinks that television has a bad effect on people.

Reading/Writing Connection

Complete each sentence to list some benefits of watching television.

1. Many nature shows on television <u>appeal</u> to _____.

2. Some television programs can <u>challenge</u> _____.

3. Family programs on television can <u>involve</u> _____.

Note-taking Guide

Use the chart to list the main reasons that MacNeil believes television is a bad influence.

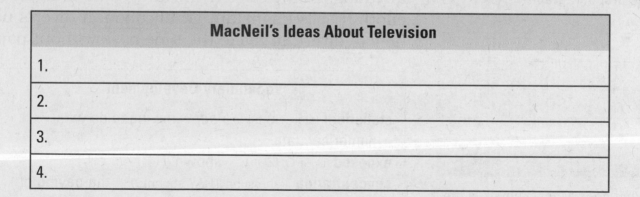

MacNeil's Ideas About Television
1.
2.
3.
4.

Think about television. How often do you watch it? What effect does television have on you? Finish the statement: "I believe that the trouble with television is . . ."

_____

_____

_____

_____

Literary Analysis

Persuasive techniques are ways a writer tries to influence the reader to agree about something. A writer might use facts, or the writer might use words to get an emotional reaction. Sometimes writers repeat ideas or phrases. What **persuasive techniques** does MacNeil use in the first paragraph?

_____

_____

_____

_____

Reading Check

What does MacNeil think is the main problem with television? Underline the sentence that tells you.

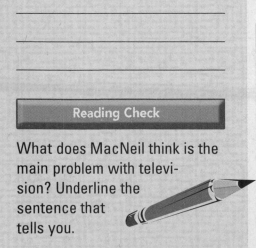

The Trouble With Television
Robert MacNeil

It is difficult to escape the influence of television. If you fit the <u>statistical</u> averages, by the age of 20 you will have been <u>exposed</u> to at least 20,000 hours of television. You can add 10,000 hours for each decade you have lived after the age of 20. The only things Americans do more than watch television are work and sleep.

◆ ◆ ◆

MacNeil points out that time spent watching television could be put to better use. For example, he says that you could earn a college degree instead. You could read classic works of literature in their original languages. Or you could walk around the world and write a book about the experience.

◆ ◆ ◆

The trouble with television is that it discourages <u>concentration</u>. Almost anything interesting and rewarding in life requires some <u>constructive</u>, consistently applied effort. The dullest, the least gifted of us can achieve things that seem miraculous to those who never concentrate on anything. But television encourages us to apply no effort. It sells us instant <u>gratification</u>. It <u>diverts</u> us only to divert, to make the time pass without pain.

Vocabulary Development

statistical (stuh TIS ti kuhl) *adj.*   having to do with numerical data

exposed (ik SPOHZD) *v.*   shown

concentration (kahn suhn TRAY shuhn) *n.*   the paying of close attention

constructive (kuhn STRUK tiv) *adj.*   leading to improvement

gratification (grat uh fuh KAY shuhn) *n.*   the act of pleasing or satisfying

diverts (duh VERTS) *v.*   distracts

Capturing your attention—and holding it—is the prime motive of most television programming and <u>enhances</u> its role as a profitable advertising vehicle. Programmers live in constant fear of losing anyone's attention—anyone's. The surest way to avoid doing so is to keep everything brief, not to strain the attention of anyone but instead to provide constant stimulation through variety, <u>novelty</u>, action and movement. Quite simply, television operates on the appeal to the short attention span.

◆ ◆ ◆

MacNeil is worried about television's effect on the values of our society. He believes that Americans have come to want "fast ideas." He also believes that television news does not accurately portray events. It does not provide viewers with enough details.

◆ ◆ ◆

I believe that TV's appeal to the short attention span is not only inefficient communication but decivilizing as well. Consider the casual assumptions that television tends to cultivate: that complexity must be avoided, that visual stimulation is a substitute for thought, that verbal precision is an anachronism[1]. It may be old-fashioned, but I was taught that thought is words, arranged in grammatically precise ways.

◆ ◆ ◆

MacNeil says that television has caused a crisis of literacy in the United States. About

---

Vocabulary Development

enhances (in HANTS iz) *v.* heightens
novelty (NAHV uhl tee) *n.* the quality of being new

---

1. **anachronism** (uh NAK ruh niz uhm) *n.* anything that seems to be out of its proper place in history.

TAKE NOTES

Literary Analysis

A **persuasive technique** MacNeil uses in this essay is to repeat ideas. Circle one word that is repeated in the first bracketed paragraph.

Reading Skill

A **fact** is information that can be proved. An **opinion** cannot be proved. Read the second bracketed passage. Underline two sentences that tell the author's opinion. Write the word that helped you know that each sentence expressed an opinion.

_____

Stop to Reflect

What do you think the author means by "fast ideas"?

_____
_____
_____
_____

Reading Check

What does MacNeil believe about television's appeal to the short attention span? Underline the text that tells you.

An **overgeneralization** is a conclusion that overstates the facts. Clue words can help you find overgeneralizations. These words may include *always, never, everything, nothing,* and *everyone.* Read the bracketed text. Underline one overgeneralization you find in the text. Then, circle the clue word that helped you identify it.

Read the bracketed text. What **persuasive technique** does MacNeil use in this paragraph? Circle words that help you identify the techniques.

_____

_____

Read the underlined sentence. Circle the most important words in this sentence. Explain why these words are the most important.

_____

_____

_____

30 million Americans cannot read and write well enough to answer a want ad or to understand instructions on a medicine bottle.

◆　◆　◆

Everything about this nation—the structure of the society, its forms of family organization, its economy, its place in the world—has become more complex, not less. Yet its dominating communications instrument, its principal form of national linkage, is one that sells neat resolutions to human problems that usually have no neat resolutions. It is all symbolized in my mind by the hugely successful art form that television has made central to the culture, the thirty-second commercial: the tiny drama of the earnest housewife who finds happiness in choosing the right toothpaste.

◆　◆　◆

In conclusion, MacNeil warns that television threatens our society's values. He believes that television negatively affects our language. He thinks it discourages our interest in complex issues. He calls on others to join him in resisting television's influence.

The Trouble With Television

1. **Connect:** MacNeil says that television shortens our attention span. How do broadcasters add to the problem with the methods they use?

   _____

   _____

2. **Evaluate:** Do you agree that much of the news on television depends on "horrifying pictures" instead of telling the full story? Explain.

   _____

   _____

3. **Reading Skill:** Complete this chart. Identify each statement as a **fact**, an **opinion**, a **generalization**, or an **overgeneralization**. Explain your choice. Follow the example given.

Statement	Type of Statement	Explanation
Almost anything interesting and rewarding in life requires some constructive . . . effort.	Opinion	It is the author's opinion based on personal observation.
But television encourages us to apply no effort.		
. . . by the age of 20 you will have been exposed to at least 20,000 hours of television.		
I think this society is being force fed with trivial fare . . .		

4. **Literary Analysis:** Why does MacNeil **repeat** the idea that television appeals to the short attention span?

   _____

SUPPORT FOR WRITING AND EXTEND YOUR LEARNING

Writing: Evaluation

Write an **evaluation** of the persuasive arguments in MacNeil's essay. Use the questions below to gather ideas for your evaluation.

- What is MacNeil's position?

  _____

  _____

- What are two of his arguments?

  _____

  _____

- What are two counterarguments for the arguments you just listed?

  _____

  _____

- How well does MacNeil deal with these counterarguments?

  _____

  _____

Listening and Speaking: Debate

You will **debate** this topic: "Television viewing for teenagers should be limited to one hour daily during the week." Use the chart to help you prepare. Write information that supports your argument in the first column. Write how you would answer opposing arguments to your research in the second column.

Information From Research	How I Would Answer Opposing Arguments

from Sharing in the American Dream • Science and the Sense of Wonder

READING SKILL

A **fact** is information that can be proved. An **opinion** is a person's judgment or belief. **Ask questions to evaluate an author's support** for his or her opinions.

- A *valid opinion* can be backed up with facts or information from experts.

- A *faulty opinion* cannot be backed up with facts. It is supported by other opinions. It often ignores facts that prove it wrong. Faulty opinions often show *bias*. This is an unfair dislike for something.

Use the chart to help you identify facts and opinions while you are reading.

LITERARY ANALYSIS

An author's **word choice** can help show an idea or feeling. Authors have different reasons for choosing their words. The following are several reasons:

- the author's audience and purpose

- **connotations** of words: the negative or positive ideas connected with words

- **denotations** of words: the dictionary definition of words

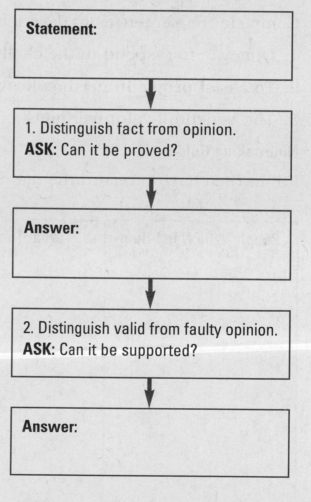

Statement:

1. Distinguish fact from opinion.
ASK: Can it be proved?

Answer:

2. Distinguish valid from faulty opinion.
ASK: Can it be supported?

Answer:

from Sharing in the American Dream

Colin Powell

Summary Former Secretary of State Colin Powell shares his beliefs about volunteer work. He encourages listeners to volunteer their time to help others in some way. He believes that this is an important part of keeping the United States strong.

Reading/Writing Connection

Complete the sentences to describe reasons why people volunteer.

1. One way to <u>respond</u> to the challenges of society is ___ _____.

2. To <u>assist</u> people in need makes volunteers feel _____.

3. The <u>benefit</u> of volunteering is _____.

Note-taking Guide

Fill in the chart to record the main points of Powell's speech.

People Who Need Help	What They Need	Who Should Help
		each and every one of us

from Sharing in the American Dream
Colin Powell

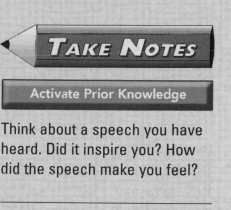
This selection is taken from a speech that Colin Powell gave. He was speaking to a meeting of government leaders in Philadelphia. He begins his speech by referring to the leaders of the American Revolution, who met in Philadelphia more than 200 years before to sign the Declaration of Independence. He quotes from the Declaration to inspire his listeners.

◆ ◆ ◆

They pledged their lives, their fortune and their sacred honor to secure <u>inalienable</u> rights given by God for life, liberty and pursuit of happiness— pledged that they would provide them to all who would inhabit this new nation.

◆ ◆ ◆

Powell says that the signers of the Declaration are present at the meeting in spirit. They are proud of what Americans have achieved, but America still has not completely achieved the dream described in the Declaration.

◆ ◆ ◆

Despite more than two centuries of moral and material progress, despite all our efforts to achieve a more perfect union, there are still Americans who are not sharing in the American Dream.

◆ ◆ ◆

Powell quotes from the poem "A Dream Deferred," by Langston Hughes. The poem asks how people react when they are not able to achieve their dreams. It suggests that such people may turn to violence.

Vocabulary Development

inalienable (in AYL yuhn uh buhl) *adj.* not capable of being taken away; nontransferable

---

Activate Prior Knowledge

Think about a speech you have heard. Did it inspire you? How did the speech make you feel?

_____

_____

_____

_____

Reading Skill

A **fact** can be proved. An **opinion** is a person's belief. What is one fact in the first paragraph?

_____

_____

_____

Stop to Reflect

"The American Dream" means different things to different people. What is your "American Dream"?

_____

_____

_____

Reading Check

To whom does Powell refer in the beginning of his speech? Underline the text that tells you.

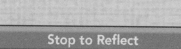

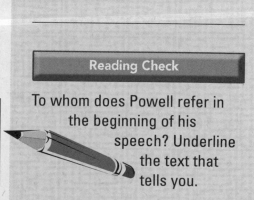

Literary Analysis

An author's **word choice** can help tell a certain idea or feeling. Read the bracketed paragraph. What ideas and feelings does Powell want the audience to have? Circle the text that supports the answer.

_____

_____

_____

Reading Skill

Read the underlined text. Is this statement a **fact** or an **opinion**? Explain your answer.

_____

_____

_____

Reading Check

To whom does Powell ask that his listeners make a commitment? Underline the text that tells you.

Powell then asks his listeners to pledge that no one in America will be denied the promise of the American Dream. He says that in order for the dream to come true, fortunate Americans must reach out to help the less fortunate.

◆ ◆ ◆

We are a <u>compassionate</u> and caring people. We are a generous people. We will reach down, we will reach back, we will reach across to help our brothers and sisters who are in need.

◆ ◆ ◆

He urges his listeners to reach out to those who most need help—America's children.

◆ ◆ ◆

As you've heard, up to 15 million young Americans today are at risk . . .

◆ ◆ ◆

Powell says that helping children in need may seem like too big a job. Actually, though, it is something we all can do because we all know what children need. They need adults who care for them, safe homes and schools, health care, skills, and opportunities.

He asks his listeners to make a commitment to American children today. He says that government, corporations, nonprofit agencies, churches, and individuals can all work together to make sure that all children get what they need.

◆ ◆ ◆

You heard the governors and the mayors, and you'll hear more in a little minute that says the real answer is for each and every one of us,

---

Vocabulary Development

compassionate (kuhm PASH uhn it) _adj._   deeply sympathetic

---

not just here in Philadelphia, but across this land—for each and every one of us to reach out and touch someone in need.

◆ ◆ ◆

Powell ends his speech by again referring to the spirit of the Declaration of Independence, which was signed in Philadelphia more than 200 years before.

◆ ◆ ◆

All of us can spare 30 minutes a week or an hour a week. All of us can give an extra dollar. . . . There is a spirit of Philadelphia that will leave Philadelphia tomorrow afternoon and spread across this whole nation—

◆ ◆ ◆

Powell says that all Americans must help spread the promise of the American Dream. It must be done in order to make the promises of the Declaration of Independence come true.

◆ ◆ ◆

Let us make sure that no child in America is left behind, no child in America has their dream deferred or denied.

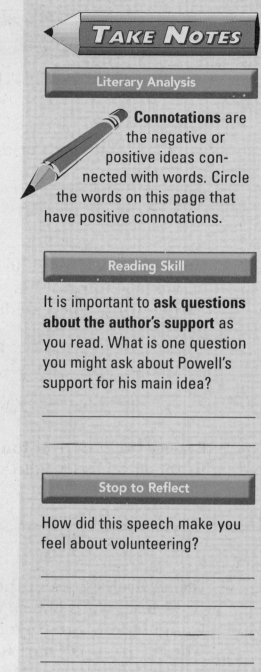

TAKE NOTES

Literary Analysis

Connotations are the negative or positive ideas connected with words. Circle the words on this page that have positive connotations.

Reading Skill

It is important to **ask questions about the author's support** as you read. What is one question you might ask about Powell's support for his main idea?

_____

_____

Stop to Reflect

How did this speech make you feel about volunteering?

_____

_____

_____

_____

Vocabulary Development

deferred (di FERD) *adj.*   delayed

from Sharing in the American Dream

1. **Respond:** Powell believes that all citizens should participate in volunteer work. Do you agree or disagree with this message? Explain.

   _____

   _____

2. **Interpret:** Powell refers to the signers of the Declaration of Independence at the beginning of his speech. What kinds of feelings do you think Powell wants to create in his audience by mentioning this group of people?

   _____

   _____

3. **Reading Skill:** An **opinion** is a judgment or belief. Identify one opinion in the speech. Explain your choice.

   _____

   _____

4. **Literary Analysis:** An author's **word choice** can help show a certain idea or feeling. Word choice can be influenced by **connotation**. Connotations are the negative or positive ideas connected with certain words. Use this chart to analyze Powell's word choice in his speech.

Powell's Purpose	Words and Phrases That Support His Purpose	Connotations

SUPPORT FOR WRITING AND EXTEND YOUR LEARNING

Writing

Write a brief **response** to Powell's statement "All of us can spare 30 minutes a week or an hour a week." The following questions will help you write your response.

- Who does Powell think needs the most help?

  _____

  _____

- Do you agree or disagree with Powell? Explain.

  _____

  _____

- Does Powell's idea apply to your own experience? Explain.

  _____

  _____

Use your notes to write your response.

Research and Technology

Take notes from Internet and library resources to make a **reference list** of local or national volunteer organizations. Use the following chart to categorize the different kinds of volunteer organizations. Add additional categories to the chart if needed.

Homeless Shelters	Animal Rescue Organizations	Children's Organizations	Food Banks	Community Cleanup Groups

Science and the Sense of Wonder

Isaac Asimov

Summary Isaac Asimov responds to a poem by Walt Whitman. In the poem, Whitman describes how the beauty of the stars moved him, while an astronomer's scientific explanation left him cold. Asimov disagrees with Whitman, and shows how knowledge of science can add to beauty.

Reading/Writing Connection

Complete the sentences to give reasons to enjoy nature and reasons to study nature scientifically.

1. The best way to <u>appreciate</u> nature is _____.

2. People who <u>investigate</u> nature _____.

3. Nature needs people to <u>focus</u> on _____.

Note-taking Guide

Use the chart to recall Asimov's reasons for why science makes watching the sky more interesting.

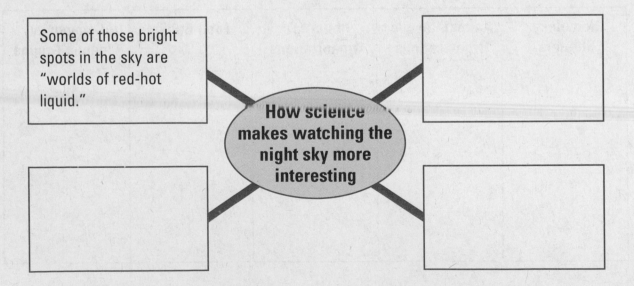

Some of those bright spots in the sky are "worlds of red-hot liquid."

How science makes watching the night sky more interesting

Science and the Sense of Wonder

1. **Analyze:** Our galaxy is small, compared with other galaxies that scientists have found. Asimov tries to explain how small our galaxy is. How does he do this?

   _____

   _____

2. **Make a Judgment:** Asimov says that knowing science makes the night sky more interesting. Whitman says that he would rather just enjoy the night sky than learn scientific explanations. Do you agree with Asimov or Whitman? Explain your choice.

   _____

   _____

3. **Reading Skill:** A **fact** is a detail that is true and can be proved. Identify one fact that is in the essay.

   _____

   _____

4. **Literary Analysis: Word choice** can help show an idea or feeling. Use this chart to analyze Asimov's word choice. Write words and phrases that support his purpose. Then, write the **connotations**.

Asimov's Purpose	Words and Phrases That Support His Purpose	Connotations
To convince people that scientific knowledge of nature adds to our appreciation of its beauty		

SUPPORT FOR WRITING AND EXTEND YOUR LEARNING

Writing: Response

Write a **response** to Asimov's idea that science helps you enjoy nature. Use the chart to list things that you like about nature. Explain whether you enjoy them as a poet would or as a scientist would. Use your notes to write your response.

Things You Like About Nature	Poet or Scientist?

Listening and Speaking: Introductory Speech

Write an **introductory speech** to present Isaac Asimov to a school assembly. Answer the questions below to help you with your presentation.

- List three things that you want to include in your speech.

  _____

  _____

  _____

- What style would be appropriate for your speech?

  _____

  _____

- What parallel wording will you use in your speech?

  _____

  _____

Use your notes to write your introductory speech.

Newspaper Articles

ABOUT NEWSPAPER ARTICLES

Newspaper articles include the *Five Ws* and an *H*: *who,* or the subject of the story; *what* the action is; and *where, when, why,* and *how* the action takes place. This information is usually included in the opening paragraph.

READING SKILL

The **organizational structure** of a text is the way information is organized. Possible ways to organize include:

- **Comparison and contrast:** Details are grouped by how they are alike and different.
- **Cause and effect:** Details are grouped to show connections, reasons, and results.
- **Chronological order:** Details are grouped in order to show what happened first, next, and last.

The information in "Lots in Space" is organized in a problem-and-solution structure. It describes a problem. It suggests a way to solve it. Use the chart to note facts that support the writer's opinions and suggested solutions.

Problem	
Facts	**Opinions**
"...a 1965 space glove that zipped around for a month at 17,000 miles per hour ... can puncture space suits and cripple satellites."	"If we don't change our ways, this could become a serious problem."

Solution 1		Solution 2	
Facts	**Opinions**	**Facts**	**Opinions**

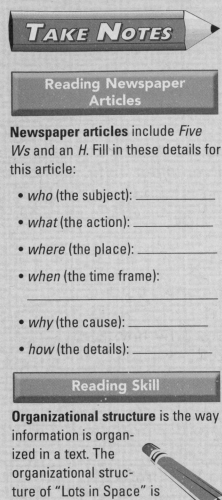

Lots in Space

Orbiting junk, from old satellites to space gloves, has scientists worried for spacecraft— and engineers working on ways to clean it up.

Peter N. Spotts

If you want to get rid of an old fridge or an obsolete TV, you could call for curbside pickup. But an obsolete satellite? Or a spent rocket?

Increasingly, the space about Earth is getting cluttered with such junk. And it's not just messy, it's dangerous. Full-size rocket bodies can destroy. Even smaller pieces—such as a 1965 space glove that zipped around for a month at 17,000 miles per hour—amount to more than a smack in the face. They can puncture space suits and cripple satellites.

Fortunately, the aerospace community is giving the problem increasing attention. Engineers are considering everything from techniques for rendering derelict satellites and boosters less harmful, to an international "space traffic control" system, to Earth-based lasers that can zap the stuff.

But the problem is expected to get worse as governments and companies prepare to triple the satellite population over the next two decades and send more people into space.

"If we don't change our ways, this could become a serious problem," says William Ailor, who heads the Center for Orbital Reentry Debris Studies at the Aerospace Corporation in El Segundo, Calif. . . .

Ever since Sputnik, humans have lobbed more than 20,000 metric tons of hardware into orbit. In addition, Dr. Ailor notes that the number of operating satellites is expected to grow from 700 today to as many as 3,000 in 2020.

This hardware can yield space junk in several ways: When satellites separate from their boosters, they shed shrouds and other bits and pieces. They can collide. Boosters can malfunction and

Space Junk Highlights

- **Oldest debris still in orbit** The U.S. Vanguard 1 satellite, which was launched on March 17, 1958, and worked for six years.
- **Most dangerous garment** U.S. astronaut Edward White's glove, lost during a Gemini-4 space-walk in 1965, orbited Earth for a month at 17,398 miles per hour.
- **Heftiest garbage disposal** The Mir space station, where cosmonauts jettisoned more than 200 objects, most of them bags full of garbage, during the station's first 10 years of operation.
- **Most debris from the destruction of a single spacecraft** The explosion in 1996 of a Pegasus rocket used in a 1994 launch. The blast generated 300,000 fragments bigger than 4 millimeters (0.15 inches). Some 700 of these objects were big enough to earn entries in catalogs of large space debris. The explosion doubled the Hubble Space Telescope's risk of colliding with a large piece of space junk.
- **Most heavily shielded spacecraft in history** The International Space Station.

explode. Or spent booster segments with still-pressurized fuel tanks can explode when hit by debris or after joints weaken from the constant freezing and thawing. Solid-fuel motors can give off "slag" as part of their exhaust plumes. . . .

All of this junk can travel at sizzling speeds and packs a wallop, according to Richard Crowther, a space consultant with the British research and development firm QinetiQ. He notes that for an object to remain in orbit at altitudes below 620 miles (1,000 km). . ., it must travel at speeds of nearly 18,000 miles per hour. It's within this region of space that critical satellites and craft, including the International Space Station and the shuttle, operate. A small coin hurtling along at

---

TAKE NOTES

Reading Newspaper Articles

A *sidebar* is chunk of text that is set apart from the body of an article. A sidebar is a good way to present a collection of facts. Read the text in the sidebar. Select one of the bulleted sections. Fill in as many of the blanks below for the section as you can.

- *who* (the subject): _____
- *what* (the action): _____
- *where* (the place): _____
- *when* (the date and/or time): _____
- *why* (the cause): _____
- *how* (the details): _____

Reading Check

What can cause fuel tanks to explode in space? Underline the answer.

Reading Newspaper Articles

The author cites statistics and makes comparisons to emphasize the seriousness of the problem. For example, the author explains how fast an object must travel to remain in orbit below a certain altitude. What risk does extreme speed pose at this altitude of space?

_____

_____

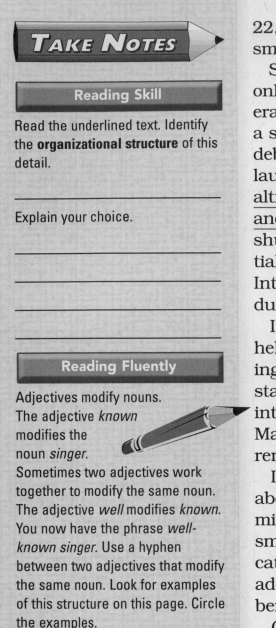

Reading Skill

Read the underlined text. Identify the **organizational structure** of this detail.

_____

Explain your choice.

_____

_____

_____

_____

Reading Fluently

Adjectives modify nouns. The adjective *known* modifies the noun *singer*. Sometimes two adjectives work together to modify the same noun. The adjective *well* modifies *known*. You now have the phrase *well-known singer*. Use a hyphen between two adjectives that modify the same noun. Look for examples of this structure on this page. Circle the examples.

Reading Check

What happens in low-earth orbit to naturally dispose of space debris? Underline the answer.

22,000 miles an hour hits with the impact of a small bus traveling at 62 miles an hour on Earth.

So far, spacecraft operators have experienced only one confirmed hit from space junk and several near misses. The hit came in July 1996, when a small French military satellite was struck by debris from an Ariane rocket that had been launched in 1986. <u>The debris hit the satellite's altitude-control arm at more than 33,500 m.p.h. and knocked the craft into a different orbit.</u> Space shuttles have been guided out of the way of potentially threatening debris at least eight times. The International Space Station has performed orbital duck-and-weave maneuvers at least three times.

In low-earth orbit, gravity and atmospheric drag help sweep a good portion of humanity's leavings—from abandoned space stations and rocket stages to astronauts' gloves and lens caps—back into the atmosphere to burn up or break up. Many more of these objects at higher orbits could remain in space for thousands of years or more.

In all, more than 9,000 objects larger than about 4 inches have been cataloged. Within 1,200 miles of Earth, some 2,200 tons of debris orbit. If smaller but still-lethal objects were included, the catalog could number more than 100,000. Ailor adds that the figure is likely to grow as the number of satellites mushrooms.

Confronted with growing space debris, the FCC is proposing that applicants for new commercial satellites show that the craft is robust enough to prevent fragmenting in the face of any remaining fuel, pressurization, or sudden discharge of the crafts batteries. Ideally, leftover fuel would be vented, as would any pressurized system. And batteries would be discharged. The proposed rules also set guidelines for moving an over-the-hill spacecraft into a disposal orbit.

But additional shielding or fuel add weight and thus cost. European Space Agency engineers, for example, calculate a $2 million price tag for the additional fuel needed to steer a 1-ton satellite

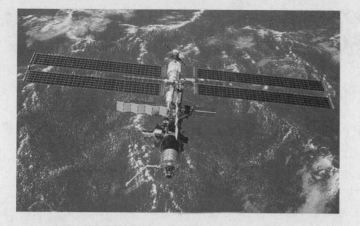

from geosynchronous orbit toward reentry into Earth's atmosphere.

Others suggest more high-tech approaches, such as using ground-based lasers to zap orbital debris—a plan that also could have space-weapon implications. The idea, which NASA reportedly pronounced workable after studying the approach in the late 1990s, relies on high-powered lasers to vaporize small bits of material from the surface of a hunk of space junk. The vapor emitted acts like a tiny rocket motor, propelling the junk either into a less threatening orbit or on a path toward a fiery reentry.

Others have proposed using space tethers, which a satellite could lower at the close of its career. Taking advantage of electrical properties induced at each end by its motion through Earth's magnetic field, the tether would slow the satellite, dropping it into ever-lower orbits toward reentry.

Even if these approaches prove practical, Ailor maintains that space debris and growing traffic raise the need for an international space-traffic control system. Currently, the U.S. Air Force maintains the 9,000-entry catalog of large objects. But it warns the relevant agency only if a manned vehicle is threatened.

<u>Unfortunately, Ailor concludes, it may take a high-profile collision to jump-start the kind of system he envisions.</u>

Stop to Reflect

Space debris is a concern for all countries on Earth. Sometimes, a solution to a problem may create another problem. How might leaders of other countries be concerned with the solution discussed in the bracketed paragraph?

_____

_____

Underline the sentence that hints at the answer.

Reading Newspaper Articles

Read the underlined text. What does the word *unfortunately* indicate?

_____

_____

Reading Informational Materials

Does the article suggest that scientists are close to solving the space debris problem? Explain your answer.

_____

_____

THINKING ABOUT THE NEWSPAPER ARTICLE

1. Why does the writer introduce both the problem and suggested solutions at the beginning of the article?

   _____

   _____

2. What is the writer's opinion about the problem of space junk? Support your answer with a detail from the article.

   _____

READING SKILL

3. What is the overall organizational structure of the article?

   _____

4. Is the following statement a fact or an opinion that supports the problem of space debris: "Full-sized rocket bodies can destroy"?

   _____

TIMED WRITING: PROBLEM-SOLUTION ESSAY (40 minutes)

Use the article as a model to write your problem-and-solution essay. Explore a problem in your school or community.

• What is the problem?

   _____

• What caused the problem?

   _____

• Whom could you ask to provide expert opinions on the problem?

   _____

• What possible solutions are there for this problem?

   _____

Describe Somebody • Almost a Summer Sky

Poetry is the most musical form of writing. People who write poems choose words for both sound and meaning. Poets use some or all of the following to do this:

- **Sensory language** is writing or speech that deals with the five senses—sight, sound, smell, taste, and touch.

- **Figurative language** is writing that is imaginative. It may mean something different than what it seems to mean. The many kinds of figurative language include these:

Figurative Language	Definition	Example
Metaphor	• describes one thing as if it were another	Her eyes were saucers, wide with expectation.
Simile	• uses *like* or *as* to compare two unlike things	The drums were as loud as a fireworks display.
Personification	• gives human qualities to something that is not human	The clarinets sang.

Sound devices add a musical quality to poetry. Some sound devices include these:

Sound Device	Definition	Example
Alliteration	• repetition of consonant sounds at the beginning of words	featured friend
Repetition	• repeated use of a sound, word, or phrase	water, water everywhere
Assonance	• repetition of a vowel sound followed by different consonants in stressed syllables	fade/hay

Other sound devices include these:

Sound Device	Definition	Example
Consonance	• repetition of a consonant sound at the end of stressed syllables with different vowel sounds	end/hand
Onomatopoeia	• use of words that imitate sounds	buzz, whack
Rhyme	• repetition of sounds at the ends of words	dear, cheer, here
Meter	• the pattern of unstressed and stressed syllables in a poem	A **horse**, a **horse**! My **king**dom **for** a **horse**!

The structure of a poem determines its form. Most poems are written in lines. These lines are grouped into stanzas. This list describes several forms of poetry.

- **Lyric** poetry describes the thoughts and feelings of one speaker. The **speaker** is the person who speaks in the poem. Lyric poetry usually seems musical.

- **Narrative** poetry tells a story in verse. It often includes some of the same things that are found in short stories.

- **Ballads** are songlike poems that tell a story. They often tell about adventure and romance.

- **Free verse** is poetry that has no set structure. It does not have to rhyme or have regular meter. Lines do not have to be a specific length. There may be no specific stanza pattern.

- **Haiku** is a three-line Japanese form. The first and third lines have five syllables each. The second line has seven syllables.

- **Rhyming couplets** are a pair of lines that rhyme. The lines usually have the same meter and length.

- **Limericks** are funny poems with five lines. They have a specific rhythm pattern and rhyme scheme.

Describe Somebody • Almost a Summer Sky

Jacqueline Woodson

Summaries In "Describe Somebody," a teacher asks her class to write a poem that describes someone. This poem describes Lonnie's thoughts as he thinks about the assignment. In "Almost a Summer Sky," Lonnie and his brother Rodney walk to the park. This poem shares Lonnie's thoughts as the two boys walk.

Note-taking Guide

Use this chart to record main ideas from the poems.

	Speaker	Characters	What the Speaker Learns or Realizes
Describe Somebody	Lonnie	Lonnie, Ms. Marcus, Eric, Miss Edna, Lamont	
Almost a Summer Sky			

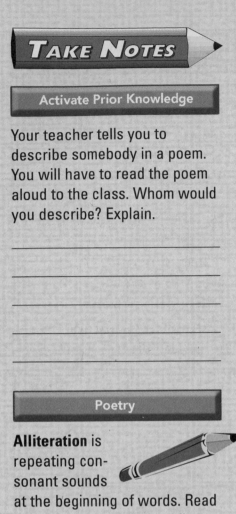

TAKE NOTES

Activate Prior Knowledge

Your teacher tells you to describe somebody in a poem. You will have to read the poem aloud to the class. Whom would you describe? Explain.

_____

_____

_____

_____

_____

Poetry

Alliteration is repeating consonant sounds at the beginning of words. Read the first set of underlined lines. Circle the words that create alliteration.

Poetry

Consonance is repeating a consonant sound at the end of two or more words. Read the second set of underlined lines. Circle the words that create consonance.

Describe Somebody
Jacqueline Woodson

Today in class Ms. Marcus said
Take out your poetry notebooks and
    describe somebody.
Think carefully, Ms. Marcus said.
You're gonna read it to the class.

5 I wrote, Ms. Marcus is tall and a little bit
    skinny.
Then I put my pen in my mouth and stared
    down
at the words.
Then I crossed them out and wrote
Ms. Marcus's hair is long and brown.

10 Shiny.
When she smiles it makes you feel all good
    inside.
I stopped writing and looked around the
    room.
Angel was staring out the window.
Eric and Lamont were having a pen fight.

15 They don't care about poetry.
Stupid words, Eric says.
Lots and lots of stupid words.
Eric is tall and a little bit mean.
Lamont's just regular.

20 Angel's kinda chubby. He's got light brown
    hair.

Sometimes we all hang out,
play a little ball or something. Angel's real
    good
at science stuff. Once he made a volcano
for science fair and the stuff that came out
    of it
25 looked like real lava. Lamont can
draw superheroes real good. Eric—nobody
at school really knows this but
he can sing. Once, Miss Edna[1] took me
to a different church than the one
30 we usually go to on Sunday.
I was surprised to see Eric up there
with a choir robe on. He gave me a mean
    look
like I'd better not
say nothing about him and his dark green
    robe with
35 gold around the neck.
<u>After the preacher preached</u>
<u>Eric sang a song with nobody else in the</u>
    <u>choir singing.</u>
<u>Miss Edna started dabbing at her eyes</u>
<u>whispering *Yes, Lord.*</u>
40 Eric's voice was like something
that didn't seem like it should belong
to Eric.
Seemed like it should be coming out of
    an angel.

Now I gotta write a whole new poem
45 'cause Eric would be real mad if I told the
    class
about his angel voice.

---

1. **Miss Edna** Lonnie's foster mother.

Describe Somebody **191**

TAKE NOTES

Poetry

Free verse is poetry without regular rhyme, rhythm, meter, or stanza pattern. Write two reasons why this poem can be said to be written in free verse.

1. _____
_____
_____
_____

2. _____
_____
_____
_____

Poetry

Narrative poetry has some story elements. Which characters are involved in the action in the set of underlined text? Circle their names. Bracket the actions in which they are involved.

Reading Check

Why does the speaker have to write a whole new poem? Underline the text that tells you.

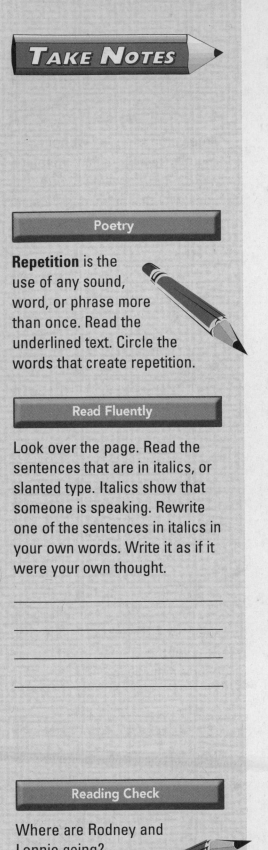

Poetry

Repetition is the use of any sound, word, or phrase more than once. Read the underlined text. Circle the words that create repetition.

Read Fluently

Look over the page. Read the sentences that are in italics, or slanted type. Italics show that someone is speaking. Rewrite one of the sentences in italics in your own words. Write it as if it were your own thought.

_____

_____

_____

_____

Reading Check

Where are Rodney and Lonnie going? Underline the text that tells you.

Almost a Summer Sky
Jacqueline Woodson

It was the trees first, Rodney[1] tells me.
It's raining out. But the rain is light and
    warm.
And the sky's not all close to us like it gets
sometimes. It's way up there with
5 some blue showing through.
Late spring sky, Ms. Marcus says. *Almost*
    summer sky.
And when she said that, I said
<u>*Hey Ms. Marcus, that's a good title*</u>
<u>*for a poem, right?*</u>
10 <u>*You have a poet's heart, Lonnie.*</u>
<u>That's what Ms. Marcus said to me.</u>
<u>I have a poet's heart.</u>
<u>That's good. A good thing to have.</u>
And I'm the one who has it.

15 Now Rodney puts his arm around my
    shoulder
We keep walking. There's a park
eight blocks from Miss Edna's house
That's where we're going.
Me and Rodney to the park.
20 Rain coming down warm
Rodney with his arm around my shoulder
Makes me think of Todd and his pigeons
how big his smile gets when they fly.
The trees upstate ain't like other trees you
    seen, Lonnie
25 Rodney squints up at the sky, shakes his
    head
smiles.

No, upstate they got maple and catalpa and
    scotch pine,[2]
all kinds of trees just standing.
Hundred-year-old trees big as three men.

---

1. **Rodney** one of Miss Edna's sons.
2. **catalpa** (kuh TAL puh) *n.* tree with heart-shaped leaves; **scotch pine** tree with yellow wood, grown for timber.

30 *When you go home this weekend,*
        Ms. Marcus said.
    Write about a perfect moment.

    Yeah, Little Brother, Rodney says.
    You don't know about shade till you lived
        upstate.
    Everybody should do it—even if it's just for
        a little while.

35 Way off, I can see the park—blue-gray sky
    touching the tops of trees.

    I had to live there awhile, Rodney said.
    Just to be with all that green, you know?
    I nod, even though I don't.
40 I can't even imagine moving away from
        here,
    from Rodney's arm around my shoulder,
    from Miss Edna's Sunday cooking,
    from Lily[3] in her pretty dresses and great
    big smile when she sees me.

45 Can't imagine moving away

    From
    Home.

    You know what I love about trees, Rodney
        says.
    It's like . . . It's like their leaves are hands
        reaching
50 *out to you. Saying Come on over here,*
        Brother.
    Let me just . . . Let me just . . .
    Rodney looks down at me and grins.
    Let me just give you some shade for a while.

---

3. Lily Lonnie's sister, who lives in a different foster home.

TAKE NOTES

Poetry

Free verse is poetry that lacks rhyme, stanzas with the same number of lines, or lines with the same number of syllables. Why is "Almost a Summer Sky" an example of free verse?

_____

_____

_____

Stop to Reflect

How does Lonnie feel about the day and his walk? How do you know?

_____

_____

_____

_____

Poetry

Personification means giving human qualities to something that is not human. How does Rodney make the trees seem human? Underline the personification in the bracketed lines.

Poetry

1. **Interpret:** The speaker says that Eric would be mad if the class knew he could sing. Why would Eric be angry?

_____

_____

_____

2. **Respond:** Do you agree that Lonnie has the heart of a poet? Explain.

_____

_____

_____

3. **Poetry:** These poems are written in **free verse**. Free verse is poetry that is not set up in any certain way. It does not have to rhyme. Why is free verse a good choice for these poems?

_____

_____

_____

4. **Poetry:** Complete the chart below. Find examples of **figurative language**, or imaginative writing, in the poems. Tell what the figurative language compares. Tell what the figurative language conveys, or means.

	Ideas Compared	Ideas Conveyed
Describe Somebody lines 40–43	Eric's voice is like something that doesn't belong to him.	
Almost a Summer Sky lines 49–53		

RESEARCH THE AUTHOR

Poetry Reading

Arrange a **poetry reading**. Follow these steps to prepare for your poetry reading.

- Read some of the author's works. Jacqueline Woodson's books include *Locomotion, Last Summer with Maizon,* and *Between Madison and Palmetto.* Be sure to read several of the poems included in *Locomotion.*

  What I learned from Woodson's writing:

  _____

  _____

  _____

  _____

- Search the Internet. Use words and phrases such as "Jacqueline Woodson article."

  What I learned about Jacqueline Woodson:

  _____

  _____

  _____

  _____

- Watch the video interview with Jacqueline Woodson. Review your source material.

  Additional information learned about the author:

  _____

  _____

  _____

  _____

  _____

Use your notes as you prepare for your poetry reading.

Poetry Collection 1 • Poetry Collection 2

READING SKILL

Context means the words and phrases around another word. Context helps you understand words you do not know. **Preview the lines of verse to identify unfamiliar words**. This means to look for words you do not know before you read the whole poem. Look for clues in the context as you read. Try to figure out the meaning of each unfamiliar word. Look for these types of clues:

- **synonyms or definitions:** words that mean the same as the unfamiliar word
- **antonyms:** words that are opposite in meaning
- **explanation:** words that give extra details, as in the chart below
- **sentence role:** the way the word is used

Using Context	
With her hair all *disheveled,* Looking like she had just awoken	
Explanation	looking like she had just awoken
Sentence Role	describes hair
Meaning *Disheveled* probably means messy, like hair looks after sleeping.	

LITERARY ANALYSIS

Sound devices are tools that poets use to make words sound musical. Sound devices help poets share ideas. Common sound devices are these:

- **alliteration:** first consonant sound is repeated, as in *big bell*
- **onomatopoeia:** word sounds like its meaning, such as *buzz*
- **rhyme:** word endings sound the same, such as *spring fling*
- **rhythm:** the pattern of strong and weak beats, such as *MAry HAD a LITtle LAMB*

Poetry Collection 1

Summaries "Cat!" uses fun language and sounds to describe a frightened and angry cat. The speaker in "Silver" creates a silvery image of a moonlit night. "Your World" challenges the reader to push past life's limitations.

Reading/Writing Connection

Complete the following paragraph to explain why imagination and creativity are important.

Being creative helps <u>enrich</u> _____.

When a person <u>generates</u> new ideas, he or she _____.

A strong imagination can help a person <u>maintain</u> _____.

Note-taking Guide

Use this chart to record the topic and actions in each poem.

Poem	Topic	Two Actions in the Poem
Cat!		
Silver	the moon	
Your World		

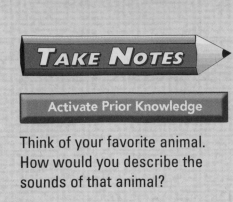

Activate Prior Knowledge

Think of your favorite animal. How would you describe the sounds of that animal?

_____

_____

_____

Reading Skill

Context is the text around a particular word. Context may include a **synonym**. This is a word that means the same as another word. Which word in the underlined passage is a synonym that helps you figure out the meaning of *git*?

_____

_____

_____

Literary Analysis

Sound devices allow poets to use the musical quality of words to express ideas. One type of sound device is **onomatopoeia**, or words that imitate sounds. Underline two made-up words that imitate cat sounds. How do they help you imagine the poem's action?

_____

_____

_____

Cat!
Eleanor Farjeon

> *Cat!*
> *Scat!*
> After her, after her,
> Sleeky <u>flatterer</u>,
> 5 Spitfire chatterer,
> Scatter her, scatter her
>   Off her mat!
>   *Wuff!*
>   *Wuff!*
> 10   Treat her rough!
> <u>Git her, git her,</u>
> <u>Whiskery spitter!</u>
> <u>Catch her, catch her,</u>
> <u>Green-eyed scratcher!</u>
> 15   Slathery
>   Slithery
>   Hisser,
>   Don't miss her!
> Run till you're dithery,[1]
> 20   Hithery
>   Thithery[2]
>   *Pftts! pftts!*
>   How she spits!
>   *Spitch! Spatch!*
> 25   Can't she scratch!
> Scritching the bark
> Of the sycamore tree,
> She's reached her ark
> And's hissing at me

Vocabulary Development

flatterer (FLAT er er) *n.*   one who praises others insincerely in order to win their approval

1. **dithery** (DITH er ee) *adj.* nervous and confused; in a dither.
2. **Hithery/Thithery** made-up words based on *hither* and *thither*, which mean "here" and "there."

<pre>
30   Pftts! pftts!
        Wuff! wuff!
            Scat,
            Cat!
            That's
35   That!
</pre>

Silver
Walter de la Mare

Slowly, silently, now the moon
Walks the night in her silver shoon;[1]
This way, and that, she peers, and sees
Silver fruit upon silver trees;
5 One by one the casements[2] catch
Her beams beneath the silvery thatch;[3]
<u>Couched in his kennel, like a log,</u>
<u>With paws of silver sleeps the dog;</u>
From their shadowy coat the white breasts
    peep
10 Of doves in a silver-feathered sleep;
A harvest mouse goes scampering by,
With silver claws, and silver eye;
And moveless fish in the water gleam,
By silver reeds in a silver stream.

TAKE NOTES

Reading Skill

Preview the lines of verse to identify unfamiliar words in "Silver." Write the words below.

_____

_____

Write the **definition** of each word and its **sentence role**, or the way each word is used.

_____

_____

Read Fluently

Read the underlined text. Then, write the lines in your own words, using sentence form. This will help you find the subject of the lines, its description, and action.

_____

_____

Reading Check

What "walks the night"? Circle the text that tells you.

Vocabulary Development

kennel (KEN uhl) *n.*   a place where dogs are kept

---

1. **shoon** (SHOON) *n.* old-fashioned word for "shoes."
2. **casements** (KAYS muhnts) *n.* windows that open out, as doors do.
3. **thatch** (THACH) *n.* roof made of straw or other plant material.

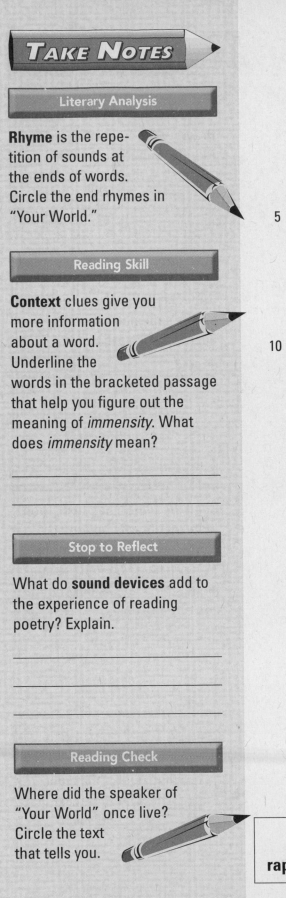

TAKE NOTES

Literary Analysis

Rhyme is the repetition of sounds at the ends of words. Circle the end rhymes in "Your World."

Reading Skill

Context clues give you more information about a word. Underline the words in the bracketed passage that help you figure out the meaning of *immensity*. What does *immensity* mean?

_____

_____

Stop to Reflect

What do **sound devices** add to the experience of reading poetry? Explain.

_____

_____

_____

Reading Check

Where did the speaker of "Your World" once live? Circle the text that tells you.

Your World

Georgia Douglas Johnson

Your world is as big as you make it.
I know, for I used to abide
In the narrowest nest in a corner,
My wings pressing close to my side.

5   But I sighted the distant horizon
Where the sky line encircled the sea
And I throbbed with a burning desire
To travel this immensity.

I battered the cordons[1] around me
10 And cradled my wings on the breeze
Then soared to the uttermost reaches
With <u>rapture</u>, with power, with ease!

Vocabulary Development

rapture (RAP cher) *n.* ecstasy

---

1. **cordons** (KAWR duhnz) *n.* lines or cords that restrict free movement.

Poetry Collection 1

1. **Draw Conclusions:** How does the speaker of "Cat!" feel about the cat?

   _____

   _____

2. **Generalize:** The silvery light of the moon in "Silver" makes everything look silver. What mood does the poet create as he describes these effects? The mood is the feeling an author creates in the reader.

   _____

   _____

3. **Reading Skill: Context** is the text around a certain word. Explain how context helps you figure out the meaning of the word *scritch* in "Cat!"

   _____

   _____

4. **Literary Analysis:** Complete the chart with examples of the **sound devices** you find in each poem. Sound devices use different sounds to make words more musical. Not all of the sound devices are used in each poem. An example of each sound device has been given to you.

	Cat!	Silver	Your World
alliteration	slithery/slathery		
onomatopoeia	scritch, scratch		
rhyme	flatterer, chatterer, scatter her		

WRITING AND EXTEND YOUR LEARNING

Writing: Introduction

Write an **introduction** for a poetry reading. Use this chart to help you decide which poem to choose for your introduction. Be sure to explain your choices as you answer the questions.

	Poem	Reason
Which poem did you like best?		
Which poem do you think will be most meaningful to others?		
Which poem is written in the most interesting way?		

Use these notes to write your introduction.

Research and Technology: Poet's Timeline

Create a **poet's timeline**. Be sure to answer the following questions in your research. Use your notes to help you complete your timeline.

- What is each author's date of birth?

  _____

- What is each author's date of death?

  _____

- List five key events that took place between 1870 and 1970. Summarize each event.

  _____

  _____

  _____

  _____

  _____

Poetry Collection 2

Summaries The speaker in "Thumbprint" is glad that no one is exactly like her. The speaker in "The Drum" describes different people in terms of drums. The speaker in "Ring Out, Wild Bells" wants the bells to ring out the bad and ring in the good.

Reading/Writing Connection

Complete these sentences to explain how the world needs to change.

1. The world can <u>achieve</u> _____.

2. Researchers should <u>dedicate</u> themselves to _____.

3. Right now, people should <u>cease</u> _____.

Note-taking Guide

Use this chart to note details about the subject of each poem.

	Thumbprint	The Drum	Ring Out, Wild Bells
Subject of the poem	the speaker's thumbprint		
Words that describe the subject			

Poetry Collection 2

1. **Respond:** Think about the way that a poem is like a song. Which of these three poems do you think would work best as a song? Explain.

   _____

   _____

2. **Interpret:** In "Thumbprint," the speaker describes her thumbprint. Why is her thumbprint so important to her?

   _____

   _____

3. **Reading Skill:** Look at the word *feud* in "Ring Out, Wild Bells." Try to figure out the meaning of *feud*. Explain the **context** clues that help you figure out the word's meaning.

   _____

   _____

4. **Liteary Analysis:** Three common **sound devices** are listed in the chart below. Complete the chart with examples of each of the sound devices in the three poems. Not all of the sound devices are used in each poem.

	Thumbprint	The Drum	Ring Out, Wild Bells
alliteration (Example: big bell)	my mark		
onomatopoeia (Example: buzz)		Pa-rum	
rhyme (Example: bad fad)			

SUPPORT FOR WRITING AND EXTEND YOUR LEARNING

Writing: Introduction

Write an **introduction** for a poetry reading. Use this chart to help you decide which poem to choose for your introduction. Be sure to explain your choices as you answer the questions.

	Poem	Reason
Which poem did you like best?		
Which poem do you think will be most meaningful to others?		
Which poem is written in the most interesting way?		

Use these notes to write your introduction.

Listening and Speaking: Group Reading

Plan to give a **group reading** of one of the poems. Use your notes from the following prompts to plan your group reading.

- What sound devices are used in the poem?

_____

_____

_____

- What mood or feelings does the poem produce?

_____

- How could you show this mood while you speak the poem aloud?

_____

_____

_____

Recipes

ABOUT RECIPES

Recipes are directions that explain how to make a type of food or drink. You will find recipes much easier to follow after you have learned the different parts of a recipe. These parts include
- a title that names the dish
- a list of ingredients
- directions that tell the steps to follow
- the number of servings the dish will make

Many recipes have other information, such as
- the amount of time it will take to make the dish
- information explaining the nutritional value of the dish
- serving ideas

READING SKILL

Sometimes recipes include words you do not know. **Use context clues to understand specialized and technical language** when this happens. Look at the words surrounding the unfamiliar word. They may help explain what the word means. Pictures can also provide context clues.

Use this chart to figure out the meanings of words you do not know. Record context clues. Guess what the unfamiliar words mean. Follow the example shown in the chart.

Unfamiliar Word	Sentence in which it is used	Context Clue	Possible Meaning
simmer	Bring to a boil, reduce heat, and simmer for 5 minutes.	reduce heat	Cook at a temperature that is not as hot as a boil.

Thumbprint Cookies

½ cup brown sugar
1 cup butter
2-3 egg yolks
2 cups flour
egg whites
1½ cups chopped nuts
raspberry preserves

> In most recipes, ingredients are listed in the order in which they are used.

To separate eggs, crack each egg in half.
Over a bowl, pour the egg back and forth between the cracked halves.
Let the egg white fall into the bowl, keeping the egg yolk intact in the shell.
Cream together sugar, butter, and egg yolks. Beat flour into this mixture.
Form balls and dip into slightly beaten egg whites. Roll balls in chopped nuts.
Put on lightly greased cookie sheet and make a thumbprint on each ball.
Bake at 350° for 8 minutes. Remove from oven and reset thumbprint.
Bake 8 to 10 minutes longer. Fill print with raspberry preserves.

Preparation: 25 min.   Yield: 30
Baking: 18 min.   Can freeze

Separating an egg

Using a teaspoon

ABOUT DROP COOKIES

Whoever invented drop cookies, which we used to call "drop cakes," deserves a medal. Except for bars, drop cookies are the easiest of all cookies to make, because shaping usually involves nothing more than dropping dough from a spoon. A few call for patting down the dough or spreading it out with the tip of a knife. In most cases, drop cookies are very forgiving: No harm is done if the mixture is slightly stiffer or softer than expected; the results will just be a little flatter or puffier than usual.

> Some recipes include information that will help cooks prepare the food successfully.

Rules for Making Great Cookies

◆ The best cookies are made from the best ingredients. Use unsalted butter, and don't stint. If possible, use unsalted nuts, and make sure they're very fresh. (Nuts are oily, and the oil can turn rancid with age.) Dried fruits such as raisins, dates, and candied citrus bits should always be plump and moist; hard, dried-out "bullets" are not only untoothsome, but will draw off moisture and make cookies dry. Don't economize on baking chocolate or on spices. Believe it or not, there is a dramatic difference between the flavor of genuine cinnamon and that of ground cassia, often sold as a cinnamon substitute. Always buy pure vanilla, almond, or other extracts, not imitation, which can taste tinny and artificial.

◆ Always use large eggs when baking. Their size is closely regulated for uniformity, one large egg weighing 2 ounces in the shell and 1.75 ounces out of the shell. It is important to note that an egg is a liquid ingredient and substituting extra-large or jumbo eggs will throw off the balance of a recipe.

◆ Baking, unlike some other forms of cooking, is not a casually improvisational art. Read each recipe all the way through before starting, always preheat the oven for 20 minutes before baking, and measure out all the ingredients carefully before you start mixing them.

◆ A cookie must have certain characteristics to earn it a place in the home-baking hall of fame: a distinctive texture, be it brittle-crisp, chewy-gooey, crunchy, silky, or melt-in-the-mouth (great cookies are rarely dry or cakey); an inviting appearance—which is not to say necessarily a picture-perfect one; a size and shape suitable to the cookie's character (oversize and sturdy for munching from a baggy in a lunch box, say, or dainty and chic for perching on a saucer at a tea); and most of all, of course, good flavor.

You can tell from the context that the specialized word *rancid* refers to food that has gone bad.

Words may have a specific meaning related to the task. Here, *uniformity* means "always the same size and weight."

THINKING ABOUT THE RECIPE

1. Why is it important to separate the eggs before you start mixing ingredients?

_____

_____

2. Think about the recipe. Describe how the finished cookies might taste, given their ingredients.

_____

_____

READING SKILL

3. What context clues help you figure out the meaning of *rancid* in the first bullet on page 208?

_____

4. List two meanings for the word *reset*. Circle the meaning that is used in this recipe in the middle of page 207.

_____

_____

TIMED WRITING: EXPLANATION (15 minutes)

Write directions for a food you know how to make.

• What ingredients are needed for this recipe?

_____

• What tools are needed?

_____

• What steps do you take in following the recipe?

_____

Poetry Collection 1 • Poetry Collection 2

READING SKILL

Context is the text around a word. These words and phrases can help you understand new or confusing words. **Reread or read ahead** for context clues when you see a word you do not know. Figure out a possible meaning. Replace the word with the possible meaning as you reread the sentence. If the sentence makes sense, your meaning is probably right. If it does not make sense, reread or read ahead again. Look up the word in a dictionary if you do not find any other clues.

The chart shows the common types of context clues.

Contrast: I *never shop* anymore, but last year, I was a shopping <u>enthusiast</u>.
Synonym: Don't *reject* our request. Your <u>veto</u> can hurt many people.
Explanation: Think of the *capacity*—this truck can carry *a lot of cargo*.
Example: She <u>agonized</u> for days, *biting her nails, sleeping poorly*, and *crying* because she was worried.

LITERARY ANALYSIS

Figurative language is writing or speech that is not to be taken literally. Figurative language includes these *figures of speech*.

- A simile uses the words *like* or *as* to compare two unlike things: His eyes were as black as coal.

- A metaphor compares two unlike things by saying that one thing *is* the other: The world is my oyster.

- Personification compares a nonhuman thing to a person by giving the nonhuman thing human qualities: The trees toss in their sleep.

Read the poems. Look for examples of figurative language.

Poetry Collection 1

Summaries Concrete mixers and elephants are compared in "Concrete Mixers." The speaker of "The City Is So Big" feels frightened by the city at night. The speaker in "Harlem Night Song" invites a loved one to enjoy the beauty of the night sky over the city.

Reading/Writing Connection

Complete the sentences to describe the typical sights and sounds someone might experience in the city.

1. City experiences appeal _____.

2. The pace and excitement of the city capture _____.

3. Cars and people circulate through _____.

Note-taking Guide

Use this chart to help you record the imagery in each poem.

	Imagery
Concrete Mixers	elephant tenders, tough gray-skinned monsters, muck up to their wheel caps
The City Is So Big	
Harlem Night Song	

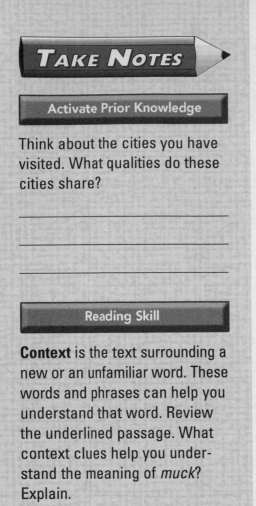

TAKE NOTES

Activate Prior Knowledge

Think about the cities you have visited. What qualities do these cities share?

_____

_____

_____

Reading Skill

Context is the text surrounding a new or an unfamiliar word. These words and phrases can help you understand that word. Review the underlined passage. What context clues help you understand the meaning of *muck*? Explain.

_____

_____

_____

_____

Literary Analysis

A **simile** compares two apparently unlike things, using the words *like* or *as*. What two things are being compared in the simile in line 7?

_____

_____

_____

Concrete Mixers
Patricia Hubbell

The drivers are washing the concrete
    mixers;
Like elephant tenders they hose them
    down.
Tough gray-skinned monsters standing
    ponderous,
Elephant-bellied and elephant-nosed,
5   Standing in muck up to their wheel-caps,
Like rows of elephants, tail to trunk.
Their drivers perch on their backs like
    mahouts,[1]
Sending the sprays of water up.
They rid the trunk-like trough of concrete,
10 Direct the spray to the bulging sides,
Turn and start the monsters moving.
        Concrete mixers
        Move like elephants
        Bellow like elephants
15   Spray like elephants,
Concrete mixers are urban elephants,
Their trunks are raising a city.

Vocabulary Development

ponderous (PAHN duh ruhs) *adj.* very heavy
urban (ER buhn) *adj.* in or relating to a town or city

---

1. **mahouts** (muh HOWTS) *n.* in India and the East Indies, elephant drivers or keepers.

The City Is So Big

Richard García

The city is so big
Its bridges quake with fear
I know, I have seen at night

The lights sliding from house to house
5 And trains pass with windows shining
Like a smile full of teeth

I have seen machines eating houses
And stairways walk all by themselves
And elevator doors opening and closing
10 And people disappear.

Reading Skill

Read the first bracketed passage. Circle the context clues that help you learn that *quake* means "tremble."

Read Fluently

Readers often confuse *its* and *it's*. *Its* is a possessive. It describes how one thing belongs to another. *It's* is a contraction that is short for *it is*. Look at *Its* in the first bracketed passage. To what do the bridges belong?

Literary Analysis

Personification is a comparison in which a non-human subject is given human characteristics. Underline an example of personification in the second bracketed passage. Then, put a box around the human characteristic that is described.

Reading Check

To what does the speaker compare a train's windows? Bracket the answer in the text.

A **simile** uses the words *like* or *as* to compare two things. A **metaphor** compares two things by saying that one thing *is* the other. Does Hughes use a simile or a metaphor to describe stars in the underlined passage? Explain.

_____

_____

_____

_____

Stop to Reflect

What example of figurative language do you find most striking In the poems you have read so far? Explain.

_____

_____

_____

Reading Check

What does the speaker urge the listener to do as they "roam the night together"? Circle the answer in the text.

Harlem Night Song
Langston Hughes

Come,
Let us <u>roam</u> the night together
Singing.

I love you.

5 Across
The Harlem roof-tops
Moon is shining.
Night sky is blue.
<u>Stars are great drops</u>
10 <u>Of golden dew.</u>

Down the street
A band is playing.

I love you.

Come,
15 Let us roam the night together
Singing.

Vocabulary Development

roam (rohm) *v.*   go aimlessly; wander

Poetry Collection 1

1. **Interpret:** What has the speaker of "The City Is So Big" actually seen?

_____

_____

_____

2. **Analyze:** Mood is the feeling that a work creates for a reader. How do the repeated phrases in "Harlem Night Song" stress the joyful mood of the poem?

_____

_____

3. **Reading Skill:** Use the **context** surrounding the word *trough* in line 9 of "Concrete Mixers" to explain what a trough looks like. What does a trough do on a concrete mixer?

_____

_____

_____

4. **Literary Analysis: Figurative language** is writing or speech that is not meant to be taken literally. Use this chart to study the **figurative language** in "The City Is So Big."

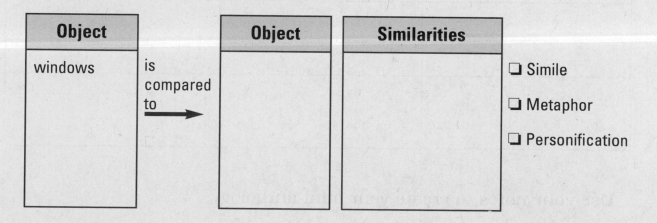

Object		Object	Similarities
windows	is compared to →		❏ Simile ❏ Metaphor ❏ Personification

WRITING AND EXTEND YOUR LEARNING

Writing: Study for a Poem

Write a **study for a poem** about a city setting. List an object, a sight, and a sound that you can find in a city. Then, use simile, metaphor, and personification to describe each item. Use this chart to begin planning your poem.

	Simile	Metaphor	Personification
Object:			
Sight:			
Sound:			

Research and Technology: Mini-Anthology

Create a **mini-anthology** by finding three poems about a similar topic. Use the chart to list your reasons for selecting each poem.

Poem Title	Why I Chose the Poem

Use your notes to create your mini-anthology.

Poetry Collection 2

Summaries The speaker of "Ode to Enchanted Light" enjoys the beauty of nature. A thunderstorm at the beach is described in "Little Exercise." The speaker of "The Sky Is Low, the Clouds Are Mean" humorously describes a dark winter day.

Reading/Writing Connection

Complete these sentences to describe nature's different sides.

1. Thunderstorms <u>display</u> _____.

2. A hot summer day can <u>dissolve</u> _____.

3. Trees cannot <u>maintain</u> _____.

Note-taking Guide

Use this chart to recall the main image in each poem.

Ode to Enchanted Light	Little Exercise	The Sky Is Low, the Clouds Are Mean
a forest with light shining through the trees		

Poetry Collection 2

1. **Infer:** Think about how Pablo Neruda describes the world in "Ode to an Enchanted Light." How do you think he feels about life?

_____

_____

2. **Interpret:** It is winter in "The Sky Is Low, the Clouds Are Mean." The writer uses the words *rut, complain,* and *mean.* What mood do these words show about the season?

_____

_____

3. **Reading Skill:** Look at the word *pile* in line 20 of "Little Exercise." The word *pile* does not mean a *heap* here. Use **context** clues to find another possible meaning.

_____

4. **Literary Analysis:** Use the chart to analyze the **figurative language** in "Ode to an Enchanted Light."

Object		Object	Similarities	
light	is compared to →		both have . . .	❏ Simile ❏ Motaphor ❏ Personification

SUPPORT FOR WRITING AND EXTEND YOUR LEARNING

Writing: Study for a Poem

Write a **study for a poem** about a natural setting. List an object, a sight, and a sound that you can find in nature. Then, describe each item through simile, metaphor, and personification. Use this chart to begin planning your poem.

	Simile	Metaphor	Personification
Object:			
Sight:			
Sound:			

Listening and Speaking: Poetry Recitation

Prepare for a **poetry recitation**. Choose one of the poems from the collection. Use the following prompts to prepare your recitation.

- Summarize the poem in your own words.

  _____

  _____

- What parts of the poem are exciting?

  _____

  _____

- How can you show this excitement while you are reciting the poem?

  _____

  _____

Poetry Collection 1 • Poetry Collection 2

READING SKILL

To **paraphrase** is to put text in your own words. Before you paraphrase a line or a passage, **reread to clarify** the writer's meaning. First, look for the most important information in each sentence. Then, start putting the whole sentence into your own words. Restate details more simply. Use synonyms for the writer's words. Synonyms are words that mean the same as the word you replace. Look up any words that you do not know. Replace unusual words and sentences with language that is more like the way people speak every day.

Use this chart to help you paraphrase poetry.

Poem:	
Line from poem	
Basic information	
Paraphrase	

LITERARY ANALYSIS

There are two main kinds of poetry. They are lyric poetry and narrative poetry.

- **Lyric poem:** tells the thoughts and feelings of a single **speaker**. The speaker is the person "saying" the poem. This type of poem gives a certain feeling or idea.

- **Narrative poem:** tells a story in verse. A narrative poem has all the parts of a short story: characters, setting, conflict, and plot.

Read the poems. Look for examples of lyric and narrative poetry.

Poetry Collection 1

Summaries In "Runagate Runagate," the speaker describes a frightening escape. "Blow, Blow, Thou Winter Wind" uses images from winter to describe a false friendship. In "Old Man," the speaker celebrates his grandfather.

Reading/Writing Connection

Describe why people read about the feelings and experiences of others.

1. People read stories to <u>perceive</u> _____.

2. Reading about the way others <u>react</u> can _____.

3. People want to know how others <u>respond</u> _____.

Note-taking Guide

Use this chart to list the emotions expressed in each poem.

	Emotion
Runagate Runagate	
Blow, Blow, Thou Winter Wind	
Old Man	

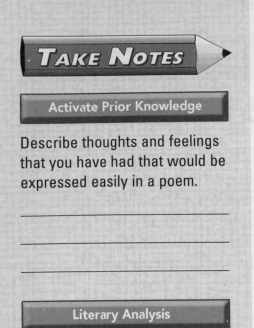

TAKE NOTES

Activate Prior Knowledge

Describe thoughts and feelings that you have had that would be expressed easily in a poem.

_____

_____

_____

Literary Analysis

A **narrative poem** tells a story in verse and has all the elements of a short story—character, setting, conflict, and plot. What historical setting and conflict are described in this narrative poem?

_____

_____

_____

Reading Check

For whom is the slaveholder looking? Underline the text that tells you.

Runagate Runagate
Robert Hayden

The poem opens with images and thoughts of an escaping slave—a "runagate"—who is being pursued by hunters and dogs.

♦ ♦ ♦

I.
Runs falls rises stumbles on from darkness
    into darkness
and the darkness thicketed with shapes of
    terror
and the hunters pursuing and the hounds
    pursuing

♦ ♦ ♦

The poem continues with more of the escaped slave's thoughts. He is determined to escape the auction block and the lash. The narrator refers to the "mythic North," where freedom is possible. Then the poem shifts to another point of view. We now hear from a slaveholder—the "subscriber"—who has placed an ad in a newspaper.

♦ ♦ ♦

If you see my Pompey, 30 yrs of age,
new breeches, plain stockings, negro
    shoes:
if you see my Anna, likely young
    mulatto
branded E on the right cheek, R on
    the left,
catch them if you can and notify
    subscriber.

♦ ♦ ♦

The slaveholder goes on to say that the slaves will be hard to catch. He says that they will do anything to escape—even that they will turn into scorpions when anyone gets close. The point of view shifts back to that of the runaway slave. The narrator expresses his determination to escape. The second section of the poem opens with a reference to Harriet Tubman. She risked her life many times to help slaves escape. Harriet Tubman shows her strength as the escaped slaves begin to doubt that they will make it.

◆ ◆ ◆

we'll never make it. *Hush that now,*
and she's turned upon us, leveled pistol
glinting in the moonlight:
Dead folks can't jaybird-talk, she says:
you keep on going now or die, she says.

◆ ◆ ◆

The poem tells about the wanted posters for Harriet Tubman. A reward is offered for her, dead or alive. The poem then shifts back to the point of view of the escaped slave. He wonders whether divine help will be offered. Then, the narrator talks about the "train" that is carrying the escaped slaves to freedom. The reader is invited to come ride the train, too. The poem ends with the narrator expressing a strong determination to be free.

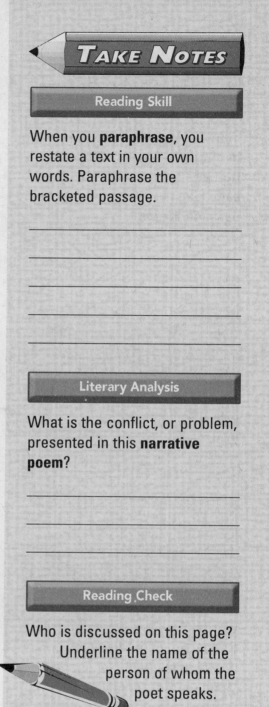

TAKE NOTES

Reading Skill

When you **paraphrase**, you restate a text in your own words. Paraphrase the bracketed passage.

_____

_____

_____

_____

_____

Literary Analysis

What is the conflict, or problem, presented in this **narrative poem**?

_____

_____

_____

Reading Check

Who is discussed on this page? Underline the name of the person of whom the poet speaks.

Blow, Blow, Thou Winter Wind
William Shakespeare

Sometimes it is helpful to **reread to clarify** the writer's meaning. Reread the first bracketed passage. Explain whom or what this passage is about.

_____

_____

Stop to Reflect

In the second bracketed passage, look at the sentence about friendship. Do you agree with this statement? Explain.

_____

_____

_____

Read Fluently

Reread the poem. Notice the words *thou, thy, art,* and *dost.* People no longer use these words in everyday language. What words would you use today to replace these words?

_____

_____

Select two lines that use these old words. Put the sentences into your own words. Use everyday language.

_____

_____

_____

Blow, blow, thou winter wind.
Thou art not so unkind
   As man's <u>ingratitude</u>.
Thy tooth is not so keen,
5 Because thou art not seen,
   Although thy breath be rude.
Heigh-ho! Sing, heigh-ho! unto the green holly.
Most friendship is feigning, most loving mere folly.[1]
   Then, heigh-ho, the holly!
10   This life is most jolly.

Freeze, freeze, thou bitter sky,
That dost not bite so nigh
   As benefits forgot.
Though thou the waters warp,[2]
15 Thy sting is not so sharp
   As friend remembered not.
Heigh-ho! Sing, heigh-ho! unto the green holly.
Most friendship is feigning, most loving mere folly.
   Then, heigh-ho, the holly!
20   This life is most jolly.

Vocabulary Development

ingratitude (in GRAT uh tood) *n.* lack of thankfulness

---

1. feigning . . . folly Most friendship is fake, most loving is foolish.
2. warp *v.* freeze.

Old Man
Ricardo Sánchez

remembrance
(smiles/hurts sweetly)
October 8, 1972

old man
with brown skin
talking of past
    when being shepherd
5   in utah, nevada, colorado and
        new mexico
was life lived freely;

old man,
    grandfather,
10 wise with time
running rivulets on face,
deep, rich furrows,[1]
    each one a legacy,
deep, rich memories of life . . .

15   "you are indio,[2]
        among other things,"
he would tell me
    during nights spent
so long ago
20   amidst familial gatherings
in albuquerque . . .

Vocabulary Development

legacy (LEG uh see) *n.*   anything handed down from an ancestor

---

1. **rivulets . . . furrows** here, the wrinkles on the old man's face.
2. **indio** (IN dee oh) *n.* Indian; Native American.

TAKE NOTES

Reading Skill

In your own words, **paraphrase** what the speaker says about the subject of this poem.

_____

_____

_____

Literary Analysis

How does the **speaker** of this poem feel about the person he is discussing?

_____

_____

_____

Reading Check

What does the poet say that the old man's *rivulets*, or wrinkles, represent? Underline the text that tells you.

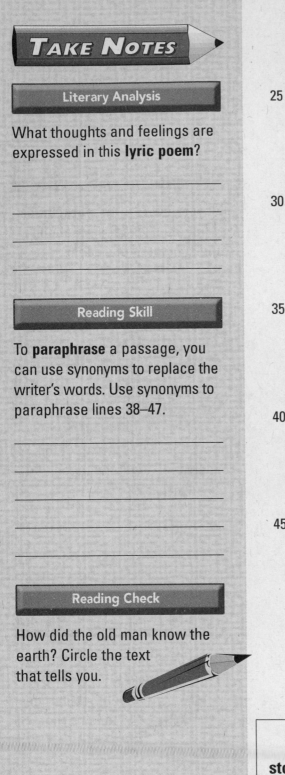

TAKE NOTES

Literary Analysis

What thoughts and feelings are expressed in this **lyric poem**?

_____

_____

_____

_____

Reading Skill

To **paraphrase** a passage, you can use synonyms to replace the writer's words. Use synonyms to paraphrase lines 38–47.

_____

_____

_____

_____

_____

Reading Check

How did the old man know the earth? Circle the text that tells you.

old man, loved and respected,
he would speak sometimes
of pueblos,[3]
25   san juan, santa clara,
        and even santo domingo,
and his family, he would say,
        came from there:
        some of our blood was here,
30   he would say,
        before the coming of coronado,[4]
other of our blood
        came with los españoles,[5]
and the mixture
35 was rich,
        though often painful . . .
old man,
who knew earth
        by its awesome aromas
40 and who felt
the heated sweetness
        of chile verde[6]
by his supple touch,
gone into dust is your body
45   with its <u>stoic</u> look and resolution,
but your reality, old man, lives on
in a mindsoul touched by you . . .

Old Man . . .

Vocabulary Development

stoic (STOH ik) *adj.*   calm in the face of suffering

---

3. **pueblos** (PWEB lohs) *n.* here, Native American towns in central and northern New Mexico.
4. **coronado** (kawr uh NAH doh) sixteenth-century Spanish explorer Francisco Vasquez de Coronado journeyed through what is today the American Southwest.
5. **los españoles** (los es pan YOH les) *n.* Spaniards.
6. **chile verde** (CHEE lay VER day) *n.* green pepper.

Poetry Collection 1

1. **Respond:** Which poem did you find most meaningful? Explain.

_____

_____

2. **Analyze:** Fill out this chart to explain what the lines mean.

	What Does It Say?	What Does It Mean?	Why Is It Important?
Runagate	(Lines 1–2)		
Blow, Blow . . .	(Line 8)		
Old Man	(Lines 8–14)		

3. **Reading Skill:** To **paraphrase** means to restate a text in your own words. Paraphrase lines 1–3 of "Blow, Blow, Thou Winter Wind."

_____

_____

4. **Literary Analysis:** What overall impression is created in the lyric poem, "Old Man"? Explain.

_____

_____

WRITING AND EXTEND YOUR LEARNING

Writing: Lyric or Narrative Poem

Write a **lyric or narrative poem** about a person whom you admire. Your subject can be a historical figure or someone you know.

Answer the following questions to help you get started. Use your notes as you write your poem.

• Why do you admire this person?

_____

_____

• What thoughts and feelings do you have about him or her?

_____

_____

• What overall impression do you want to express about this person?

_____

_____

Research and Technology: Source List

Create a **source list** that provides factual background for "Runagate Runagate." Answer these questions first.

• Where can you find *primary sources* about the Underground Railroad?

_____

_____

• Where can you find *secondary sources* about the Underground Railroad?

_____

_____

• What search words can you use to find Internet sources?

_____

_____

Poetry Collection 2

Summaries In "The New Colossus," the speaker describes the Statue of Liberty. In "Paul Revere's Ride," the speaker tells the story of the man who warned American colonists about a British raid. In "Harriet Beecher Stowe," the speaker praises Harriet Beecher Stowe, who helped people understand the fight against slavery.

Reading/Writing Connection

Fill in the sentences. List reasons for remembering and celebrating people from history.

1. Historical figures did things that <u>affect</u> _____.

2. They would often <u>contribute</u> to _____.

3. Their efforts <u>define</u> _____.

Note-taking Guide

Use this chart to recall the key parts of the poems.

	The New Colossus	**Paul Revere's Ride**	**Harriet Beecher Stowe**
Main Subject	The Statue of Liberty		
Main Idea		Paul Revere rode a horse all night to warn people that the British troops were coming.	
Why is the poem's subject important?			Her book helped bring about the end of slavery.

Poetry Collection 2

1. **Respond:** Which poem's subject interests you most? Explain.

_____

_____

_____

2. **Interpret:** Fill out the chart below. Tell the meaning of the lines indicated. Follow the example given to you.

Poem	What Does It Say?	What Does It Mean?	Why Is It Important?
The New Colossus	(Line 9)	Ancient cultures, continue to celebrate your magnificent achievements.	The United States is not interested in remaking the achievements of the past. It wants to make something new.
Harriet Beecher Stowe	(Lines 9–10)		

3. **Reading Skill:** Reread lines 3–5 of "The New Colossus." **Paraphrase** the lines. Use a sentence structure that is more like everyday speech.

_____

_____

4. **Literary Analysis:** "Paul Revere's Ride" is a **narrative poem**. What are the setting and conflict of the poem?

_____

_____

SUPPORT FOR WRITING AND EXTEND YOUR LEARNING

Writing: Lyric or Narrative Poem

Write a **lyric or narrative poem** about a person whom you admire. The person can be someone you know or someone from history. Use the following prompts to revise your lyric or narrative poem.

- Write the lines of your poem.

_____

_____

_____

_____

- Circle words that you could change to make your poem more musical.

- What musical words could you use to replace your circled words?

_____

_____

Listening and Speaking: Evaluation Form

Prepare an **evaluation form** for poetry reading. Use the chart to list qualities you think a good poetry reader should have. Write why you think the quality is important. Then, explain how you could evaluate each quality. Use your notes to create your evaluation form.

Quality	Why It Is Important	How to Evaluate It

Poetry Collection 1 • Poetry Collection 2

READING SKILL

Paraphrasing is restating something in your own words. Poets sometimes use words in patterns that are unlike the word patterns in everyday speech. Paraphrasing can help you understand a poem better. Use the following steps to paraphrase:

- First, **read aloud fluently according to punctuation**. As you read, pause briefly at commas (,), dashes (—), and semicolons (;). Pause longer after end marks, such as periods (.). Paying attention to punctuation will help you group words for meaning. It will also help you see complete thoughts.

- Next, restate the meaning of each complete thought in your own words. Use synonyms for the writer's words. Synonyms are words that have the same meaning as another word. Write unusual or difficult phrases in simple words.

As you read, pause every now and then. Paraphrase what you have just read. Make sure you understand what it means.

LITERARY ANALYSIS

Poets use **imagery** to describe things that appeal to the five senses. Imagery helps readers imagine sights, sounds, textures, tastes, and smells.

- **With imagery:** The train thundered past, roaring, screaming.

- **Without imagery:** The train went by.

Use this chart to note the imagery used in each poem.

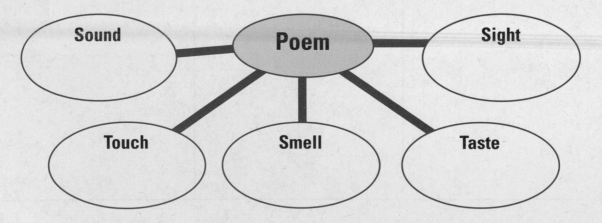

Poetry Collection 1

Summaries In "January," the speaker describes images connected with winter. "New World" shares different parts of the day in nature. In "For My Sister Molly Who in the Fifties," the speaker talks about her relationship with her sister.

Reading/Writing Connection

Complete the following paragraph. Explain why you have positive feelings about a person or place.

I <u>appreciate</u> _____. This person

or place helps <u>evoke</u> _____. I can

always <u>generate</u> _____.

Note-taking Guide

Use this chart to record the main image or images in each poem.

January	New World	For My Sister Who . . .
snowy footsteps		

January
John Updike

The days are short,
    The sun a spark
Hung thin between
    The dark and dark.

5 Fat snowy footsteps
    Track the floor,
And parkas pile up
    Near the door.

The river is
10   A frozen place
Held still beneath
    The trees' black lace.

The sky is low.
    The wind is gray.
15 The radiator
    Purrs all day.

Activate Prior Knowledge

Think about your relationship with the natural world. What in nature inspires you?

_____

_____

_____

_____

_____

Literary Analysis

Imagery is language that appeals to the senses. Underline one example of imagery in this poem. Is the imagery effective? Explain.

_____

_____

_____

_____

_____

Reading Check

What things does the speaker associate with the month of January? Underline two examples.

New World

N. Scott Momaday

1.

First Man,
behold:
the earth
glitters
5 with leaves;
the sky
glistens
with rain.
Pollen
10 is borne
on winds
that low
and lean
upon
15 mountains.
Cedars
blacken
the slopes—
and pines.

2.

20 At dawn
eagles
hie and
hover[1]
above
25 the plain
where light
gathers
in pools.
Grasses

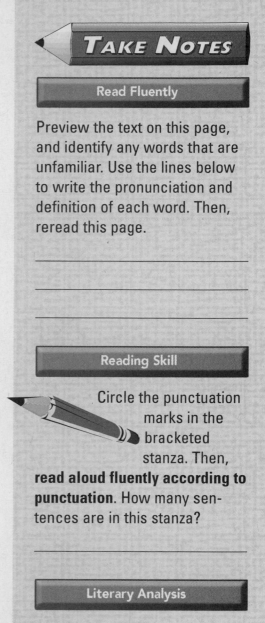

Vocabulary Development

glistens (GLI suhnz) _v._ shines; sparkles

---

1. hie and hover fly swiftly and then hang as if suspended in the air.

Reading Skill

Paraphrase lines 37–45. Remember to use your own words to rewrite the passage.

_____

_____

_____

_____

Literary Analysis

In the fourth stanza, what **imagery** creates a feeling of temperature?

_____

_____

_____

_____

Reading Check

What times of day does the speaker mention? Circle the words that signal each time of day.

30   shimmer
and shine.
Shadows
withdraw
and lie
35   away
like smoke.

3.

At noon
turtles
enter
40   slowly
into
the warm
dark loam.[2]
Bees hold
45   the swarm.
Meadows
recede
through planes
of heat
50   and pure
distance.

4.

At dusk
the gray
foxes
55   stiffen
in cold;
blackbirds
are fixed
in the
60   branches.

Vocabulary Development

recede (ri SEED) *v.*   move away

---

2. **loam** (lohm) rich, dark soil.

Rivers
follow
the moon,
the long
65 white track
of the
full moon.

For My Sister Molly
Who in the Fifties

Alice Walker

FOR MY SISTER MOLLY WHO IN THE
    FIFTIES
Once made a fairy rooster from
Mashed potatoes
Whose eyes I forget
5 But green onions were his tail
And his two legs were carrot sticks
A tomato slice his crown.
Who came home on vacation
When the sun was hot
10 and cooked
and cleaned
And minded least of all
The children's questions
A million or more
15 Pouring in on her
Who had been to school
And knew (and told us too) that certain
Words were no longer good
And taught me not to say us for we
20 No matter what "Sonny said" up the
road.

Literary Analysis

Reread the first stanza of Walker's poem. What does the **imagery** in these lines tell you about Molly?

_____

_____

_____

Stop to Reflect

Do the descriptions in the first stanza effectively appeal to your senses? Explain.

_____

_____

_____

Reading Check

What does Molly make? Underline the answer in the poem.

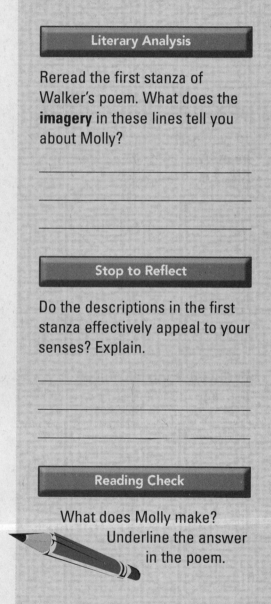

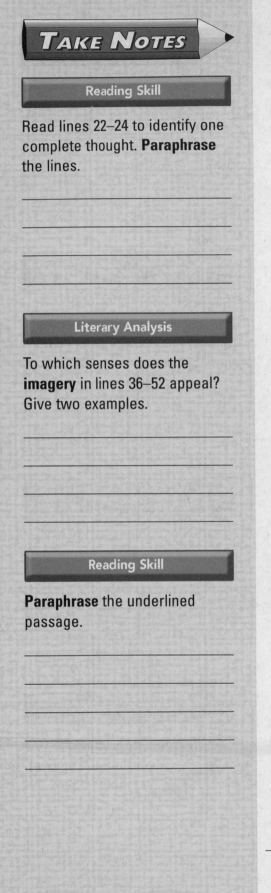

Reading Skill

Read lines 22–24 to identify one complete thought. **Paraphrase** the lines.

_____

_____

_____

_____

Literary Analysis

To which senses does the **imagery** in lines 36–52 appeal? Give two examples.

_____

_____

_____

_____

Reading Skill

Paraphrase the underlined passage.

_____

_____

_____

_____

_____

FOR MY SISTER MOLLY WHO IN THE
    FIFTIES
Knew Hamlet[1] well and read into the night
And coached me in my songs of Africa
25 A continent I never knew
But learned to love
Because "they" she said could carry
A tune
And spoke in accents never heard
30 In Eatonton.
Who read from Prose and Poetry
And loved to read "Sam McGee from
    Tennessee"[2]
On nights the fire was burning low
And Christmas wrapped in angel hair[3]
35 And I for one prayed for snow.

WHO IN THE FIFTIES
Knew all the written things that made
Us laugh and stories by
The hour   Waking up the story buds
40 Like fruit. Who walked among the flowers
And brought them inside the house
And smelled as good as they
And looked as bright.
Who made dresses, braided
45 Hair. Moved chairs about
Hung things from walls
Ordered baths
Frowned on wasp bites
And seemed to know the endings
50 Of all the tales
I had forgot.

---

1. **Hamlet** play by William Shakespeare.
2. **"Sam McGee from Tennessee"** reference to the title character in the Robert Service poem, "The Cremation of Sam McGee."
3. **angel hair** fine, white, filmy Christmas tree decoration.

WHO OFF INTO THE UNIVERSITY
Went exploring   To London and
To Rotterdam
55 Prague and to Liberia
Bringing back the news to us
Who knew none of it
But followed
crops and weather
60 funerals and
Methodist Homecoming;
easter speeches,
groaning church.

WHO FOUND ANOTHER WORLD
65 Another life   With gentlefolk
Far less trusting
And moved and moved and changed
Her name
And sounded precise
70 When she spoke   And frowned away
Our sloppishness.

WHO SAW US SILENT
Cursed with fear   A love burning
Inexpressible
75 And sent me money not for me
But for "College."
Who saw me grow through letters
The words misspelled   But not
The longing   Stretching
80 Growth
The tied and twisting
Tongue
Feet no longer bare
Skin no longer burnt against
85 The cotton.

Reading Skill

Paraphrase the complete thought expressed in the bracketed passage.

_____
_____
_____
_____
_____

Literary Analysis

What **images** describe the feelings of growing up?

_____
_____
_____
_____
_____

Reading Check

To what places does Molly go? Circle the names of those places in the poem.

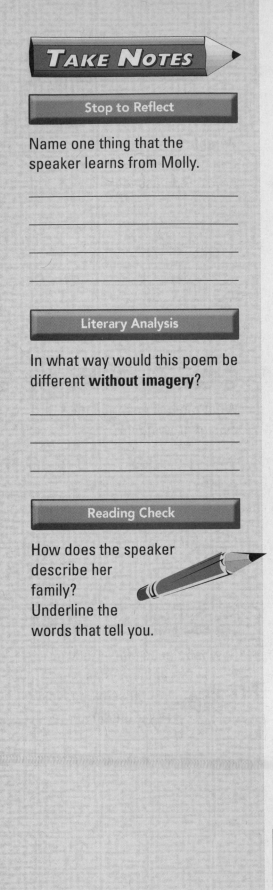

TAKE NOTES

Stop to Reflect

Name one thing that the speaker learns from Molly.

_____

_____

_____

_____

Literary Analysis

In what way would this poem be different **without imagery**?

_____

_____

_____

Reading Check

How does the speaker describe her family? Underline the words that tell you.

WHO BECAME SOMEONE OVERHEAD
A light   A thousand watts
Bright and also blinding
And saw my brothers cloddish

90 And me destined to be
Wayward[4]
My mother <u>remote</u>   My father
A wearisome farmer
With heartbreaking

95 Nails.

FOR MY SISTER MOLLY WHO IN THE
      FIFTIES
Found much
Unbearable
Who walked where few had

100 Understood   And sensed our
Groping after light
And saw some extinguished
And no doubt mourned.

FOR MY SISTER MOLLY WHO IN THE
      FIFTIES
Left us.

Vocabulary Development

remote (ri MOHT) *adj.*   aloof; cold; distant

---

4. **wayward** (WAY werd) *adj.* headstrong; disobedient.

Poetry Collection 1

1. **Draw Conclusions:** The speaker in "January" describes things as he has seen them in winter. Basing your opinion on these descriptions, do you think the speaker has good or bad feelings about winter? Explain.

_____

_____

2. **Interpret:** In "New World," the speaker talks about three parts of the day. What do you think the times of the day represent?

_____

_____

3. **Reading Skill:** To **paraphrase** is to restate something in your own words. Use this chart to paraphrase lines from two of the poems.

Original Lines	Paraphrase
January (Lines 13–16)	The cloudy sky seems close to Earth, and even the wind is gray. The radiator makes a comforting humming sound.
New World (Lines 37–45)	
For My Sister Molly . . . (Lines 16–18)	

4. **Literary Analysis:** List one image that stands out from "For My Sister Molly Who in the Fifties." What mood, or feeling, does this image create?

_____

_____

SUPPORT FOR WRITING AND EXTEND YOUR LEARNING

Writing: Review

A review of a literary work is an evaluation of its strengths and weaknesses. Write a **review** of this three-poem collection. Use the following chart to write notes for your review.

	Poem's Strengths	Poem's Weaknesses	Opinion of Poem
January			
New World			
For My Sister . . .			

Research and Technology: Profile

Write a **profile** of one of the poets featured in this collection. Gather information about the poet's life, writings, and influences. Write notes about the following information.

- Describe two important experiences in the poet's life. How did these experiences affect the poet?

_____

_____

- Who or what influenced the poet and his or her work? In what way?

_____

_____

_____

Poetry Collection 2

Summaries In "Grandma Ling," the speaker travels to Taiwan to meet her grandmother. She and her grandmother do not speak the same language. They still feel close to each other. In "Drum Song," the lines flow like the beat of a drum. The speaker tells how a turtle, a woodpecker, a snowhare, and a woman move through the world to their own beat. The speaker in "your little voice/Over the wires came leaping" talks to a special person on the telephone. Her voice makes him dizzy. He thinks of flowers. He feels as though he is dancing.

Reading/Writing Connection

Complete this paragraph by describing a memory that includes more than one sensory detail.

I <u>appreciate</u> the sound of _____. When I hear that sound, I <u>perceive</u> _____. The sounds <u>evoke</u> a feeling of _____.

Note-taking Guide

Use this chart to help you note the events of each poem.

Grandma Ling	Drum Song	your little voice/Over the wires came leaping
The speaker visits her grandmother in Taiwan.		

1. **Speculate:** The grandmother and the granddaughter in "Grandma Ling" do not speak the same language. What might they want to tell each other if they could speak the same language?

_____

_____

2. **Analyze:** Think about what the animals and women are doing in "Drum Song."How do they interact with the world around them?

_____

_____

3. **Reading Skill:** To **paraphrase** means to restate in your own words. Read the lines listed in this chart. Paraphrase the lines.

Original Lines	Paraphrase
Grandma Ling (Lines 15–16)	My likeness stood in front of me, though aged by fifty years.
Drum Song (Lines 8–13)	
your little voice . . . (Lines 1–6)	

4. **Literary Analysis: Imagery** helps readers picture what the author is describing. Write one image from "your little voice . . . ." To what sense does this image appeal?

_____

_____

_____

SUPPORT FOR WRITING AND EXTEND YOUR LEARNING

Writing: Review

Write a **review** of the poems in this collection. Use these questions to write notes for your review.

	Grandma Ling	Drum Song	your little voice . . .
How does the rhythm match the subject?			
How do the words match the subject?			
Which lines have vivid imagery?			

Listening and Speaking: Dramatic Reading

Present a **dramatic reading** of one of the poems in the collection. Select music that matches the mood of the poem. Use the chart below to choose music that will go with each poem.

	Mood	Type of Music
Grandma Ling		
Drum Song		
your little voice		

Use your ideas to present a dramatic reading of one of the poems.

Manuals

ABOUT MANUALS

A **manual** is a set of directions. It tells how to use a tool or product. Most manuals have these parts:

- a drawing or picture of the product with the parts and features labeled
- step-by-step directions for putting the item together and using it
- safety information
- a guide that tells how to fix common problems
- customer service information, such as telephone numbers, addresses, and Web site addresses

READING SKILL

A manual is a type of informational material. It is something that you **read in order to perform a task**. To perform the task

- notice each detail
- complete the tasks in order

You can restate information in your own words, or **paraphrase**. Paraphrasing is one way to make sure that you understand the directions. You can use a checklist like this one to get the most information from manuals and other technical documents.

Checklist for Using Technical Manuals

❑ Read all directions completely before performing a task.

❑ Look for clues, such as bold type or capital letters, that point out specific sections or important information.

❑ Use diagrams to locate and name the parts of the product.

❑ Follow each step in the proper order.

❑ Do not skip a step.

Using Your Answering Machine

Displays number of messages and other information

Adjust volume

Set and hear time/day

Use with other buttons to change/hear settings

Turn system on or off

Delete all or selected messages

Record and play outgoing announcement / Skip all or part of a message

Microphone

Record a memo / Repeat all or part of a message

Play/Stop messages

PLAY Light indicates messages

Setting the Clock

You'll need to set the clock so that it can announce the day and time that each message is received. Press $\boxed{PLAY/STOP}$ to exit Setting the Clock at any time.

1. Press and hold $\boxed{CLOCK}$ until the Message Window displays $\boxed{CLOCK}$, and the default day is announced.

2. To change the day setting, hold down $\boxed{MEMO/REPEAT}$ or $\boxed{ANNC/SKIP}$ until the correct day is announced. Then release the button.

3. Press and release $\boxed{CLOCK}$. The current hour setting is announced.

4. To change the hour setting, hold down $\boxed{MEMO/REPEAT}$ or $\boxed{ANNC/SKIP}$ until the correct hour is announced. Then release the button.

5. Press and release $\boxed{CLOCK}$. The current minutes setting is announced.

6. To change the minutes setting, hold down $\boxed{MEMO/REPEAT}$ or $\boxed{ANNC/SKIP}$ until the correct minutes setting is announced. Then release the button.

7. Press and release $\boxed{CLOCK}$. The new day and time are announced.

To check the clock, press and release $\boxed{CLOCK}$.

NOTE: In the event of a power failure, see the instructions on the bottom of the unit to reset the clock.

Recording Your Announcement

Before using this answering system, you should record the announcement (up to one minute long) that callers will hear when the system answers a call. If you choose not to record an announcement, the system answers with a prerecorded announcement: *"Hello. Please leave a message after the tone."*

1. Press and hold $\boxed{ANNC/SKIP}$. The system beeps. Speak toward the microphone normally, from about nine inches away. While you are recording, the Message Window displays —.

2. To stop recording, release $\boxed{ANNC/SKIP}$. The system automatically plays back your announcement.

To review your announcement, press and release $\boxed{ANNC/SKIP}$.

Turning the System On/Off

Use $\boxed{ON/OFF}$ to turn the system on and off. When the system is off, the Message Window is blank.

Volume Control

Use volume buttons ($\boxed{\blacktriangle}$ and $\boxed{\blacktriangledown}$) to adjust the volume of the system's speaker. Press the top button ($\boxed{\blacktriangle}$) to increase volume. Press the bottom button ($\boxed{\blacktriangledown}$) to decrease volume. The system beeps three times when you reach the maximum or minimum volume setting.

2

Announcement Monitor

You can choose whether to hear the announcement when your system answers a call, or have it silent (off) on your end (your caller will still hear an announcement).

1   Press and hold SET UP. After the Ring Select setting is announced, continue to press and release SET UP until the system announces "*Monitor is on (or off).*"

2   Press and release ANNC/SKIP or MEMO/REPEAT until the system announces your selection.

3   Press and release PLAY/STOP or SET UP to exit.

Listening to Your Messages

As the system plays back messages, the Message Window displays the number of the message playing. Before playing each message, the system announces the day and time the message was received. After playing the last message, the system announces "*End of messages.*"

Play all messages — Press and release PLAY/STOP. If you have no messages, the system announces "*No messages.*"

Play new messages only — Hold down PLAY/STOP for about two seconds, until the system begins playing. If you have no new messages, the system announces "*No new messages.*"

Repeat entire message — Press and release MEMO/REPEAT.

Repeat part of message — Hold down MEMO/REPEAT until you hear a beep, then release to resume playing. The more beeps you hear, the farther back in the message you will be when you release the button.

Repeat previous message — Press MEMO/REPEAT twice, continue this process to hear other previous messages.

Skip to next message — Press and release ANNC/SKIP.

Skip part of a message — Hold down ANNC/SKIP until you hear a beep, then release to resume playing. The more beeps you hear, the farther into the message you will be when you release the button.

Stop message playback — Press and release PLAY/STOP.

Saving Messages

The system automatically saves your messages if you do not delete them. The system can save about 12 minutes of messages, including your announcement, for a total of up to 59 messages. When memory is full, you must delete some or all messages before new messages can be recorded.

Deleting Messages

Delete all messages — Hold down DELETE. The system announces "*Messages deleted*" and permanently deletes messages. The Message Window displays **0**. If you haven't listened to all of the messages, the system beeps five times, and does not delete messages.

Delete selected messages — Press and release DELETE while the message you want to delete is being played. The system beeps once, and continues with the next message. If you want to check a message before you delete it, you can press MEMO/REPEAT to replay the message before deleting it.

When the system reaches the end of the last message, the messages not deleted are renumbered, and the Message Window displays the total number of messages remaining in memory.

Recording a Memo

You can record a memo to be stored as an incoming message. The memo can be up to three minutes long, and will be played back with other messages.

1   Press and hold MEMO/REPEAT. After the beep, speak toward the microphone.

2   To stop recording, release MEMO/REPEAT.

3   To play the memo, press PLAY/STOP.

When Memory is Full

The system can record approximately 12 minutes of messages, including your announcement, for a total of up to 59 messages. When memory is full, or 59 messages have been recorded, the Message Window flashes **F**. Delete messages to make room for new ones.

When memory is full, the system answers calls after 10 rings, and sounds two beeps instead of your announcement.

4

THINKING ABOUT THE MANUAL

1. You may use some of the answering machine features more than others. Which features do you think are most important? Explain.

   _____

   _____

2. Look at the diagram. How does it make the text easier to follow?

   _____

   _____

READING SKILL

3. **Paraphrase** the first sentence of "Recording Your Announcement."

   _____

   _____

4. **Paraphrase** the steps for recording an announcement. Be sure to keep the steps in the correct order.

   _____

   _____

TIMED WRITING: EXPLANATION (15 minutes)

Choose a function listed in the manual. Explain the directions in your own words. Use these questions to help organize your steps.

1. What is the first step? _____

2. What is the last step? _____

Number all of the steps in between to make sure that they are in the right order.

Reading Informational Materials **249**

ADDING -*ED* AND -*ING*

Adding a suffix to a word can change its spelling. Knowing the rules can help you spell words with suffixes correctly.

RULES FOR ADDING -*ED* AND -*ING*

- The base word sometimes does not change. (*answer + ed = answered*)
- If the base word ends in *e*, drop the *e*. (*decide + ed = decided; decide + ing + deciding*)
- If a two-syllable word ends with a stressed syllable, often double the final consonant. (*omit + ed = omitted; omit + ing = omitting*)
- If the base word ends in *y*, change the *y* to *i* before adding -*ed*. (*satisfy + ed = satisfied*)
- If the base word ends in *y*, keep the *y* before adding -*ing*. (*satisfy + ing = satisfying*)

Word List

controlled
controlling
imitated
imitating
qualified
qualifying
receiving
researched
traveled
traveling

Practice Read the following paragraph. Circle any word that is misspelled. Then, write the misspelled word correctly on the lines.

During our summer vacation, my family travelled by car to California. It was a long drive from Ohio. My brother annoyed everyone by imitateing a rock star for hours. My sister seemed to be receiveing messages from outer space. I was sure that they were controling her brain. We finally got there. Travveling by car is not my favorite way to go.

_____

_____

_____

_____

from Anne Frank & Me

Drama is written to be performed, or acted out. Dramas, or plays, can include elements of fiction such as plot, conflict, and setting. They also use some elements that occur only in dramas, or plays. These special elements include those listed in the chart below.

Element	Definition	Example
Playwright	• author of a play	William Shakespeare
Script	• written form of a play	*Romeo and Juliet*
Acts	• units of the action in a play	Act III
Scenes	• parts of an act	Act III, scene ii
Characterization	• the playwright's technique of creating believable characters	A character hangs his head to show that he is ashamed.
Dialogue	• words that characters say • words that characters speak appear next to their names • much of what you learn about the play is revealed through dialogue	JIM: When did you recognize me? LAURA: Oh, right away.
Monologue	• a long, uninterrupted speech that is spoken by a single character	HAMLET: To be, or not to be . . .
Stage Directions	• bracketed information that tells the cast, crew, and readersof the play about sound effects, actions, and sets • this information can also describe a character's gestures or emotions	*[whispering]*
Set	• scenery on stage that suggests the time and place of the action	a kitchen, a park
Props	• small, portable items that make actions look realistic	plates, a book

There are different types of drama. Several types are listed below.

Comedy is a drama that has a happy ending. Comedies often have normal characters in funny situations. Comedies can be written to amuse their audiences. They can also point out what is wrong in a society.

Tragedy is often contrasted with comedy. Events in a tragedy lead to the downfall of the main character. This character can be an average person. More often the main character is an important person. He or she could be a king or queen or another type of heroic figure.

Drama is often used to describe plays that talk about serious things. Some dramas are not acted on a stage. These types of drama are listed below.

- **Screenplays** are scripts for films. They include instructions for the person using the camera. A screenplay usually has many more scene changes than a stage play.

- **Teleplays** are scripts for television. They often contain the same elements that screenplays have.

- **Radio plays** are scripts for radio broadcasts. They include sound effects. A radio play does not have a set.

from Anne Frank & Me

Cherie Bennett

Summary An American teenager named Nicole travels back in time to Paris in 1942. Her family is arrested for being Jewish. They are put on a train going to a prison camp. Nicole recognizes Anne Frank on the train. She tells Anne details about Anne's life. Both girls are shocked by what Nicole knows.

Note-taking Guide

Use this diagram to compare and contrast the main characters.

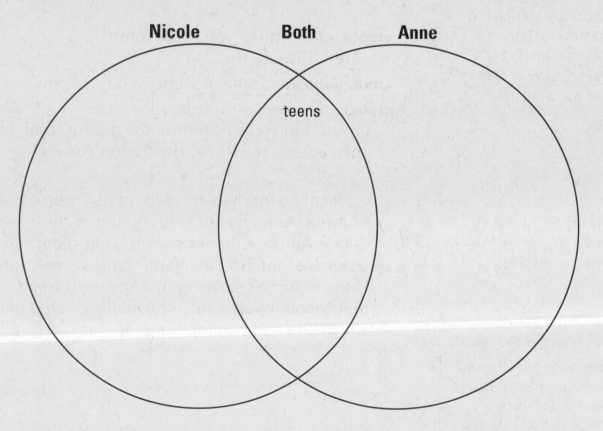

Nicole   Both   Anne

teens

from Anne Frank & Me
Cherie Bennett

Activate Prior Knowledge

Imagine that you are arrested because of something you believe. How would you feel?

_____

_____

_____

_____

During this monologue, which takes place in a cattle car, Nazis push people onto the car. The pre-recorded voice of Nicole explains that the car is in Westerbork, Holland, the date is September 3, 1944, and she expects the war to be over soon.

Nicole approaches a girl who is sitting in front of the toilet bucket with her back to the audience. Nicole explains that she needs to use the bucket and the girl offers to shield Nicole with her coat. Nicole tells the girl that she boarded the train just outside Paris and has been traveling for 17 days.

Nicole explains that, although she is from Paris and the other girl is from Amsterdam, Nicole somehow knows the girl.

Read Fluently

The two sentences in the brack-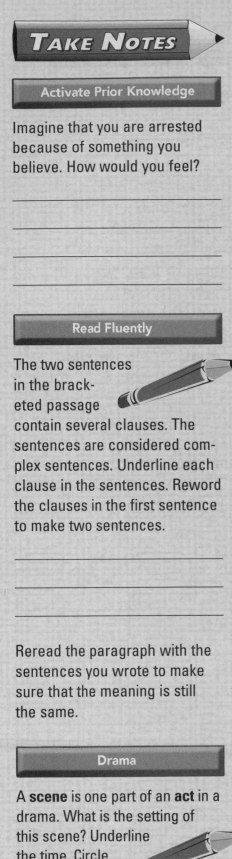eted passage contain several clauses. The sentences are considered complex sentences. Underline each clause in the sentences. Reword the clauses in the first sentence to make two sentences.

_____

_____

_____

Reread the paragraph with the sentences you wrote to make sure that the meaning is still the same.

♦ ♦ ♦

NICOLE. I do know you. Your name is . . . Anne Frank.[1]

ANNE. *(shocked)* That's right! Who are you?

NICOLE. Nicole Bernhardt. I know so much about you...you were in hiding for a long time, in a place you called . . . the Secret Annex[2]—

♦ ♦ ♦

Nicole continues describing her memories of Anne. Anne has been in hiding in the Secret Annex with her parents, her older sister Margot, and the Van Daans, whose son, Peter, is Anne's boyfriend. Anne is shocked that Nicole knows this information, some of which she has confided only to her diary.

♦ ♦ ♦

Drama

A **scene** is one part of an **act** in a drama. What is the setting of this scene? Underline the time. Circle the place.

1. **Anne Frank** a young German Jewish girl who wrote a diary about her family's hiding in The Netherlands during the Holocaust. The Holocaust was the mass killing of European Jews and others by the Nazis during World War II.
2. **Secret Annex** name given to the space in an Amsterdam office building, where in 1942, thirteen-year-old Anne Frank and her family went into hiding.

NICOLE. You kept a <u>diary</u>. I read it.

ANNE. But . . . I left my diary in the Annex when the Gestapo[3] came. You couldn't have read it.

NICOLE. But I did.

◆ ◆ ◆

Anne believes that this very strange conversation the two girls are having may be a practical joke that Peter or Anne's father came up with as a distraction. Nicole denies that she is playing a joke on Anne.

◆ ◆ ◆

NICOLE. Do you believe in time travel?

ANNE. I'm to believe that you're from the future? Really, I'm much more <u>intelligent</u> that I look.

NICOLE. I don't know how I know all this. I just do.

ANNE. Maybe you're an angel.

NICOLE. That would certainly be news to me.

Vocabulary Development

diary (DY uh ree) *n.*   book in which a person writes important or interesting things that happen in his or her life

intelligent (in TEL uh juhnt) *adj.*   having a high level of ability to learn, understand, and think about things

---

3. **Gestapo** German security police under the Nazis.

TAKE NOTES

Drama

Look at the chart on page 251. What **element of drama** would you call the conversation between Anne and Nicole?

_____

Stop to Reflect

Do you have trouble believing in this drama? Explain your answer.

_____

_____

_____

_____

_____

_____

Reading Check

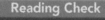

What does Anne believe that Nicole is? Circle the text that tells you.

Drama

1. **Respond:** How would you feel if someone you had never met knew details about you and your life?

_____

_____

2. **Generalize:** What is it like for Anne and Nicole on the train?

_____

_____

3. **Drama:** A **comedy** is a drama that has a happy ending. Events in a **tragedy** lead to the downfall of the main character. A **drama** is often used to describe plays that talk about serious things. How would you characterize this play? Explain your answer.

_____

_____

4. **Drama:** A **character** is a person or an animal that takes part in the action of a story. The author makes Anne and Nicole believable characters. List details that make them seem real.

Character Description	
Anne	**Nicole**
huge eyes	anxious, confused
speaks Dutch	speaks French

RESEARCH THE AUTHOR

Bulletin Board Display

Create a **bulletin board display**. Following these tips will help prepare you to create a bulletin board display.

- Read some of the author's works. Cherie Bennett's books include *Zink, Life in the Fat Lane, Searching for David's Heart,* and *A Heart Divided.*

  What I learned from Bennett's writing:

  _____

  _____

  _____

  _____

- Search the Internet. Use words and phrases such as "Cherie Bennett."

  What I learned about Cherie Bennett:

  _____

  _____

  _____

  _____

- Watch the video interview with Cherie Bennett. Add what you learn from the video to what you have already learned about the author.

  Additional information learned about the author:

  _____

  _____

  _____

  _____

  Use your notes to create your bulletin board display.

The Governess

READING SKILL

Drawing conclusions means making decisions and forming opinions after thinking about the facts and details in a text. Look at what characters say and do to draw conclusions from a play. Look at what characters say that shows their ideas and attitudes. Think about the way that characters treat each other. Notice actions that show a pattern of behavior.

Make connections among these items to decide what they show about the characters. Use this chart to record the things that you notice and the conclusions you reach.

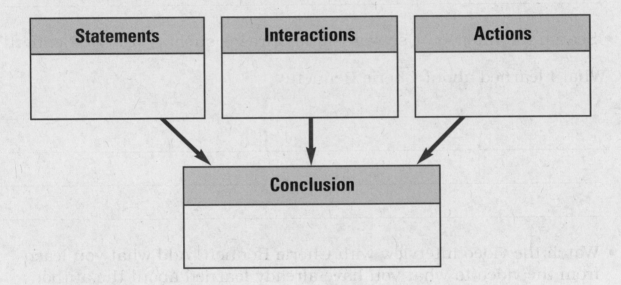

LITERARY ANALYSIS

Stage directions are notes that tell how a play should be performed. They describe the scenery, costumes, lighting, and sound. Stage directions also describe how characters feel, move, or speak. They are usually printed in italics and set in brackets, or parentheses. Here is an example:

> (It is late evening. The stage is dark, except for the glow of a small lamp beside the bed.)

Use stage directions to form a picture in your mind of how the play would look and sound.

The Governess

Neil Simon

Summary A wealthy mistress plays a joke on her shy employee, Julia. The mistress subtracts money from Julia's pay. Julia is left with much less money than she is owed. The mistress hopes that Julia will become angry and stand up for herself.

Reading/Writing Connection

Complete each sentence to describe why some people have trouble speaking up for themselves.

1. Some people may not <u>assert</u> themselves when _____.

2. A shy person might have trouble trying to <u>convince</u> _____.

3. Some people are afraid to <u>challenge</u> _____.

Note-taking Guide

Use this chart to record the actions of the mistress and the way the governess responds to these actions.

Mistress's Action	Governess's Response

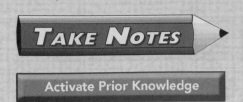

Think about a time when you felt you were being treated unfairly. Explain what you did or what you wish you had done in the situation.

_____

_____

_____

Reading Skill

Drawing conclusions means using the facts and details in the text to form opinions. Read the bracketed passage. What conclusion can you draw about the relationship between Julia and the Mistress?

_____

_____

Literary Analysis

Stage directions describe the details of the play's setting. They also tell how the characters move, feel, and sound. Underline the stage directions on this page. What effect do they have on the reader?

_____

_____

The Governess
Neil Simon

The play opens as a woman calls out to Julia, the young governess who has been hired to teach the woman's children. When Julia enters, she curtsies and keeps her head down. The woman keeps telling Julia to keep her head up, but Julia finds this difficult. The woman asks Julia how the children's lessons in French and mathematics are coming along. Julia assures her that the children are doing well. The woman tells Julia again to keep her head up. She says that if Julia thinks of herself as inferior, people will treat her that way. Then the woman announces that she wants to pay Julia for the past two months of work.

◆ ◆ ◆

MISTRESS. Let's see now, we agreed on thirty rubles a month, did we not?

JULIA. *(Surprised)* Forty, ma'am.

MISTRESS. No, no, thirty. I made a note of it. *(Points to the book)* I always pay my governess thirty . . . Who told you forty?

◆ ◆ ◆

The woman insists that the rate of pay is thirty rubles a month. Julia accepts this. They then discuss how long Julia has been there. The woman says it has been two months exactly, but Julia says it has been two months and five days. The woman says she has made a note of it, and Julia accepts this. Then the woman wants to subtract nine Sundays, saying that they had agreed earlier on this.

Vocabulary Development

rubles (ROO buhlz) *n.* Russian currency; similar to U.S. dollars

governess (GUV uhr nes) *n.* a female teacher who lives with a family and teaches its children at home

Although Julia does not remember this, she says she does. The woman then subtracts three holidays: Christmas, New Year's, and Julia's birthday. Even though Julia worked on her birthday, she agrees to what the woman says.

◆ ◆ ◆

MISTRESS. Now then, four days little Kolya was sick, and there were no lessons.

JULIA. But I gave lessons to Vanya.

MISTRESS. True. But I <u>engaged</u> you to teach two children, not one. Shall I pay you in full for doing only half the work?

JULIA. No, ma'am.

MISTRESS. So we'll deduct it . . . Now, three days you had a toothache and my husband gave you permission not to work after lunch. Correct?

JULIA. After four. I worked until four.

MISTRESS. *(Looks in the book)* I have here: "Did not work after lunch." We have lunch at one and are finished at two, not at four, correct?

JULIA. Yes, ma'am. But I—

MISTRESS. That's another seven rubles . . . Seven and twelve is nineteen . . . Subtract . . . that leaves . . . forty-one rubles . . . Correct?

JULIA. Yes, ma'am. Thank you, ma'am.

◆ ◆ ◆

Now the woman wants to subtract more money to cover a teacup and saucer that Julia broke, even though Julia broke only the saucer. She also wants to deduct money because her son climbed a tree and tore his jacket, even though Julia had told him not to climb the tree. Julia also gets charged for the son's shoes that had been stolen by the

---

Vocabulary Development

engaged (en GAJD) *v.* employed

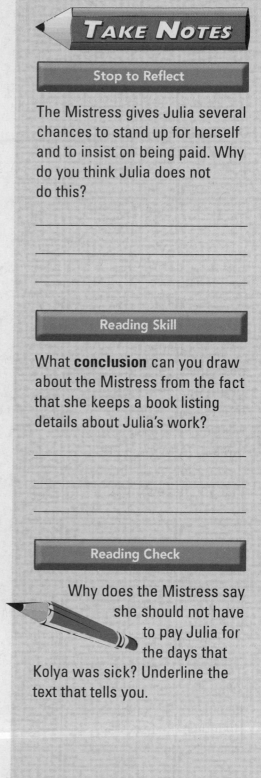

TAKE NOTES

Stop to Reflect

The Mistress gives Julia several chances to stand up for herself and to insist on being paid. Why do you think Julia does not do this?

_____

_____

_____

Reading Skill

What **conclusion** can you draw about the Mistress from the fact that she keeps a book listing details about Julia's work?

_____

_____

_____

Reading Check

Why does the Mistress say she should not have to pay Julia for the days that Kolya was sick? Underline the text that tells you.

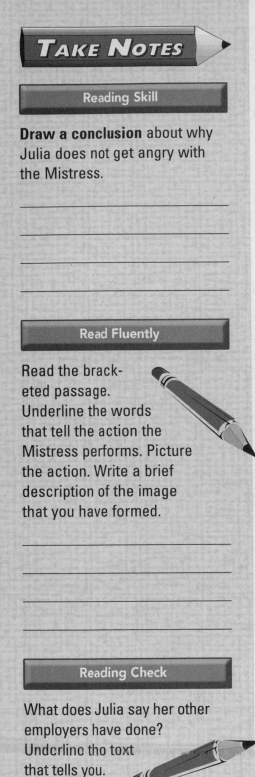

Reading Skill

Draw a conclusion about why Julia does not get angry with the Mistress.

_____

_____

_____

_____

Read Fluently

Read the bracketed passage. Underline the words that tell the action the Mistress performs. Picture the action. Write a brief description of the image that you have formed.

_____

_____

_____

_____

Reading Check

What does Julia say her other employers have done? Underline the text that tells you.

maid. The reason for this is that the woman says Julia is paid to "watch everything." More deductions are made for money the woman claims she gave to Julia earlier. Julia objects weakly, saying she never got any money. Finally, the woman pays Julia, saying she is giving her eleven rubles. When Julia counts only ten, the woman says she must have dropped one on the floor. Julia accepts this, thanks the woman for the money, and starts to leave. She is called back by the woman.

◆ ◆ ◆

MISTRESS. Why did you thank me?

JULIA. For the money, ma'am.

MISTRESS. For the money? . . . But don't you realize what I've done? I've cheated you . . . _Robbed_ you! I have no such notes in my book. I made up whatever came into my mind. Instead of the eighty rubles which I owe you, I gave you only ten. I have actually stolen from you and you still thank me . . . Why?

JULIA. In the other places that I've worked, they didn't give me anything at all.

MISTRESS. Then they cheated you even worse than I did . . . I was playing a little joke on you. A cruel lesson just to teach you. You're much too trusting, and in this world that's very dangerous . . . I'm going to give you the entire eighty rubles. _(Hands her an envelope)_ It's all ready for you. The rest is in this envelope. Here, take it.

JULIA. As you wish, ma'am.

◆ ◆ ◆

Julia turns to leave, but the woman calls her back again. The woman asks her why she does not speak up for herself. She asks if it is possible to be "such a simpleton." Julia tells her yes, that it is possible. Julie curtsies and leaves. The woman looks after her, completely baffled.

The Governess

1. **Connect:** Julia works as a governess to the Mistress's children. Why does this make her discussion with the Mistress difficult?

_____

_____

2. **Analyze:** The Mistress withholds money from Julia's pay to try to teach her a lesson. Do you think the Mistress is being kind, or cruel, or both? Explain.

_____

_____

3. **Reading Skill:** Think about the way that Julia answers her Mistress's questions. She is quiet and polite. What **conclusions** can you draw about the way governesses were treated at the time of this play?

_____

_____

_____

4. **Literary Analysis:** Write **stage directions** from *The Governess* in the chart below. Give one example for each type of direction.

Describing an Action	Showing How a Character Feels
(Points to the book)	*(Surprised)*

WRITING AND EXTEND YOUR LEARNING

Writing: Problem-Solution Essay

Write a **problem-solution essay** that discusses Julia's inability to stand up for herself. The essay should explain Julia's problem and propose a solution different from the solution the Mistress tried.

Think about how you would define Julia's problem.

- What negative consequences does Julia's problem cause her?

_____

_____

- What solution might work better than the Mistress's solution?

_____

_____

Use your notes to help you draft your essay.

Listening and Speaking: Group Discussion

Organize a **group discussion** about how Julia should have handled her situation with the Mistress. Answer the following questions to help you get started. Use your notes as you plan the discussion.

- To what class of society do you think the Mistress belongs?

_____

_____

- To what class of society do you think Julia belongs?

_____

_____

- How might the difference in social classes affect the way in which the two women behave toward each other?

_____

_____

Public Documents

ABOUT PUBLIC DOCUMENTS

Public documents are government records or documents. They could also deal with citizens' rights and responsibilities according to the law. Some examples of public documents are:

- laws
- legal notices
- government publications
- notes taken at public meetings

READING SKILL

A **generalization** is a broad statement or rule that applies to many examples. Make generalizations by

- noticing what things have in common
- using what you already know

Generalizations can help you organize information. Make sure that your generalizations are true for all of the situations they describe.

Use this chart to help you make generalizations.

Making Generalizations

Information		Information		Generalization
Youth can work three hours on school days and eight hours on non-school days.	+	School days are Monday through Friday.	=	Youth can work longer hours on weekends.

Wage and Hour Division
Basic Information

U.S. Department of Labor
Employment Standards Administration

The U. S. Department of Labor's Wage and Hour Division (WHD) is responsible for administering and enforcing laws that establish minimally acceptable standards for wages and working conditions in this country, regardless of immigration status.

Fair Labor Standards Act

The Fair Labor Standards Act (FLSA) affects most private and public employment. The FLSA requires employers to pay covered employees who are not otherwise exempt at least the federal **minimum wage** and **overtime pay** for all hours worked over 40 in a workweek.

Covered employees must be paid for all hours worked in a workweek. In general, compensable hours worked include all time an employee is on duty or at a prescribed place of work and any time that an employee is suffered or permitted to work. This would generally include work performed at home, travel time, waiting time, training, and probationary periods.

- **Federal Minimum Wage = $5.15 per hour**
- **Tipped employees may be paid $2.13 per hour; if an employee's tips combined with cash wage does not equal $5.15, the employer must make up the difference**
- **Overtime after 40 hours in a week = 1 1/2 times an employee's regular rate of pay**

Migrant and Seasonal Agricultural Worker Protection Act

The Migrant and Seasonal Agricultural Worker Protection Act (MSPA) requires farm labor contractors, agricultural employers, and agricultural associations who "employ" workers to:

1) Pay workers the wages owed when due

2) Comply with federal and state safety and health standards if they provide housing for migrant workers

3) Ensure that vehicles that they use to transport workers are properly insured, operated by licensed drivers and meet federal and state safety standards

4) Provide written disclosure of the terms and conditions of employment

Wage and Hour Division
Basic Information

U.S. Department of Labor
Employment Standards Administration

Youth Employment

The FLSA also regulates the employment of youth.

Jobs Youth Can Do:

- 13 or younger: baby-sit, deliver newspapers, or work as an actor or performer
- Ages 14–15: office work, grocery store, retail store, restaurant, movie theater, or amusement park
- Age 16–17: Any job not declared hazardous
- Age 18: No restrictions

Hours Youth Ages 14 and 15 Can Work:

- After 7 A.M. and until 7 P.M.
- (Hours are extended to 9 P.M. June 1–Labor Day)
- Up to 3 hours on a school day
- Up to 18 hours in a school week
- Up to 8 hours on a non-school day
- Up to 40 hours in a non-school week

Note: Different rules apply to youth employed in agriculture. States also regulate the hours that youth under age 18 may work. To find State rules, log on to
www.youthrules.dol.gov

THINKING ABOUT THE PUBLIC DOCUMENT

1. Young people cannot work in some jobs. In others, they can work only a few hours each day. Why do you think young people have these limits?

_____

2. Think about the rules about migrant and seasonal workers. These rules discuss the safety of housing and vehicles. What conclusions can you draw based on these rules?

_____

READING SKILL

3. Look at these **generalizations**. Circle the most accurate one.

   Young people should be in school, not at work.
   The United States has special rules for young workers.

   Explain your choice.

_____

4. Make a **generalization** about working hours and school days for people who are 14 and 15 years old.

_____

TIMED WRITING: EXPLANATION (15 minutes)

Think about laws for wages and working conditions. Explain why these laws are important. Include problems that people could have if these laws were not in place.

_____

_____

_____

The Diary of Anne Frank, Act I

READING SKILL

A **cause** is an event, an action, or a feeling. An **effect** is the result that a cause produces. You can **use background information to link historical causes with effects**. Background information includes the work's introduction, information in footnotes, facts learned in other classes, and information you already know.

Use a chart like the one shown to connect background information with a cause and an effect.

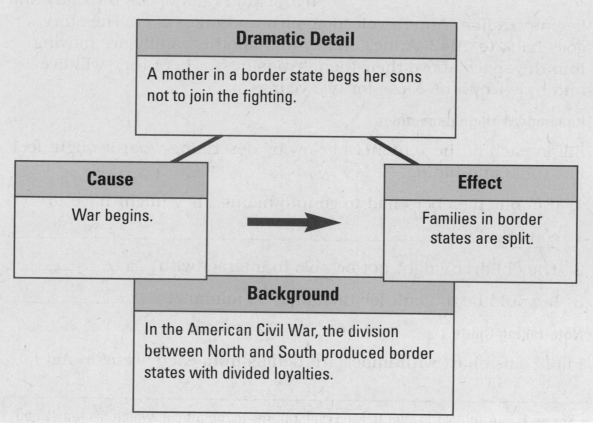

Dramatic Detail

A mother in a border state begs her sons not to join the fighting.

Cause

War begins.

Effect

Families in border states are split.

Background

In the American Civil War, the division between North and South produced border states with divided loyalties.

LITERARY ANALYSIS

Dialogue is the characters' conversation. Lines of dialogue follow the name of each character in the *script*, or text, of a play. Writers use dialogue to reveal character traits and relationships, move the plot forward, and show the conflict between characters or between the main character and outside forces.

The Diary of Anne Frank, Act I

Frances Goodrich and Albert Hackett

Summary World War II is over. Anne Frank's father returns to Amsterdam to say goodbye to a friend, Miep Gies. Gies gives him his daughter's diary. Mr. Frank opens the diary and begins reading. Anne's voice joins his and takes over. The story goes back to 1942. Anne's family and another family are moving into the space above their friends' business. There they will live and hide from the Nazis for two years.

Reading/Writing Connection

Fill in each of the sentences below by describing what it might feel like to go into hiding.

1. If family members had to go into hiding, they might have to confine _____.

2. The children might not be able to interact with _____.

3. It would be difficult for the family to minimize _____.

Note-taking Guide

Fill in this chart with important details from each scene in Act I.

Scene 1	After World War II, Mr. Frank returns to the attic in which his family had hidden from the Nazis. Miep shows him Anne's diary. He begins to think back to those terrible days.
Scene 2	
Scene 3	

The Diary of Anne Frank

Frances Goodrich and Albert Hackett

Act I, Scene 1

The Diary of Anne Frank is a play based on a diary kept during World War II by Anne Frank. The Nazis were hunting down Jews and sending them to prison camps during the war. The Franks and the Van Daans—both Jewish families—spent two years in hiding from the Nazis. In the small, cramped rooms where they are hiding, the families try to cope with their constant fear and lack of privacy. Thirteen-year-old Anne records her innermost thoughts and feelings in her diary.

The play opens in November 1945, several months after the end of World War II. Mr. Frank has returned to the upstairs rooms above his old factory—the place where his family and the Van Daans hid during the war. Miep, a loyal employee, watched over the family during those years. She is helping Mr. Frank to sort through some old papers.

◆ ◆ ◆

MIEP. *(Hurrying to a cupboard)* Mr. Frank, did you see? There are some of your papers here. *(She brings a bundle of papers to him.)* We found them in a heap of rubbish on the floor after . . . after you left.

MR. FRANK. Burn them. *(He opens his rucksack to put the glove in it.)*

MIEP. But, Mr. Frank, there are letters, notes . . .

MR. FRANK. Burn them. All of them.

MIEP. Burn this? *(She hands him a paper-bound notebook.)*

MR. FRANK. *(quietly)* Anne's diary. *(He opens the diary and begins to read.)* "Monday, the sixth of July, nineteen forty-two." *(To* MIEP*)*

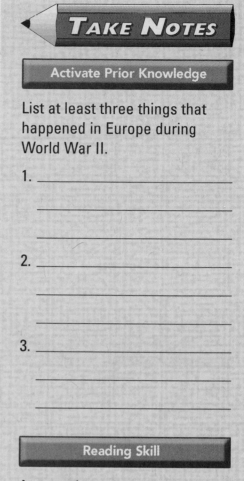

TAKE NOTES

Activate Prior Knowledge

List at least three things that happened in Europe during World War II.

1. _____

_____

_____

2. _____

_____

_____

3. _____

_____

_____

Reading Skill

A **cause** is an event, an action, or a feeling that produces a result, or an **effect**. Two families plus a man named Mr. Dussel share the upstairs rooms as they hide from the Nazis. What might **cause** so many people to share such a small space?

_____

_____

_____

Reading Check

What is the setting of the play? Circle the answer.

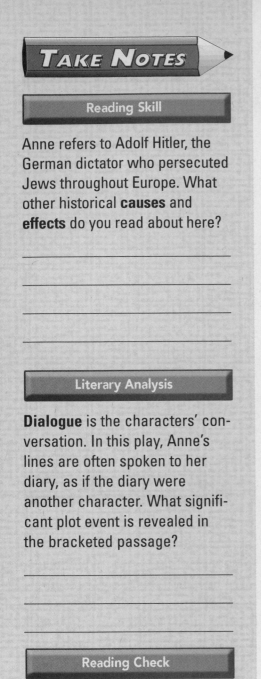

TAKE NOTES

Reading Skill

Anne refers to Adolf Hitler, the German dictator who persecuted Jews throughout Europe. What other historical **causes** and **effects** do you read about here?

_____

_____

_____

_____

Literary Analysis

Dialogue is the characters' conversation. In this play, Anne's lines are often spoken to her diary, as if the diary were another character. What significant plot event is revealed in the bracketed passage?

_____

_____

_____

Reading Check

When does Scene 2 take place? Underline the answer.

Nineteen forty-two. Is it possible, Miep? . . . Only three years ago. (*As he continues his reading, he sits down on the couch.*) "Dear Diary, since you and I are going to be great friends, I will start by telling you about myself. My name is Anne Frank. I am thirteen years old. I was born in Germany the twelfth of June, nineteen twenty-nine. As my family is Jewish, we emigrated to Holland when Hitler came to power."

(*As* MR. FRANK *reads on, another voice joins his, as if coming from the air. It is* ANNE'S VOICE.)

MR. FRANK and ANNE. "My father started a business, importing spice and herbs. Things went well for us until nineteen forty. Then the war came, and the Dutch capitulation,[1] followed by the arrival of the Germans. Then things got very bad for the Jews. . . . (The Nazis) forced Father out of his business. We had to wear yellow stars.[2] I had to turn in my bike. I couldn't go to a Dutch school anymore. I couldn't go to the movies, or ride in an automobile, or even on a streetcar, and a million other things. . . .

◆　◆　◆

Act I, Scene 2

In Scene 2, the action flashes back to July 1942. The Franks and Van Daans are moving into hiding in their cramped upstairs rooms. Mr. Frank explains to everyone that when the employees are working in the factory below, everyone must remain very quiet. People cannot run water in the sink or use the toilet. They must speak only in whispers. They must walk without shoes.

---

1. **capitulation** (kuh pich uh LAY shuhn) *n.* surrender.
2. **yellow stars:** Stars of David, which are six-pointed stars that are symbols of Judaism. The Nazis ordered all Jews to wear them sewn to their clothing so that Jews could be easily identified.

As the families are getting settled, Anne, thirteen, starts to talk to Peter, sixteen. She notices that he is taking off his yellow star. She asks him why he is doing that.

◆   ◆   ◆

ANNE. What are you doing?

PETER. Taking it off.

ANNE. But you can't do that. They'll arrest you if you go out without your star.

(He tosses his knife on the table.)

PETER. Who's going out?

ANNE. Why, of course, You're right! Of course we don't need them any more. *(She picks up his knife and starts to take her star off.)* I wonder what our friends will think when we don't show up today?

PETER. I didn't have any dates with anyone.

ANNE. Oh, I did. I had a date with Jopie to go and play ping-pong at her house. Do you know Jopie de Waal?

PETER. No.

ANNE. Jopie's my best friend. I wonder what she'll think when she telephones and there's no answer? . . . Probably she'll go over to the house . . . I wonder what she'll think . . . we left everything as if we'd suddenly been called away . . . breakfast dishes in the sink . . . beds not made . . . *(As she pulls off her star, the cloth underneath shows clearly the color and form of the star.)* Look! It's still there!

(PETER goes over to the stove with his star.)

What are you going to do with yours?

PETER. Burn it.

ANNE. *(She starts to throw hers in, and cannot.)* It's funny, I can't throw mine away. I don't know why.

PETER. You can't throw . . . ? Something they branded you with . . . ? That they made you wear so they could spit on you?

© Pearson Education, Inc., publishing as Pearson Prentice Hall.

Stop to Reflect

Jews in Europe were forced to sew a yellow Star of David onto their clothing. It was intended to identify them as Jews. What do you think it was like for people to wear the patch on their clothes?

_____

_____

Reading Skill

What **effect** does the Star of David have on Anne's clothing?

_____

_____

Read Fluently

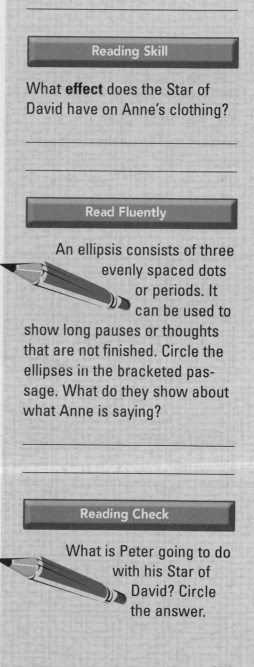

An ellipsis consists of three evenly spaced dots or periods. It can be used to show long pauses or thoughts that are not finished. Circle the ellipses in the bracketed passage. What do they show about what Anne is saying?

_____

_____

Reading Check

What is Peter going to do with his Star of David? Circle the answer.

The Diary of Anne Frank, Act I **273**

Think about the **background information that causes** Anne to answer Peter in the underlined passage. How does Anne's answer show her view about the Star of David?

_____

_____

_____

Writers use **dialogue** to help move the plot or story. How do Anne's reactions in the bracketed passage show the seriousness of their situation?

_____

_____

_____

What does Anne's father give Anne? Underline the answer.

Why might a diary be a wonderful gift for a thirteen-year-old girl who is forced to hide away for an unknown period of time?

_____

_____

_____

ANNE. <u>I know. I know. But after all, it is the Star of David, isn't it?</u>

◆　◆　◆

Mr. Frank gives Anne a diary that she can write in. She is very excited. She has always wanted to keep a diary, and now she has the chance. She starts to run down to the office to get a pencil to write with, but Mr. Frank pulls her back.

◆　◆　◆

MR. FRANK. Anne! No! *(He goes after her, catching her by the arm and pulling her back.)*

ANNE. *(Startled)* But there's no one in the building now.

MR. FRANK. It doesn't matter. I don't want you ever to go beyond that door.

ANNE. *(Sobered)* Never . . . ? Not even at nighttime, when everyone is gone? Or on Sundays? Can't I go down to listen to the radio?

MR. FRANK. Never. I am sorry, Anneke.[3] It isn't safe. No, you must never go beyond that door.

(For the first time Anne realizes what "going into hiding" means.)

◆　◆　◆

Mr. Frank tries to comfort Anne by telling her that they will be able to read all sorts of wonderful books on all sorts of subjects: history, poetry, mythology. And she will never have to practice the piano. As the scene ends, Anne comments, in her diary, about the families' situation.

◆　◆　◆

---

3. **Anneke** (AN uh kuh) nickname for Anne.

ANNE'S VOICE. . . . Friday, the twenty-first of August, nineteen forty-two. Today I'm going to tell you our general news. <u>Mother is unbearable. She insists on treating me like a baby, which I loathe.</u> Otherwise things are going better. . . .

Act I, Scene 3

> Two months have passed. All is quiet for the time being. As the scene opens, the workers are still downstairs in the factory, so everyone is very quiet in the upstairs rooms where the families are hiding. Peter and Anne are busy with their schoolwork. After the last worker leaves the downstairs factory, Mr. Frank gives the signal that the families can start to move around and use the bathroom.

◆ ◆ ◆

ANNE. *(Her pent-up energy explodes.)* WHEE!

MR. FRANK. *(Startled, amused)* Anne!

MRS. VAN DAAN. I'm first for the w.c.[4] . . .

MR. FRANK. Six o'clock. School's over.

◆ ◆ ◆

Anne teases Peter by hiding his shoes. They fall to the floor in playful wrestling. Anne asks him to dance, but he says he must go off to feed his cat, Mouschi, which he keeps in his room.

◆ ◆ ◆

ANNE. Can I watch?

PETER. He doesn't like people around while he eats.

ANNE. Peter, please.

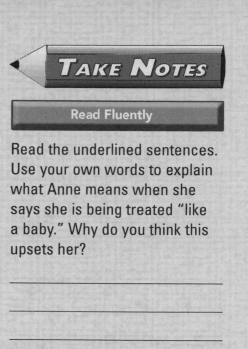

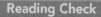

Vocabulary Development

loathe (lohth) *v.* to dislike something or someone greatly

---

4. **w.c.** water closet; bathroom.

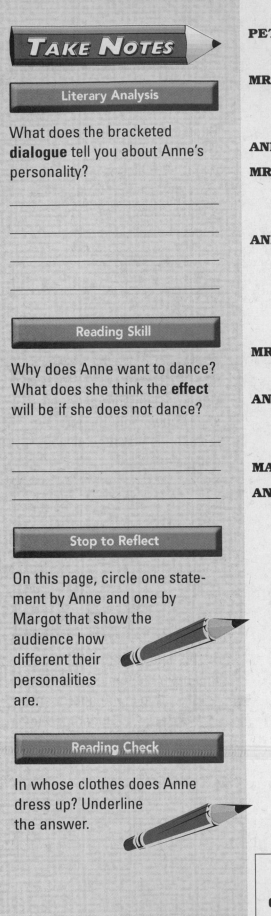

TAKE NOTES

Literary Analysis

What does the bracketed **dialogue** tell you about Anne's personality?

_____

_____

_____

_____

Reading Skill

Why does Anne want to dance? What does she think the **effect** will be if she does not dance?

_____

_____

_____

Stop to Reflect

On this page, circle one statement by Anne and one by Margot that show the audience how different their personalities are.

Reading Check

In whose clothes does Anne dress up? Underline the answer.

PETER. No! *(He goes into his room.* ANNE *slams his door after him.)*

MRS. FRANK. Anne, dear, I think you shouldn't play like that with Peter. It's not dignified.

ANNE. Who cares if it's dignified? . . .

MRS. FRANK. *(To* ANNE*)* You complain that I don't treat you like a grownup. But when I do, you resent it.

ANNE. I only want some fun . . . someone to laugh and clown with . . . After you've sat still all day and hardly moved, you've got to have some fun. I don't know what's the matter with that boy.

MR. FRANK. He isn't used to girls. Give him a little time.

ANNE. Time? Isn't two months time? I could cry. *(Catching hold of* MARGOT*)* Come one, Margot . . . dance with me. Come on, please.

MARGOT. I have to help with supper.

ANNE: You know we're going to forget how to dance . . . When we get out we won't remember a thing. . . .

◆　◆　◆

They hear a car screeching to a stop on the street. All of them freeze with fear. When the car moves away, they relax again. Anne appears. She is dressed in some of Peter's clothes, and he teases her back. He calls her Mrs. Quack! Quack! because of her constant talking.

Mrs. Frank feels Anne's forehead. She wonders if Anne is sick. Mrs. Frank asks to see her tongue. Anne objects but then obeys.

Vocabulary Development

dignified (DIG ni fyd) *v.*　deserving esteem or respect

Mr. Frank thinks Anne is not sick. He thinks she is just tired of being cooped up in the apartment. They find out that they will have beans again for dinner. They all say that they are sick of the beans.

After a brief discussion of Anne's progress with her schoolwork, they turn to a more personal subject.

◆ ◆ ◆

ANNE. Mrs. Van Daan, did you have a lot of boyfriends before you were married?

MRS. FRANK. Anne, that's a personal question. It's not courteous to ask personal questions.

MRS. VAN DAAN. Oh I don't mind. *(To* ANNE*)* Our house was always swarming with boys. When I was a girl we had . . .

MR. VAN DAAN. Oh, no. Not again!

MRS. VAN DAAN. *(Good-humored)* Shut up! *(Without a pause, to* ANNE, MR. VAN DAAN *mimics* MRS. VAN DAAN, *speaking the first few words in unison with her.)*

One summer we had a big house in Hilversum. The boys came buzzing round like bees around a jam pot. And when I was sixteen! . . . We were wearing our skirts very short those days, and I had good-looking legs. . . .

MR. VAN DAAN. Look at you, talking that way in front of her! Don't you know she puts it all down in that diary?

◆ ◆ ◆

The talk then turns to Peter's uneven progress with his schoolwork. Mr. Frank generously offers to tutor Peter as well as his own daughters. Anne spreads out on the floor to try to hear the radio downstairs. Mr. Van Daan complains that Anne's behavior is not ladylike. Mrs. Van Daan claims he is so bad-tempered from smoking cigarettes.

◆ ◆ ◆

TAKE NOTES

Literary Analysis

What does the **dialogue** on this page say about Mrs. Van Daan's character? List three words or phrases to describe her.

1. _____

2. _____

3. _____

Read Fluently

The underlined text is a sentence fragment. It is not a complete sentence. Sometimes writers use sentence fragments in dialogue to show how people really speak. On the lines below, show one way that the fragment could be rewritten as a complete sentence.

_____

_____

_____

Reading Check

Why does Anne stretch out on the floor? Underline the answer.

TAKE NOTES

Stop to Reflect

Circle the comment by Anne that shows one way that her family is different from the Van Daans. Explain the difference below.

_____

_____

_____

_____

_____

Reading Skill

What **effect** does the situation seem to be having on the characters?

_____

_____

_____

_____

Reading Check

What does Anne want to do when she grows up? Underline the answer.

MRS. VAN DAAN. You're smoking up all our money. You know that, don't you?

MR. VAN DAAN. Will you shut up? (. . . MR. VAN DAAN *turns to see* ANNE *staring up at him.*) And what are you staring at?

ANNE. I never heard grownups quarrel before. I thought only children quarreled.

MR. VAN DAAN. This isn't a quarrel! It's a discussion. And I never heard children so rude before.

ANNE *(Rising, indignantly)* I, rude!

MR. VAN DAAN. Yes!

MRS. FRANK. *(Quickly)* Anne, will you get me my knitting. . . .

◆   ◆   ◆

Anne continues to argue with Mr. Van Daan. He accuses her of doing nothing but talking all the time. He asks her why she is not nice and quiet like her sister, Margot. He says that men prefer quiet girls who love to cook and sew and follow their husband's orders. But Anne tells him that kind of life is not for her.

◆   ◆   ◆

ANNE. I'd cut my throat first! I'd open my veins! I'm going to be remarkable! I'm going to Paris . . .

MR. VAN DAAN. *(Scoffingly)* Paris!

ANNE. . . . to study music and art.

MR. VAN DAAN. Yeah! Yeah!

◆   ◆   ◆

Anne then makes a sweeping gesture. She knocks her glass of milk on Mrs. Van

Vocabulary Development

indignantly (in DIG nuhnt lee) *adv.*   in a manner that expresses anger over something unjust or unfair

scoffingly (SCOFF ing lee) *adv.*   in a mocking manner

Daan's precious fur coat. Even though Anne apologizes, Mrs. Van Daan remains very angry. Mrs. Frank tells Anne that she needs to be more calm and respectful toward the adults. She says that Anne shouldn't answer back so much. But Anne says that she will not let people walk all over her.

◆ ◆ ◆

MRS. FRANK. I'm not afraid that anyone is going to walk all over you, Anne. I'm afraid for other people, that you'll walk on them. I don't know what happens to you, Anne. You are wild, self-willed. If I had ever talked to my mother as you talk to me . . .

ANNE. Things have changed. People aren't like that anymore. "Yes, Mother." "No, Mother." "Anything you say, Mother." I've got to fight things out for myself! Make something of myself!

MRS. FRANK. It isn't necessary to fight to do it. Margot doesn't fight, and isn't she . . . ?

ANNE. (*Violently rebellious*) Margot! Margot! Margot! That's all I hear from everyone . . . how wonderful Margot is . . . "Why aren't you like Margot?"

◆ ◆ ◆

Mr. Kraler, along with Miep, is helping to hide the families. He arrives with supplies. Mr. Kraler announces that he has brought a man named Dussel, a Jewish dentist who also needs a hiding place. Mr. Frank tells Mr. Kraler to bring him up. Mr. Frank then tells Mr. Van Daan about the new arrival.

◆ ◆ ◆

MR. FRANK. Forgive me. I spoke without consulting you. But I knew you'd feel as I do.

MR. VAN DAAN. There's no reason for you to consult anyone. This is your place. You have a right to do exactly as you please. The only thing I feel . . . there's so little food as it is . . . and to take in another person . . .

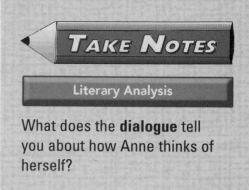

TAKE NOTES

Literary Analysis

What does the **dialogue** tell you about how Anne thinks of herself?

_____

_____

_____

_____

Read Fluently

Exclamation marks are used to show a lot of feeling. Circle the exclamation marks on this page. What do they tell you about the conversation between Anne and Mrs. Frank?

_____

_____

Reading Skill

Use background information to link historical causes with effects and answer the question: What kind of trouble is Mr. Dussel in?

_____

_____

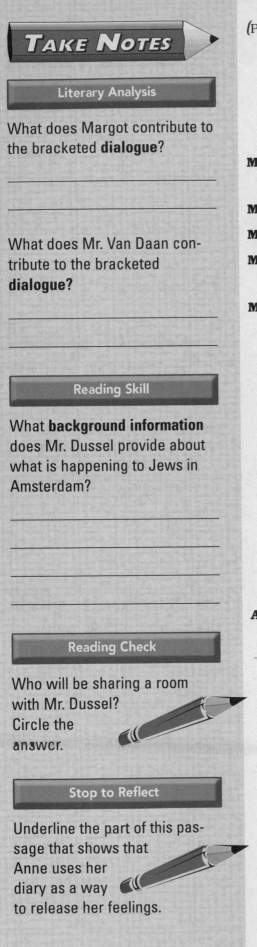

What does Margot contribute to the bracketed **dialogue**?

_____

_____

What does Mr. Van Daan contribute to the bracketed **dialogue?**

_____

_____

What **background information** does Mr. Dussel provide about what is happening to Jews in Amsterdam?

_____

_____

_____

_____

Who will be sharing a room with Mr. Dussel? Circle the answer.

Underline the part of this passage that shows that Anne uses her diary as a way to release her feelings.

(PETER *turns away, ashamed of his father.*) . . .

◆ ◆ ◆

  After they agree that Mr. Dussel will share a room with Anne, Mrs. Van Daan finds out about Dussel.

◆ ◆ ◆

MRS. VAN DAAN. What's happening? What's going on?

MR. VAN DAAN. Someone's moving in with us.

MRS. VAN DAAN. In here? You're joking.

MARGOT. It's only for a night or two . . . until Mr. Kraler finds another place.

MR. VAN DAAN. Yeah! Yeah!

◆ ◆ ◆

  Dussel tells the families that things have gotten much worse for the Jews of Amsterdam. They are being rounded up everywhere. Even Anne's best friend, Jopie, has been taken to a concentration camp. Anne is very upset to hear this.
  Dussel is a very stiff and proper man. He doesn't seem like a good roommate for a spirited girl like Anne. Sure enough, several weeks later, Anne writes about their disagreements in her diary.

◆ ◆ ◆

ANNE'S VOICE. . . . Mr. Dussel and I had another battle yesterday. Yes, Mr. Dussel! According to him, nothing, I repeat . . . nothing, is right about me . . . my appearance, my character, my manners. While he was going on at me I thought . . . sometime I'll give you such a smack that you'll fly right up to the ceiling! Why is it that every grownup thinks he knows the way to bring up children? . . .

The Diary of Anne Frank, Act I

1. **Respond:** The families must obey strict rules to avoid being discovered by the Nazis. Which rules would be hardest for you to follow? Why?

   _____

   _____

2. **Reading Skill:** Think about the reason the Franks are in hiding. What is the historical **cause** that forces the Franks to go into hiding?

   _____

   _____

3. **Reading Skill:** Think about how the families' lives have changed while they have been living in the apartment. What **effects** have these changes **caused** in their daily lives?

   _____

   _____

4. **Literary Analysis: Dialogue** shows characters' personalities, moves the action of the story, and develops the conflict. Fill in the blanks below with examples of **dialogue** from the play that achieve each purpose.

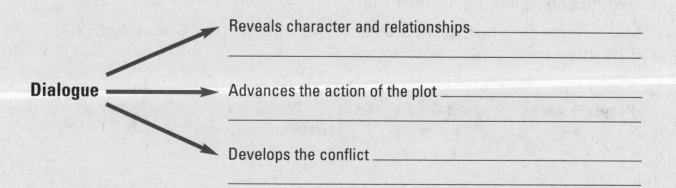

Dialogue

Reveals character and relationships _____

_____

Advances the action of the plot _____

_____

Develops the conflict _____

_____

SUPPORT FOR WRITING AND EXTEND YOUR LEARNING

Writing: Diary Entries

Write two **diary entries** from the perspective of two characters other than Anne. Answer the following questions to help you organize your thoughts.

- Select an event in Act 1 about which to write. Which two characters might have different viewpoints about the event?

  _____

- Describe the first character's perspective on the event.

  _____

  _____

- Describe the second character's perspective on the event.

  _____

  _____

- List two adjectives that describe the first character's feelings.

  _____

- List two adjectives that describe the second character's feelings.

  _____

Use your notes to write your diary entries.

Listening and Speaking: Guided Tour

Make notes for your **guided tour** of daily life in the "Secret Annex." Fill in this chart to plan your tour.

People in Annex	Food and Supplies	Rooms and Living Arrangements	Rules

The Diary of Anne Frank, Act II

READING SKILL

Cause-and-effect relationships explain the connections between events. These connections are not always simple. Look at the chart below. It shows one possible pattern of cause-and-effect relationships.

Ask questions to analyze cause-and-effect relationships:

- What could have caused the event?

- What effects could result from this cause?

- Are the events really related? The fact that one event follows another in a story does not necessarily show that the two events are connected as cause and effect.

Use the graphic organizer below to show a pattern of cause and effect in the story.

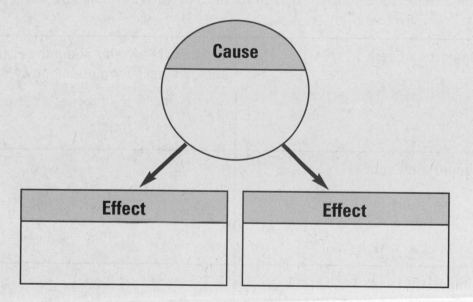

LITERARY ANALYSIS

A **character's motivation** is the reason that he or she does something. The motivation may be internal, external, or both.

- *Internal motivations:* feelings such as loneliness and jealousy

- *External motivations:* events and situations such as a fire

As you read, think about each character's possible motivations.

The Diary of Anne Frank, Act II

**Frances Goodrich
and Albert Hackett**

Summary The Franks, the Van Daans, and Mr. Dussel have been hiding for a year and a half. The eight of them have managed to live together, but they do not always get along. Food is scarce, and they are constantly afraid. Anne and Peter have become close friends. Soon, they learn that the Allies have invaded Europe, and they become excited.

Note-taking Guide

Use this chart to list four important events in Act II.

Act II: Important Event 1	Carl asks Mr. Kraler about the Franks and then asks for more money.
Act II: Important Event 2	
Act II: Important Event 3	
Act II: Important Event 4	

The Diary of Anne Frank, Act II

1. **Connect:** Mr. Kraler says that the worker might be blackmailing him. What hint does this information give about the ending of the play?

_____

_____

2. **Interpret:** How have the characters changed since the end of Act I?

_____

_____

3. **Reading Skill:** A **cause** is an event or action that produces a result. An **effect** is the result produced. Mrs. Frank wanted the Van Daans to leave, but she changed her mind. Name a cause and an effect that are related to this situation.

_____

_____

4. **Literary Analysis: Motivation** is the reason a character does something. Look at the chart. List a possible motivation for each action.

Character	Action	Motivation
Miep	brings flowers and cake to the attic rooms	
Peter Van Daan	brings Anne her cake	

SUPPORT FOR WRITING AND EXTEND YOUR LEARNING

Writing: Letter

Answer the questions below to plan a **letter** asking a local theater manager to present *The Diary of Anne Frank*.

- Why would your community benefit from seeing the play? List at least three reasons.

_____

_____

_____

- What parts of the play support your reasons?

_____

_____

_____

Research and Technology: Bulletin Board Display

Prepare a **bulletin board display** about the experiences of Jewish individuals during World War II. Fill in the following chart to organize your thoughts.

Purpose of Display	Audience	Five Questions I Want to Research
		1.
		2.
		3.
		4.
		5.

Web Sites

ABOUT WEB SITES

A Web site is a certain place on the Internet. Sponsors create and update Web sites. Sponsors can be groups, companies, or individuals. Think about whether the information on a Web site is likely to be true. Look at the Web site's sponsor to assess credibility. Most Web sites have these parts:

- The **Web address**: where you can find the site on the Internet.
- A **Web page**: one screen within the Web site.
- **Navigation bars** and **links**: tools to help you go to other Web pages.

Three pages from **www.annefrank.com** are shown here. This historical Web site is maintained by the Anne Frank Center.

READING SKILL

Sometimes you scan printed documents. Scanning is running your eyes over the page. Scanning can help you find information quickly. You can also **scan online documents** to find information. Look for the following things when you scan an electronic page:

- headings
- links to other pages or sites
- words that tell useful information

Look at the chart below. It tells you where to look when you scan a Web page.

Where to Look	What It Is	What It Does
Banner	a panel at the top of an electronic page	It shows links to other pages on the site.
Body	the main part of the Web page	It provides highlighted or underlined links to other pages of interest.
Visuals	small images	They may lead to maps, photos, or other text pages.

Welcome to the Anne Frank Center, USA Website

about us

membership

our exhibits

NEW! bookstore

students

teachers

anne frank life & times

news & media updates

spirit of anne frank awards

support our programs

Anne Frank: A Private Photo Album

Anne Frank Center, USA Online

| the anne frank house, amsterdam | the anne frank center, berlin | the anne frank educational trust, london | the anne frank fonds, basel |

membership   anne frank life   news & media   bookstore   teachers   students   about us   exhibits   spirit of anne frank

| 1889 - 1919 | 1920 - 1932 | 1933 - 1939 | 1940 - 1943 | 1944 - 1945 | 1946 - today |

1940 - 1943

Frank Family

1940

December 1 - Otto Frank's company moves into the premises at number 263 Prinsengracht.

1941 May 8 - Opekta-Werke changes its name to Messrs. Gies & Company.

Summer - Anne and Margot attend the Jewish School Amsterdam.

1942 January - Death of Grandmother Hollander.

June 12 - Anne receives a diary for her thirteenth birthday.

July 5 - Margot Frank, 16, receives a call-up notice to report for deportation to a labor camp.
The family goes into hiding the next day.

July 6 - The Frank family leaves their home forever and moves into the 'Secret Annex'.

July 13 - The van Pels family, another Jewish family originally from Germany, joins the Frank family in hiding.

November 16 - Fritz Pfeffer, the eighth and final resident of the Secret Annex, joins the Frank and van Pels families.

1943

Nazi Movement

April, May - Germany invades Denmark and Norway, the Netherlands, France, Belgium, and Luxembourg.

July 31 - Hermann Goering authorizes Reinhard Heydrich to find a 'Final Solution' to the Jewish question.

December 11 - Germany declares war on the United States.

January 20 - Heydrich, at the Wannsee Conference, mobilizes Nazi bureaucratic support for a 'Final Solution'.

February, March, April - Auschwitz, Belzec and Sobibor all become fully operational death camps.

February 2 - The encircled German Sixth Army surrenders to Soviet forces at Stalingrad, Russia. The tide of the war begins to turn against Germany.

June - SS leader Heinrich Himmler orders the complete liquidation of all Jewish ghettos in the Soviet Union and Poland.

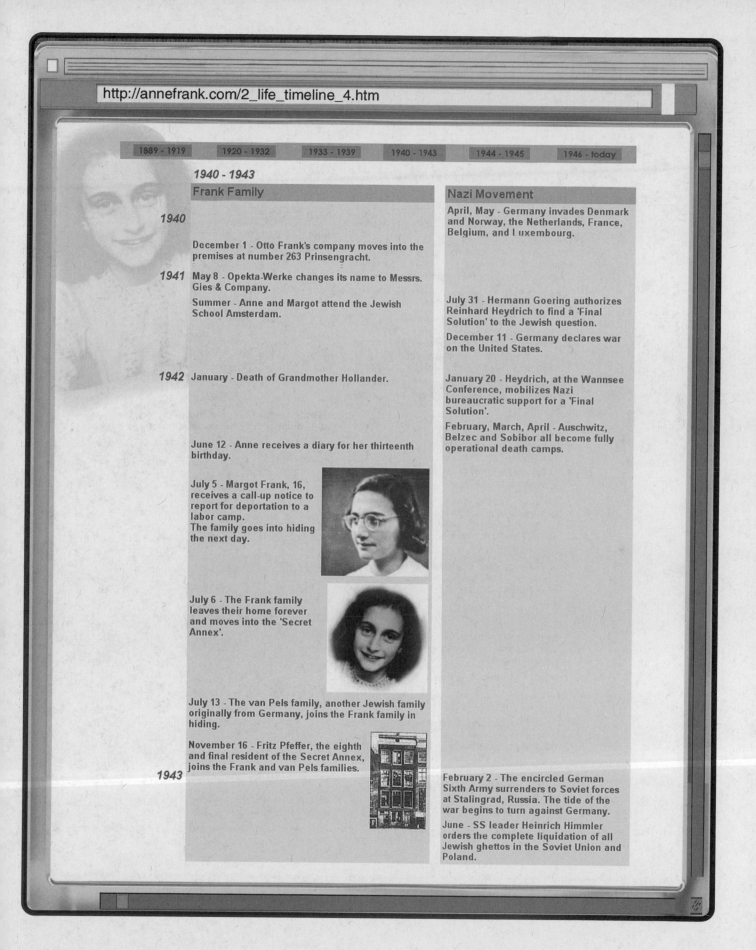

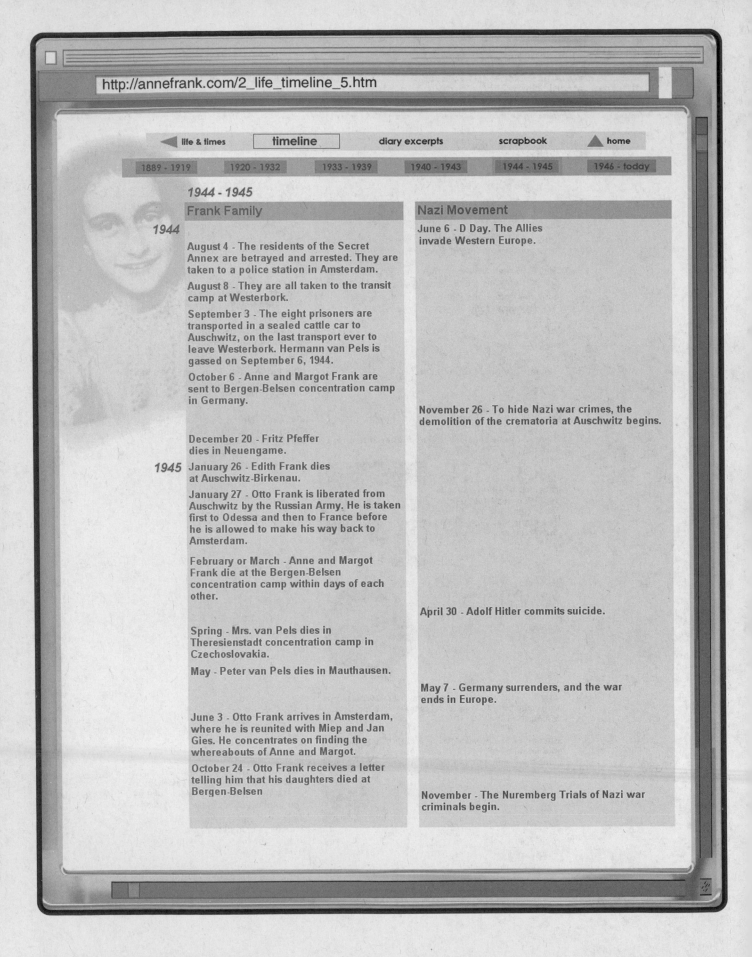

life & times   **timeline**   diary excerpts   scrapbook   ▲ home

| 1889 - 1919 | 1920 - 1932 | 1933 - 1939 | 1940 - 1943 | 1944 - 1945 | 1946 - today |

1944 - 1945

Frank Family

1944

August 4 - The residents of the Secret Annex are betrayed and arrested. They are taken to a police station in Amsterdam.

August 8 - They are all taken to the transit camp at Westerbork.

September 3 - The eight prisoners are transported in a sealed cattle car to Auschwitz, on the last transport ever to leave Westerbork. Hermann van Pels is gassed on September 6, 1944.

October 6 - Anne and Margot Frank are sent to Bergen-Belsen concentration camp in Germany.

December 20 - Fritz Pfeffer dies in Neuengame.

1945 January 26 - Edith Frank dies at Auschwitz-Birkenau.

January 27 - Otto Frank is liberated from Auschwitz by the Russian Army. He is taken first to Odessa and then to France before he is allowed to make his way back to Amsterdam.

February or March - Anne and Margot Frank die at the Bergen-Belsen concentration camp within days of each other.

Spring - Mrs. van Pels dies in Theresienstadt concentration camp in Czechoslovakia.

May - Peter van Pels dies in Mauthausen.

June 3 - Otto Frank arrives in Amsterdam, where he is reunited with Miep and Jan Gies. He concentrates on finding the whereabouts of Anne and Margot.

October 24 - Otto Frank receives a letter telling him that his daughters died at Bergen-Belsen

Nazi Movement

June 6 - D Day. The Allies invade Western Europe.

November 26 - To hide Nazi war crimes, the demolition of the crematoria at Auschwitz begins.

April 30 - Adolf Hitler commits suicide.

May 7 - Germany surrenders, and the war ends in Europe.

November - The Nuremberg Trials of Nazi war criminals begin.

THINKING ABOUT THE WEB SITE

1. How is using a Web site different from looking up information in a magazine or book?

_____

_____

2. What parts of a Web site would be most useful to students who want to learn more about Anne Frank?

_____

READING SKILL

3. **Scan** the Anne Frank Web site to find two events that happened in 1944.

_____

4. **Scan** the site. Which page of the Web site shows the topics covered on the Web site?

_____

TIMED WRITING: EVALUATION (15 minutes)

Think about the Anne Frank Web site. Then, answer the following questions.

• Is it useful?

_____

• Is the information included on the Web site credible?

_____

• Does the site meet its goal?

_____

_____

PLURALS

Most plural forms of English nouns follow basic rules. Learning these few rules will help you to correctly spell most of the plurals.

RULES

- Add *s* to most nouns to form plurals: *effect / effects*.
- Add *es* to nouns that end in **s**, **ss**, **sh**, **ch**, and **x** to form plurals: *clash / clashes*
- Add *es* to most nouns that end in a **consonant and o**: *potato / potatoes*
- Change *y* to *i* and add *es* to nouns that end in the **consonant–y** combination: *analogy / analogies*
- Do not change the *y*, just add *s* to nouns that end in the **vowel–y** combination: *key / keys*
- For some nouns ending in **fe**, change *fe* to *ve* and add *s*: *life / lives*

Word List
hero / heroes
box / boxes
class / classes
wife / wives
patch / patches
theory / theories
variety / varieties
toy / toys
tooth / teeth
deer / deer

IRREGULAR PLURALS

- Some nouns have the same spelling in both forms: *scissors / scissors, pants / pants, fish / fish*
- Some nouns require basic spelling changes in the plural form: *foot / feet, child / children, crisis / crises*

Practice Read the following paragraph. Circle any word that is misspelled. Then, write the misspelled word correctly on the lines.

How many theoryes do you think there are about the best kinds of toyies for small childs? There are many varietys of dolls and superheros. You probably should not give little kids scissor or stuffed animals with sharp teeths. Whatever you do give them, little children often like the boxs best.

_____

_____

Water Names

The **oral tradition** is stories that were once told out loud. These stories were passed down from older people to younger people. Stories in the oral tradition have these elements:

- **Theme:** a central message about life. Some themes are **universal**. Universal themes appear in many cultures and many time periods.

- **Heroes** and **heroines:** men and women who do great and often impossible things.

Storytellers tell their stories aloud. They need to hold their listeners' attention. Look at the chart for some ways that storytellers make stories more interesting and entertaining for their audiences.

Technique	Definition	Example
Hyperbole	exaggeration or overstatement, often to make people laugh	That basketball player was as tall as the Empire State Building.
Personification	human qualities or characteristics given to animals or things	The clouds shed tears.
Idioms	expressions in a language or culture that do not mean exactly what they say	"a chip off the old block" "as easy as pie"

American folk literature is a living tradition. This means that it is always changing. Many of the subjects and heroes from American folk literature can be found in the movies, sports heroes, or even politics of today.

There are different types of stories in the oral tradition.

- **Myths:** stories about the actions of gods, goddesses, and heroes. Some myths tell how things came to be. Every culture has its own **mythology**. A mythology is a collection of myths.

- **Fables:** short stories that usually have a moral. A moral is a lesson. The characters in fables are often animals that act like humans.

- **Tall tales:** stories that use exaggeration to make them funny. This kind of exaggeration is called **hyperbole**. Heroes of tall tales often do impossible things. Tale tales are one kind of **legend**. A legend is a story that is based on fact but that becomes less true with each telling.

- **Epics:** long poems about great heroes. These heroes go on dangerous journeys called **quests**. The quests are an important part of the history of a culture or nation.

Water Names

Lan Samantha Chang

Summary Three girls sit on a back porch on the prairie. Their grandmother Waipuo reminds them of how important China's longest river was in the lives of their ancestors. She tells them a story in Chinese about a girl who falls in love with a water ghost.

Note-taking Guide

Use this chart to record details about the story within the story.

In the present

Who:
three girls and their grandmother

Where:

What happens:

1200 years ago

Who:
Wen Zhiqing and his daughter

Where:

What happens:

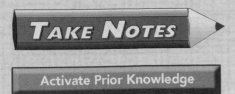

Water Names
Lan Samantha Chang

During summer evenings, the sisters would sit on the back porch. They would fight and argue with one another. Their grandmother scolded the girls for fighting. The sisters would stop their arguing immediately. Some nights their grandmother sat quietly in her chair. Other times, she would tell stories about China.

♦ ♦ ♦

"In these prairie crickets I often hear the sound of rippling waters, of the Yangtze River," she said. "Granddaughters, you are descended on both sides from people of the water country, near the mouth of the great Chang Jiang, as it is called, where the river is so grand and broad that even on clear days you can scarcely see the other side."

♦ ♦ ♦

The grandmother tells the girls that they are related to great men and women. The family has lived through floods and bad times. It runs together like rain. It has the spirit of the river. But even people of the river must be careful of water.

When the grandmother was young, her own grandmother told her a story. Twelve hundred years ago, Wen Zhiqing lived near the Yangtze River. He trained birds to catch fish for him. The birds would sit on the side of the boat. Then they would dive into the water.

Wen Zhiqing had a beautiful daughter. She loved the river. She also loved to go out in the boat to fish. She did not worry about the dangers of the river.

♦ ♦ ♦

"One clear spring evening, as she watched the last bird dive off into the blackening waters, she said, 'If only this catch would bring back something more than another fish!'

"She leaned over the side of the boat and looked at the water. The stars and moon reflected back at her. And it is said that the spirits living underneath the water looked up at her as well. And the spirit of a young man who had drowned in the river many years before saw her lovely face."

❖ ❖ ❖

The bird was gone for a long time. It came back with a very large fish. Inside the fish Wen found a pearl ring.

Wen's daughter was happy that her wish came true. In the evenings she stared at the water. Sometimes she thought she saw a young man looking back. She longed for the young man. She became sad and afraid. She knew that she would leave her family soon.

Her father told her that she was seeing only the moon's reflection in the water. The daughter told him that there was a kingdom in the river. The prince wanted to marry her. The ring was a gift to her father. Wen did not believe his daughter. He told her to stay away from the water.

For a year, nothing happened. Then a terrible flood came in the spring. The flood destroyed almost everything.

❖ ❖ ❖

"In the middle of the <u>torrential</u> rain, the family noticed that the daughter was missing. She had taken advantage of the confusion to hurry to the

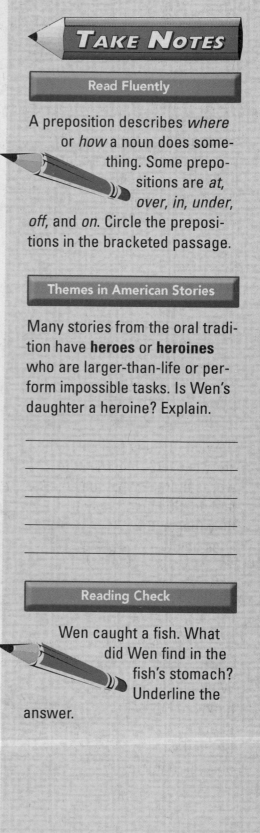

Vocabulary Development

torrential (tuh REN shuhl) *adj.* describing large amounts of water moving very quickly in a particular direction

Water Names **297**

TAKE NOTES

Themes in American Stories

Theme is a central message about life. One theme in this story is about the desire for a treasure, or something better. How is this theme shown by Wen's daughter?

_____
_____
_____
_____
_____

Stop to Reflect

How do the girls feel when the story is over? Underline the words that tell what they think and do. Summarize what they feel on the lines below.

_____
_____

Reading Check

What did the people think happened to Wen's daughter? Circle the answer in the text.

river to visit her beloved. The family searched for days but they never found her."

♦ ♦ ♦

The grandmother stopped talking. One of the sisters asked what happened to the girl.

♦ ♦ ♦

"Who knows?" Waipuo said. "They say she was seduced by a water ghost. Or perhaps she lost her mind to desiring."

♦ ♦ ♦

The grandmother answered no more questions. She rose from her chair. Soon the light went on in her bedroom.

The sisters stayed on the porch. They did not talk. They were thinking about Wen Zhiqing's daughter. They wondered what she looked like. They wondered how old she was. They wondered why no one remembered her name.

♦ ♦ ♦

While we weren't watching, the stars had emerged. Their brilliant pinpoints mapped the heavens. They glittered over us, over Waipuo in her room, the house, and the small city we lived in, the great waves of grass that ran for miles around us, the ground beneath as dry and hard as bone.

Vocabulary Development

seduced (si DOOST) *v.* persuaded someone to do something by making it seem very attractive or interesting
emerged (i MERJD) *v.* appeared after being hidden

Themes in American Stories

1. **Infer:** The girls learn how important the great river was in their family's past. How do they and their grandmother feel about the river?

_____

_____

_____

2. **Interpret:** Two unusual events from the story are listed in the first column of the chart. List different ways to explain these events in the second column. Then, use the third column to explain why you agree or disagree with each explanation.

Event	Explanation	Why You Agree or Disagree
Face in the water	The reflection of the moon	
Ring in the fish		

3. **Themes in American Stories:** A **theme** is a central idea or message that is revealed in a story. What do you think is the theme of this story?

_____

_____

4. **Themes in American Stories:** Think about the way the story is told. Identify one example of a storytelling technique or detail that is part of the **oral tradition**.

_____

_____

RESEARCH THE AUTHOR

Storytelling Hour

Plan a **storytelling hour** during which you will retell a variety of Chinese folk tales. Follow these steps to gather information for your storytelling hour.

- Go to the library and search the online catalog for collections of Chinese folklore. Record the titles and short summaries of stories that you think will interest the class.

  What I found: _____

  _____

  _____

- Search the Internet. Search for "Chinese folklore" or "Chinese folk tales." Record short summaries of the stories that you find.

  What I found: _____

  _____

  _____

- Watch the video interview with Lan Samantha Chang. Review your source material. Use this information to record additional information for your storytelling hour.

  Additional information: _____

  _____

  _____

  _____

  _____

  _____

  _____

  _____

Use your notes to prepare your storytelling hour.

Why the Waves Have Whitecaps • Coyote Steals the Sun and Moon

READING SKILL

A **summary** presents the main ideas of a text. It is much shorter than the original work. To write a summary, you must focus on the most important information. This helps you remember the main point of the story. Use these steps to summarize:

- **Reread to identify main events or ideas** in the story.

- Put the main ideas in order.

- Use your notes to write a summary that has the main ideas.

- Use as few words as possible.

Remember that summaries do not have details. Reading a summary cannot replace the experience of reading the whole work.

LITERARY ANALYSIS

A **myth** is an ancient story. It tells the beliefs or customs of a culture. A culture is a group of people. Every culture has its own **mythology**. A mythology is a group of myths. Myths explain events in nature or in a people's history. They often describe the actions of gods. Some have animals that act like people. Myths often have natural forces, such as wind and rain, that act like people.

It is helpful to know about a culture to understand its myths. Use this chart to find cultural connections that help explain the myths in this section.

Detail from Mythology	Cultural Connections
Prometheus steals fire from Zeus, king of the gods, and gives it to humans.	To ancient Greeks, fire was essential for cooking, forging weapons, and providing warmth.

Why the Waves Have Whitecaps

Zora Neale Hurston

Summary The story is an African American folk tale. Mrs. Wind brags about her children. Mrs. Water grows tired of it and drowns the children. Mrs. Wind looks for her children but sees only white feathers on the water. That is why there are whitecaps. Storms at sea are the wind and water fighting over the children.

Reading/Writing Connection

Complete the sentence to compare waves to something else.

1. Waves <u>approach</u> the shore like _____.

2. Waves <u>persist</u> in hitting the beach like _____.

3. After a storm, waves <u>subside</u> as if they _____.

Note-taking Guide

Record the sequence of events of "Why the Waves Have Whitecaps" in this chart.

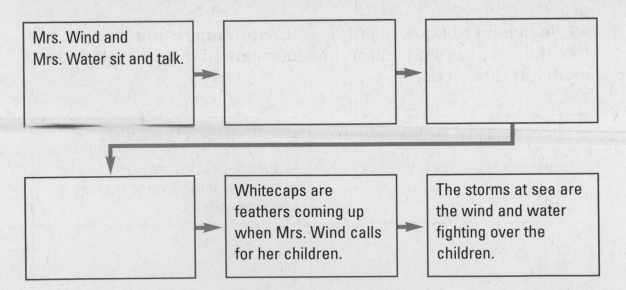

Mrs. Wind and Mrs. Water sit and talk.		

	Whitecaps are feathers coming up when Mrs. Wind calls for her children.	The storms at sea are the wind and water fighting over the children.

Why the Waves Have Whitecaps

1. **Infer:** Mrs. Wind and Mrs. Water were friends at the beginning of the story. Why did they start fighting?

_____

_____

2. **Cause and Effect:** What happens because of their fight?

_____

_____

3. **Reading Strategy:** The chart shows the three parts of the story. Use this chart to **summarize** each part of the story. Use your own words.

Section	Summary
Mrs. Water and Mrs. Wind Compete	
Mrs. Water's Revenge	
Whitecaps and Storms	

4. **Reading Strategy:** A **summary** includes the most important facts of a text. Use your chart to summarize this myth. Use only a few sentences. Do not include small details.

_____

_____

5. **Literary Analysis: Myths** explain things in life. What does this myth explain?

_____

_____

SUPPORT FOR WRITING AND EXTEND YOUR LEARNING

Writing: Myth

Create your own **myth**. In it, explain something that takes place in nature. For example, you could explain a rainbow, the seasons, or an animal behavior. Begin by thinking of a list of possible ideas. Use the graphic organizer below to help you choose your subject.

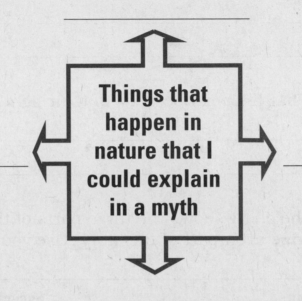

Choose one of your ideas to explain in your myth.

Listening and Speaking: Oral Presentation

Prepare an **oral presentation** about African myths and folk tales that were brought to the Americas. Do your research in the library or on the Internet. Look for ways in which history and traditional stories have affected African Americans. Make a list of topics you could use to search for information.

_____

_____

_____

Use your list to help you find information for your oral presentation.

Coyote Steals the Sun and Moon

Zuñi Myth, Retold by Richard Erdoes and Alfonso Ortiz

Summary This myth tells about how the sun and the moon got into the sky. Coyote and Eagle team up to steal the sun and moon to light up their dark world. Coyote's curious nature causes them to lose both. The sun and moon escape into the sky.

Reading/Writing Connection

Complete each sentence to explain a way people might use a myth to understand something in nature.

1. Myths <u>enable</u> parents to _____.

2. Myths help people <u>comprehend</u> _____.

3. One reason people <u>conceive</u> myths is _____.

Note-taking Guide

Use this chart to write the explanations this myth gives for questions about nature.

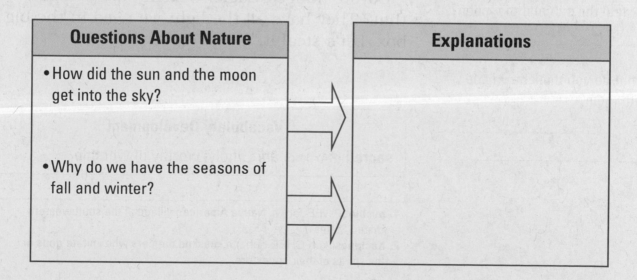

Questions About Nature	Explanations
• How did the sun and the moon get into the sky?	
• Why do we have the seasons of fall and winter?	

Describe an animal in a folk tale or fairy tale you read when you were younger. What human qualities did the animal have?

_____

_____

_____

Literary Analysis

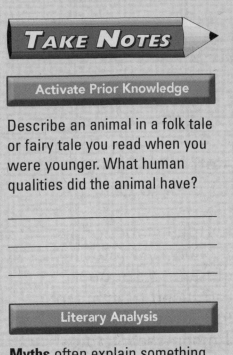

Myths often explain something in nature. What do you think this tale will explain? Underline a sentence in the bracketed passage that helps you figure out the answer. Then, write the answer below.

_____

_____

Stop to Reflect

Why do you think Coyote wants to steal the sun and the moon?

_____

What do you think he will do with them?

_____

_____

Coyote Steals the Sun and Moon
Zuñi Myth, Retold by Richard Erdoes and Alfonso Ortiz

The main characters of this story are two animals: Coyote, an eager but bad hunter, and Eagle, a very good hunter. Eagle catches many rabbits, but Coyote only catches little bugs because he has trouble seeing in the dark. So Coyote decides to team up with Eagle to get more food. Eagle agrees.

So the two hunters begin to look for the light. They set out to find the sun and the moon.

◆ ◆ ◆

At last they came to a pueblo,[1] where the Kachinas[2] happened to be dancing. The people invited Eagle and Coyote to sit down and have something to eat while they watch the <u>sacred</u> dances. Seeing the power of the Kachinas, Eagle said, "I believe these are the people who have light."

◆ ◆ ◆

Coyote sees two boxes, one large and one small. The Kachinas open these boxes whenever they want light. The big box gives off more light than the small box.

◆ ◆ ◆

Coyote nudged Eagle. "Friend, did you see that? They have all the light we need in the big box. Let's steal it."

Vocabulary Development

sacred (SAY krid) *adj.* holy; worthy of worship

---

1. **pueblo** (PWEB loh) *n.* Native American village in the southwestern United States.
2. **Kachinas** (kuh CHEE nuhz) *n.* masked dancers who imitate gods or the spirits of their ancestors.

"You always want to steal and rob. I say we should just borrow it."

"They won't lend it to us."

"You may be right," said Eagle. "Let's wait till they finish dancing and then steal it."

❖ ❖ ❖

After the Kachinas go to sleep, Eagle scoops up the large box and flies off. Coyote runs along as fast as he can, but he can't keep up. Coyote begs Eagle to let him carry the box a little way. But Eagle refuses.

❖ ❖ ❖

"No, no," said Eagle, "you never do anything right."

He flew on, and Coyote ran after him. After a while Coyote shouted again: "Friend, you're my chief, and it's not right for you to carry the box; people will call me lazy. Let me have it."

"No, no, you always mess everything up." And Eagle flew on and Coyote ran along.

❖ ❖ ❖

Coyote keeps begging to carry the box. Finally, Eagle agrees to let him carry the box for a while. But first he makes Coyote promise not to open it. Coyote gives his promise not to open the box. But as Eagle flies ahead, Coyote gets more and more curious. He hides behind a hill and sneaks a look inside the box. Coyote finds that Eagle has put both the sun and the moon in a single box.

When Coyote opens the box, the moon flies high into the sky. All the plants shrivel up and turn brown. The leaves fall off the trees. Winter comes. Then the sun flies out into the sky. All the fruits of the earth shrivel up and turn cold.

❖ ❖ ❖

TAKE NOTES

Read Fluently

A dialogue is a conversation between characters. Quotation marks often point out a dialogue. Circle any sentences spoken by Eagle in the first bracketed passage. Underline any sentences spoken by Coyote.

Reading Skill

A **summary** is a short statement that presents the key ideas and main points of a text. Read the second bracketed paragraph. Write the numbers 1, 2 and 3 next to the three sentences that tell the main points of this paragraph. Then, summarize the paragraph.

_____

_____

_____

Reading Check

What were the Kachinas doing when Coyote and Eagle stole their light? Bracket the sentence that tells you.

TAKE NOTES

Reading Skill

When you **summarize** a story, you explain its main points in your own words. Summarize how the world changes in this myth after Coyote opens the box.

_____

_____

_____

_____

Literary Analysis

Many animal characters in **myths** have human qualities. Describe one human quality that you see in each of the animals.

_____

_____

_____

Reading Check

Whose fault is it that we have winter every year? Circle the name in the story.

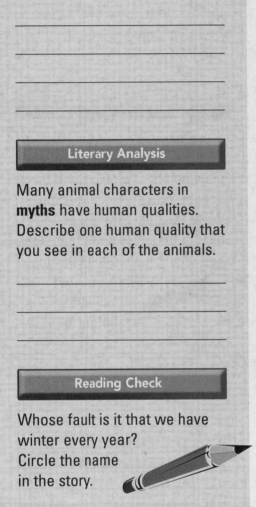

Eagle turned and flew back to see what had delayed Coyote. "You fool! Look what you've done!" he said. "You let the sun and moon escape, and now it's cold." Indeed, it began to snow, and Coyote shivered. "Now your teeth are chattering," Eagle said, "and it's your fault that cold has come into the world."

It's true. If it weren't for Coyote's curiosity and mischief making, we wouldn't have winter; we could enjoy summer all the time.

Coyote Steals the Sun and Moon

1. **Compare and Contrast:** Explain one way that Coyote and Eagle are the same. Explain one way that they are different.

_____

_____

_____

2. **Infer:** What does the way Coyote acts in this story tell you about him?

_____

_____

3. **Reading Skill:** The graphic organizer below splits this story up into four parts. In the blank next to each part, list the most important events in that part. This will help you **summarize** the story. **The Hunt** has been summarized for you.

Detail	Cultural Connections
The Hunt	Eagle catches many rabbits. Coyote catches only bugs.
At the Kachinas' Dance	
Running Away	
Coyote's Mistake	

4. **Literary Analysis:** Most **myths** explain something in nature. What event in nature does this myth explain?

_____

_____

SUPPORT FOR WRITING AND EXTEND YOUR LEARNING

Writing: Myth

A **myth** is a story that often explains something in nature. Write your own myth that answers a question about the natural world.

- What is something in nature that interests you? _____

- What is a possible explanation for your choice? _____
  _____

- Write a brief description of the characters you will use. Tell whether they are humans or animals. List the qualities they have. _____
  _____
  _____

- What is a good title for this myth? _____

Listening and Speaking: Oral Presentation

Prepare an **oral presentation** about Zuñi culture. Use the Internet and library references to gather information.

Make a list of questions you will need to answer for your report. Use this list to help focus your research.

1. _____
   _____

2. _____
   _____

3. _____
   _____

4. _____
   _____

5. _____
   _____

Reviews

ABOUT REVIEWS

A **book review** gives a feeling or opinion about a book. You can find book reviews in different places, such as newspapers, magazines, television, or online.

Some book review writers know a great deal about a book's topic or author. Most book reviews have these parts:

- basic information such as author, price, and publisher
- a summary of the book
- opinions about the book's good and bad points
- an opinion about whether the book is worth reading

READING SKILL

An **author's message** is what the author wants the reader to know. You can read a review to help you decide whether you want to read the book. You will have to understand the author's message. You can then decide for yourself what you think. Use clues to help you figure out what the author's message is. These clues can be:

- adjectives that the author uses to describe the book
- description of the book's contents
- the author's opinion about the book

Use this chart to help you figure out an author's purpose

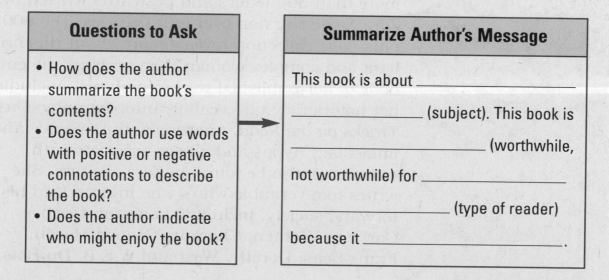

Questions to Ask	Summarize Author's Message
• How does the author summarize the book's contents? • Does the author use words with positive or negative connotations to describe the book? • Does the author indicate who might enjoy the book?	This book is about _____ _____ (subject). This book is _____ (worthwhile, not worthwhile) for _____ _____ (type of reader) because it _____.

A **book review** includes basic information about a book. You can use this information to find the book. Circle the title, editor, publisher, and publication date for *A Life in Letters*. Why would these pieces of information be useful to a reader?

_____

_____

A book review talks about one book in depth. However, it often names other books by the same author. Titles of books are usually written in italics. Skim through the review to find all book titles. Circle the title of the other book that is talked about in this review.

How many of Hurston's letters and postcards are included in the book?

A Life in Letters

**Book Review
by Zakia Carter**

**Zora Neale Hurston:
A Life in Letters.**

Edited by Carla Kaplan
Doubleday; October 2002;
896 pages

Within days of having *Zora Neale Hurston: A Life in Letters* in my possession, I was inspired to devote the total of my lunch hour to selecting beautiful blank cards and stationery, a fine ink pen and a book of stamps. By the end of the day, I had penned six letters, the old-fashioned way, to friends and relatives—something I haven't done since summer camp. In our haste to save time, we check our inboxes with an eagerness that was once reserved for that moment before pushing a tiny silver key into a mailbox door. E-mail has replaced paper and pen, so much so that the U.S. Postal Service is losing business. But the truth of the matter is, folks will neither salvage nor cherish e-mail as they might a handwritten letter.

And so *A Life in Letters* is a gift. It includes more than 500 letters and postcards written by Zora Neale Hurston over four decades. The 800-plus-page collection reveals more about this brilliant and complex woman than perhaps the entire body of her published works combined, including her notoriously unrevealing autobiography, *Dust Tracks on the Road*. Amazingly, the urgency and immediacy (typos and all) we associate with e-mail can also be found in Zora's letters. She writes to a veritable who's who in American history and society, including Langston Hughes, Carl Van Vechten, Charlotte Osgood Mason, Franz Boas, Dorothy West and W.E.B. Du Bois among others, sometimes more than once or twice a day. In these, her most intimate writings, Zora comes to life.

While we are familiar with Zora the novelist, essayist, playwright and anthropologist, *A Life in Letters* introduces us to Zora the filmmaker; Zora the Barnard College undergrad and Columbia University student; Zora the two-time Guggenheim fellow; Zora the chicken specialist; Zora the thrice-married wife; and Zora the political pundit. Zora's letters are at times flip, ironic, heartbreaking and humorous. They are insightful, biting and candid as journal entries. One can only wish for responses to Zora's words, but the work is not incomplete without them.

A treasure trove of information, in addition to the annotated letters, a chronology of Zora's life, a glossary of the people, events, and institutions to which she refers in her letters, and a thorough bibliographical listing are generously included by editor Carla Kaplan. Each decade of writing is introduced by an essay on the social, political, and personal points of significance in Zora's life. Kaplan's is a fine, well edited and utterly revealing work of scholarship into the life of one of the greatest and often most misunderstood American writers. In many ways, *A Life in Letters* is, in fact, a long love letter for Zora. It is a reminder to salvage and cherish what should not be forgotten and an admonishment to write what you love on paper.

—Zakia Carter is an editor at Africana.com.

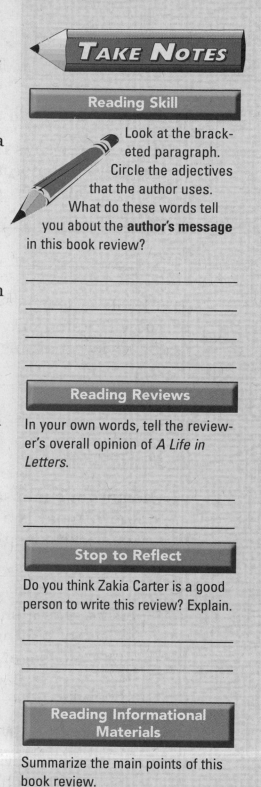

TAKE NOTES

Reading Skill

Look at the bracketed paragraph. Circle the adjectives that the author uses. What do these words tell you about the **author's message** in this book review?

_____

_____

_____

_____

Reading Reviews

In your own words, tell the reviewer's overall opinion of *A Life in Letters*.

_____

_____

Stop to Reflect

Do you think Zakia Carter is a good person to write this review? Explain.

_____

_____

Reading Informational Materials

Summarize the main points of this book review.

_____

_____

_____

_____

_____

THINKING ABOUT THE BOOK REVIEW

1. The reviewer says that there is some information in *A Life in Letters* that is not in Hurston's other books. What kind of information would not be found in other books?

   _____

   _____

2. A **book review** gives an opinion about a book. Some readers know Hurston only as a novelist and storywriter. What is in the review that might surprise these readers?

   _____

   _____

READING SKILL

3. The **author's message** is what the author wants the reader to know. What is a strength of *Zora Neale Hurston: A Life in Letters* besides the letters themselves?

   _____

4. A summary is a short statement that presents the main ideas in a piece of writing. Complete this sentence to summarize the **author's message**:

   The book is _____.

TIMED WRITING: SUMMARY (20 minutes)

Summarize the **review**. Include the author's main points and opinions. Use this chart to get started.

What does Carter think about *A Life in Letters*?	
What does Carter think readers will gain from reading *A Life in Letters*?	

Chicoria • from The People, Yes • Brer Possum's Dilemma • John Henry

READING SKILL

A **summary** is a short statement. It gives the main points of a piece of writing. Summaries do not include the minor details. They are a quick way to preview or review a work. Follow these steps to create a summary:

- Decide which events are important enough to be included.
- **Use graphics** to help you put the information in order. You could use a timeline to put the events of a story in order.

LITERARY ANALYSIS

Storytellers pass on legends, songs, folk tales, tall tales, and stories in the **oral tradition**. This means that they are passed from generation to generation by word of mouth. These stories are written down later. They are written in a **dialect**. A dialect is the language and grammar of a certain region. Reading these tales can help you learn about the values of a culture. As you read, use this chart to note characteristics of the oral tradition.

Oral Tradition	Story Detail
Repetition and exaggeration	
Heroes who are brave, clever, or strong	
Animal characters that act like human beings	
Dialect and informal speech	
Traditions of a culture	

Chicoria • from The People, Yes • Brer Possum's . . .

Chicoria • from The People, Yes

Summaries In "Chicoria," a rancher invites a poet to dinner. The poet is asked to share poetry, but not to eat. The poet uses a folk tale to point out the rancher's rude behavior. In the selection from *The People, Yes*, the speaker talks about his love for America. He describes the adventures of famous characters from American folklore, such as Paul Bunyan and John Henry.

Reading/Writing Connection

Complete this paragraph to describe characteristics of folk tales you have heard.

Folk tales <u>illustrate</u> _____. Folk tales can

<u>enrich</u> _____. Folk tales can <u>enhance</u> your

understanding of _____.

Note-taking Guide

Use this graphic organizer to record how "Chicoria" and the selection from *The People, Yes* have some of the same folk story traits. Put one example in each box.

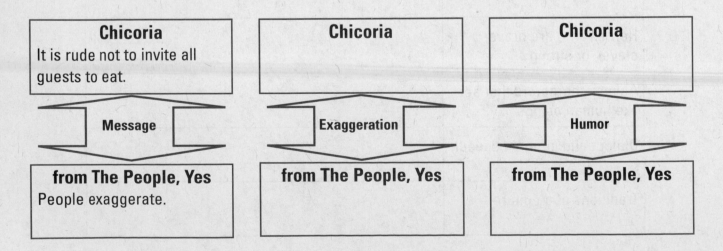

Chicoria	**Chicoria**	**Chicoria**
It is rude not to invite all guests to eat.		
Message	Exaggeration	Humor
from The People, Yes	**from The People, Yes**	**from The People, Yes**
People exaggerate.		

Chicoria • from The People, Yes

1. **Analyze:** Why is Chicoria so sure that he will eat at the rancher's table?

_____

_____

2. **Evaluate:** Identify two characters in the selection from *The People, Yes*. Tell how their abilities help them survive in a wild, new country.

_____

_____

3. **Reading Skill:** Fill in the cluster diagram below. **Summarize** images in the selection from *The People, Yes*. State the main idea behind the images.

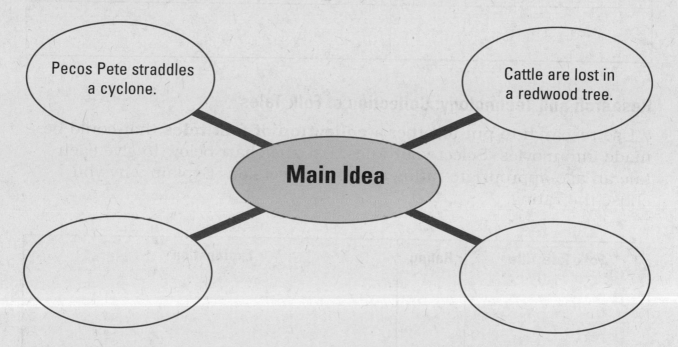

Pecos Pete straddles a cyclone.

Cattle are lost in a redwood tree.

Main Idea

4. **Literary Analysis:** Why might people from New Mexico like the story of Chicoria enough to pass it on through the **oral tradition**?

_____

_____

SUPPORT FOR WRITING AND EXTEND YOUR LEARNING

Writing: Critical Analysis

Write a **critical analysis** to explain how language and idioms affect the tone and mood in folk stories. Be sure to give examples from "Chicoria" and the selection from *The People, Yes*. Use the chart below to write notes for your critical analysis.

Example of Language or Idiom Used	How It Affects Mood of Work

Research and Technology: Collection of Folk Tales

Use research to put together a **collection of folk tales** that could be made into movies. Select your tales. Use the chart below to give each tale an age-appropriate rating for a movie version. Explain why you chose the rating.

Folk Tale Title	Rating	Explanation

Brer Possum's Dilemma • John Henry

Summary In "Brer Possum's Dilemma," Brer Snake asks Brer Possum for help. "John Henry" is a ballad, or song, that tells the story of an African American hero who tries to hammer a railroad spike faster than a steam drill can.

Reading/Writing Connection

Complete each sentence to describe how folk tales can teach lessons.

1. Folk tales <u>instruct</u> people _____.

2. Animals in folk tales <u>display</u> _____.

3. The ending of a folk tale <u>emphasizes</u> _____.

Note-taking Guide

Folk tales often pass along important life lessons. Use this chart to

Folk Tale	What Lesson It Taught
Brer Possum's Dilemma	
John Henry	Nothing is impossible when you set your mind to it.

Describe a time when you were fooled by someone. What did you learn from the experience?

_____

_____

_____

_____

Reading Skill

A **summary** presents the main points of a story. It does not include minor details. What events from this page of the story would you include in a summary?

_____

_____

_____

Reading Check

What are Brer Possum and Brer Snake like? Circle the paragraph that describes Brer Possum. Put a box around the paragraph that describes Brer Snake.

Brer Possum's Dilemma
Jackie Torrence

Back in the days when the animals could talk, there lived ol' Brer[1] Possum. He was a fine feller. Why, he never liked to see no critters[2] in trouble. He was always helpin' out, a-doin' somethin' for others.

♦　♦　♦

While walking one day, Brer Possum saw a big hole in the road. He looked in. He saw Brer Snake in the bottom of the hole. Brer Snake had a brick on his back. Brer Possum decided to leave. He knew that Brer Snake might bite him. He began to walk away.

Brer Snake called out for help. Brer Possum went back. Brer Snake asked Brer Possum to help get the brick off his back.

♦　♦　♦

Brer Possum thought.

"Now listen here, Brer Snake. I knows you. You's mean and evil and lowdown, and if'n I was to git down in that hole and git to liftin' that brick offa your back, you wouldn't do nothin' but bite me."

Ol' Brer Snake just hissed.

"Maybe not. Maybe not. Maaaaaaaybe not."

♦　♦　♦

Brer Possum saw a dead branch hanging from a tree. He climbed up the tree and broke off the branch. He poked the brick off Brer Snake's back. Then he ran away.

Brer Snake called for help again. Brer Possum went back to the hole. Brer Snake said that he could not get out of the hole. He asked Brer Possum to help. Brer Possum again said that he was afraid that Brer Snake

---

1. **Brer** (brer) dialect for "brother," used before a name.
2. **critters** dialect for "creatures"; animals.

would bite him. Brer Snake said that he might not bite him. Brer Possum pushed the dead branch under Brer Snake. He lifted Brer Snake out of the hole and tossed him into the tall grass. Then Brer Possum ran away.

Brer Snake called for help once more. Good-hearted Brer Possum once again went back to the hole. Brer Snake said that he was cold. He asked Brer Possum to put him in Brer Possum's pocket.

Brer Possum refused. If he put Brer Snake in his pocket, Brer Snake would bite him. Brer Snake said that he might not bite him. Brer Possum began to feel sorry for him.

◆ ◆ ◆

"All right," said Brer Possum. "You must be cold. So jist this once I'm a-goin' to put you in my pocket."

◆ ◆ ◆

Brer Snake was quiet and still. Brer Possum forgot about him. Suddenly, Brer Snake crawled out of the pocket. He hissed at Brer Possum.

◆ ◆ ◆

"I'm a-goin' to bite you."

But Brer Possum said, "Now wait a minute. Why are you a-goin' to bite me? I done took that brick offa your back, I got you outa that hole, and I put you in my pocket to git you warm. Why are you a-goin' to bite me?"

Brer Snake hissed.

"You knowed I was a snake before you put me in you pocket."

And when you're mindin' your own business and you spot trouble, don't never trouble trouble 'til trouble troubles you.

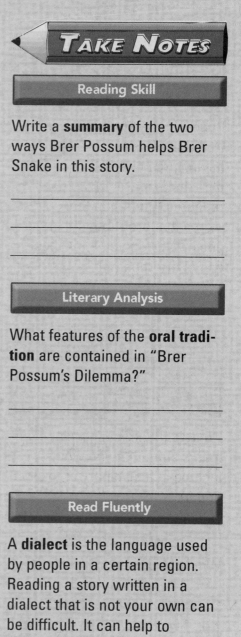

TAKE NOTES

Reading Skill

Write a **summary** of the two ways Brer Possum helps Brer Snake in this story.

_____

_____

_____

Literary Analysis

What features of the **oral tradition** are contained in "Brer Possum's Dilemma?"

_____

_____

_____

Read Fluently

A **dialect** is the language used by people in a certain region. Reading a story written in a dialect that is not your own can be difficult. It can help to rewrite passages written in dialect in your own words. Rewrite the bracketed passage in your own words below.

_____

_____

_____

_____

_____

_____

Poems in the **oral tradition** often have words or phrases that are repeated. Underline the words that are repeated in the poem. Why do you think these words are repeated?

_____

_____

_____

Reading Skill

What is the first important event in this story that you would include in a **summary** of this poem?

_____

Why is this event important?

_____

_____

Stop to Reflect

What qualities do you think a hero should have?

_____

_____

_____

John Henry

Henry

John Henry was a lil baby,
Sittin' on his mama's knee,
Said: 'The Big Bend Tunnel on the
    C. & O. road[1]
Gonna cause the death of me,
5 Lawd, Lawd, gonna cause the death of me.'

Cap'n says to John Henry,
'Gonna bring me a steam drill 'round,
Gonna take that steam drill out on the job,
Gonna whop that steel on down,
10 Lawd, Lawd, gonna whop that steel
    on down.'

John Henry tol' his cap'n,
Lightnin' was in his eye:
'Cap'n, bet yo' las, red cent on me,
Fo' I'll beat it to the bottom or I'll die,
15 Lawd, Lawd, I'll beat it to the bottom or
    I'll die.'

Sun shine hot an' burnin',
Wer'n't no breeze a-tall,
Sweat ran down like water down a hill,
That day John Henry let his hammer fall,
20 Lawd, Lawd, that day John Henry let his
    hammer fall.

John Henry went to the tunnel,
An' they put him in the lead to drive,
The rock so tall an' John Henry so small,
That he lied down his hammer an' he cried,
25 Lawd, Lawd, that he lied down his hammer
    an' he cried.

---

1. **C. & O. road** Chesapeake and Ohio Railroad. The C&O's Big Bend railroad tunnel was built in the 1870s through a mountain in West Virginia.

John Henry started on the right hand,
The steam drill started on the lef'—
'Before I'd let this steam drill beat
   me down,
I'd hammer my fool self to death,
30 Lawd, Lawd, I'd hammer my fool self
   to death.'

John Henry had a lil woman,
Her name were Polly Ann,
John Henry took sick an' had to go to bed,
Polly Ann drove steel like a man,
35 Lawd, Lawd, Polly Ann drove steel like
   a man.

John Henry said to his shaker,
Shaker, why don' you sing?
I'm throwin' twelve poun's from my hips
   on down,
Jes' listen to the col' steel ring,
40 Lawd, Lawd, jes' listen to the col' steel ring.'

Oh, the captain said to John Henry,
'I b'lieve this mountain's sinkin' in.'
John Henry said to his captain, oh my!
'Ain' nothin' but my hammer suckin' win',
45 Lawd, Lawd, ain' nothin' but my hammer
   suckin' win'.'

John Henry tol' his shaker,
'Shaker, you better pray,
For, if I miss this six-foot steel,
Tomorrow'll be yo' buryin' day,
50 Lawd, Lawd, tomorrow'll be yo' buryin' day.'

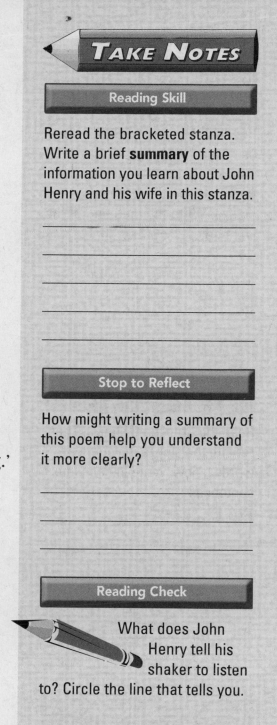

TAKE NOTES

Reading Skill

Reread the bracketed stanza. Write a brief **summary** of the information you learn about John Henry and his wife in this stanza.

_____

_____

_____

_____

_____

Stop to Reflect

How might writing a summary of this poem help you understand it more clearly?

_____

_____

_____

Reading Check

What does John Henry tell his shaker to listen to? Circle the line that tells you.

Vocabulary Development

shaker (SHAY kuhr) *n.*   person who sets the spikes and places the drills for a steel-driver to hammer

Poems in the **oral tradition** often use dialect to show the ways that different people speak. Reread the underlined text in the first stanza. Write the meaning of the lines below.

_____

_____

_____

_____

Read Fluently

Read the bracketed stanza. Then, rewrite the stanza in your own words below. Write in complete sentences.

_____

_____

_____

_____

_____

_____

Reading Check

How does John Henry die? Circle the lines that tell you.

John Henry tol' his captain,
'Look yonder what I see—
Yo' drill's done broke an' yo' hole's
   done choke,
An' you cain' drive steel like me,
55 Lawd, Lawd, an' you cain' drive steel
    like me.'

The man that invented the steam drill,
Thought he was mighty fine.
John Henry drove his fifteen feet,
An' the steam drill only made nine,
60 Lawd, Lawd, an' the steam drill only
    made nine.

The hammer that John Henry swung,
It weighed over nine pound;
He broke a rib in his lef'-han' side,
An' his intrels[2] fell on the groun',
65 Lawd, Lawd, an' his intrels fell on
    the groun'.

All the womens in the Wes',
When they heared of John Henry's death,
Stood in the rain, flagged the eas'-boun
    'train,
Goin' where John Henry fell dead,
70 Lawd, Lawd, goin' where John Henry
    fell dead.

John Henry's lil mother,
She was all dressed in red,
She jumped in bed, covered up her head,
Said she didn' know her son was dead,
75 Lawd, Lawd, didn' know her son was dead.

2. **intrels** (IN trelz) *n.* dialect for entrails—internal organs.

Dey took John Henry to the graveyard,
An' they buried him in the san',
An' every locomotive come roarin' by,
Says, 'There lays a steel-drivin' man,
80   Lawd, Lawd, there lays a steel-drivin' man.'

Literary Analysis

Which features of stories in the **oral tradition** are present in this poem?

_____

_____

_____

Reading Skill

Summarize the ending of this poem.

_____

_____

_____

Reading Check

What comes by the graveyard that John Henry was buried in? Circle the word in the text.

Brer Possum's Dilemma • John Henry

1. **Infer:** Brer Possum helps Brer Snake even though he does not trust the snake. Is Brer Possum meant to look foolish or very kind in the story? Explain.

   _____

   _____

   _____

2. **Deduce:** Brer Possum does not help Brer Snake right away. Why might Brer Possum think it is safe to trust Brer Snake?

   _____

   _____

3. **Reading Skill:** A **summary** tells the main points of a story. Knowing the important events in a story can help you summarize it. Complete this timeline to help you summarize "John Henry."

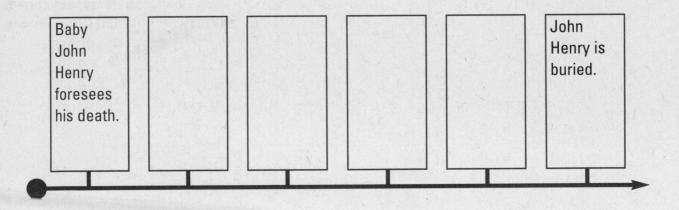

| Baby John Henry foresees his death. | | | | | John Henry is buried. |

4. **Literary Analysis:** Think about how John Henry is described in this ballad. Why do you think "John Henry" has been passed down from generation to generation in the **oral tradition**?

   _____

   _____

SUPPORT FOR WRITING AND EXTEND YOUR LEARNING

Writing: Writing a Critical Analysis

Write a **critical analysis** to explain how language and idioms affect mood and tone in folk literature. Use this chart to help you list certain dialect or idioms from the stories. Note their meanings. Use your notes to help you write your critical analysis.

Dialect and Folk Idioms	Meaning

Listening and Speaking: Storytelling Workshop

Prepare for a **storytelling workshop**. Select a tale to perform. The following prompts will help prepare you to perform your tale.

- How will you use your voice and body to dramatize the action? Give specific examples of what you will do at different points in the tale.

  _____

  _____

- What informal language or dialect can you add to your performance?

  _____

  _____

- In which parts of the story will you make eye contact? _____

  _____

Ellis Island • from Out of the Dust

READING SKILL

Setting a purpose for reading helps you pay attention when you read. Think about when you read about people from a different time and place. Your purpose might be to learn about the way they see the world and the problems they face.

One way to set a purpose for reading is to **ask questions**. The "K-W-L" chart can help you organize your thoughts. Fill in the first two boxes before you begin to read "Ellis Island." Fill in the last box after you are done reading.

K	W	L
What I already **k**now about the topic	Questions that explore what I **w**ant to know	Answers that show what I **l**earned

LITERARY ANALYSIS

Each work of literature has a **cultural context**. The cultural context is the society and point in history in which the characters live. Cultural contexts are shaped by many things, such as war and money issues.

Knowing about the cultural context helps you understand the characters better. As you read, look for things that characters say or do that are based on a cultural issue.

Ellis Island

Joseph Bruchac

Summary The poet imagines his Slovak grandparents as they arrive in the United States. Their first stop in the land of their dreams was Ellis Island in New York. He then writes of his Native American grandparents. He points out that they had always lived in America. Their way of life was destroyed when the Europeans came.

Reading/Writing Connection

Describe the risks and challenges that immigrants in the 1890s faced.

Immigrants came to America hoping to <u>maximize</u> their

_____. They had to <u>adapt</u> to new ways so that they

_____. They also tried to <u>maintain</u> some of _____.

Note-taking Guide

Some of the phrases in the poem are hard to understand. They use words that paint pictures and stand for other things. Use this graphic organizer to record some of the hidden messages.

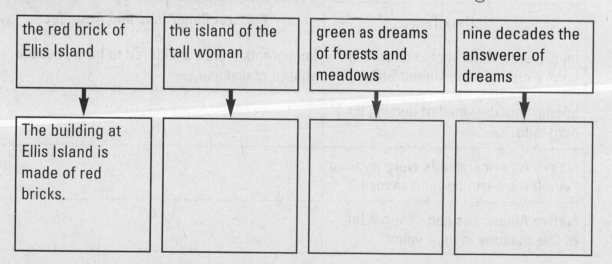

| the red brick of Ellis Island | the island of the tall woman | green as dreams of forests and meadows | nine decades the answerer of dreams |

| The building at Ellis Island is made of red bricks. | | | |

Ellis Island

1. **Interpret:** The word "native" means to be a member of or belong to the first group of people. The speaker uses the phrase "native lands within this nation." What does the phrase mean?

_____

2. **Analyze:** The speaker had one set of grandparents who came from Europe. He had another set who were Native American. How do his grandparents affect his feelings about Ellis Island?

_____

_____

3. **Reading Skill:** Your **purpose** for reading is the reason you read a text. What was your purpose for reading "Ellis Island"?

_____

_____

_____

4. **Literary Analysis:** The **cultural context** shows the setting in which the characters lived. What did you learn about the cultural context in the late 1800s? To answer, fill in the rest of the chart.

Detail	Cultural Conditions and Attitudes
Immigrants were kept in quarantine before entering the United States.	Immigrants were considered to be a possible source of disease.
Immigrants dreamed of owning their own land.	
Native American lands were invaded "when the earth became owned."	
Native Americans had "knowledge of the seasons in their veins."	

SUPPORT FOR WRITING AND EXTEND YOUR LEARNING

Writing: Research Proposal

Write a short **research proposal** for a report on immigrants' experiences as they passed through Ellis Island in the 1890s and early 1900s. A research proposal is an outline or description of information you plan to research. Complete these steps to help you organize your proposal.

Title of the report: _____

List at least two sources for your report: _____

_____

_____

Explain what you will describe first in your report: _____

_____

Explain what you will describe last in your report: _____

_____

Use your observations to help you get ideas for a research proposal.

Research and Technology: Letter

Write a **letter** to a friend back home as if you are an immigrant at Ellis Island. Use the list below to help you choose what information to include in your letter.

- Where I am coming from: _____

- Reasons for leaving the "old country": _____

_____

- What the journey to America was like: _____

_____

- What I felt when I first saw land: _____

_____

- How I was treated when I arrived: _____

_____

from Out of the Dust

Karen Hesse

Summary "Out of the Dust" includes three poems. The speaker in "Debts" describes the faith her father has that it will rain again. "Fields of Flashing Light" describes a dust storm on the prairie. In "Migrants," people leave their dried-up farms behind.

Reading/Writing Connection

Complete these sentences to describe how weather affects daily life.

1. Bad weather <u>complicates</u> life because _____.

2. The weather has an <u>impact</u> on _____.

3. Jobs in farming and building <u>involve</u> _____.

Note-taking Guide

Use this chart to list the ways that dust and drought affect the people in each of the three poems.

Effects of Dust and Drought		
Debts	**Fields of Flashing Light**	**Migrants**

Debts

Daddy is thinking
of taking a loan from Mr. Roosevelt and his
men,[1] . . .

◆ ◆ ◆

Daddy will use the money to plant new wheat. His winter crop has dried up and died. He will not have to repay the money until he harvests the crop. He is sure that it will soon rain and the wheat will grow.

Ma worries that it might not rain. Daddy disagrees. Ma tells Daddy that there has not been enough rain in the last three years.

Daddy is angry. He goes to the barn. He does not want to argue with Ma. The speaker asks Ma why Daddy is sure that it will rain. Ma says that it rains just enough to give people hope.

◆ ◆ ◆

But even if it didn't
your daddy would have to believe.
It's coming on spring,
and he's a farmer."

March 1934

---

1. **. . . . a loan from Mr. Roosevelt and his men.** In 1933, President Franklin D. Roosevelt began a series of government programs, called the New Deal, to help Americans suffering from the effects of the Great Depression. Among these programs were government loans to help Dust Bowl farmers.

TAKE NOTES

Activate Prior Knowledge

Describe a time when bad weather affected your life.

_____

_____

_____

_____

Reading Skill

Setting a purpose for reading helps you focus your attention as you read a literary work. Read the title and the first three lines of this poem. What will your purpose be in reading this poem?

_____

_____

Literary Analysis

The **cultural context** of a literary work is the social and historical environment in which the characters live. Underline three words and/or phrases that tell you about what life is like for the people in this poem. Explain one choice below.

_____

_____

_____

_____

Fields of Flashing Light

The wind woke the speaker from sleep. The speaker went outside to watch the lightning. Then the speaker heard the dust coming. It destroyed the fields of winter wheat.

♦   ♦   ♦

I watched the plants,
surviving after so much <u>drought</u> and so much wind,
I watched them fry, . . .

♦   ♦   ♦

The dust began to blow at the house. The speaker ran back inside the house. When the dust blew against the windows, Daddy woke up. He quickly went out into the storm.

♦   ♦   ♦

his overalls half-hooked over his union suit.
"Daddy!" I called. "You can't stop dust."

♦   ♦   ♦

Ma asked the speaker to cover the beds. The speaker pushed rugs against the doors and wet the rags around the windows. Ma made coffee and biscuits. She waited for Daddy to return.

After four in the morning, Ma sat down. She covered her face. Daddy was gone for many hours. It started to snow. At first, they were glad to see the snow. But the wind blew the snow away. All that was left was dust. Daddy returned. He sat down and blew his nose.

♦   ♦   ♦

Mud streamed out.
He coughed and spit out
mud.
If he had cried,
his tears would have been mud too,
but he didn't cry.
And neither did Ma.

March 1934

Migrants

The neighbors say that they will return when it rains again. They fill their cars with everything they own. The springs on their cars sag with heavy loads. They ask the speaker's family to remember them.

◆　◆　◆

And so they go,
Fleeing the blowing dust, . . .

◆　◆　◆

The neighbors say that they will come back. Some of them will travel to Texas or to Arkansas. They hope to rent a farm and start over. Still, they promise to come back when it rains. They take everything they own. Some of them are going to California. They might stay there if life is better.

◆　◆　◆

Don't forget us, they say.
But there are so many leaving,
how can I remember them all?

April 1935

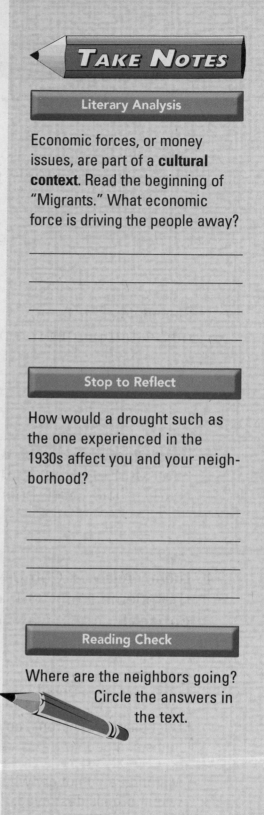

TAKE NOTES

Literary Analysis

Economic forces, or money issues, are part of a **cultural context**. Read the beginning of "Migrants." What economic force is driving the people away?

_____

_____

_____

_____

Stop to Reflect

How would a drought such as the one experienced in the 1930s affect you and your neighborhood?

_____

_____

_____

_____

Reading Check

Where are the neighbors going? Circle the answers in the text.

from Out of the Dust

1. **Cause and Effect:** The storm in "Fields of Flashing Light" destroys the wheat that the family planted. How will this affect the family's income?

_____

_____

2. **Speculate:** The family's neighbors move away in "Migrants." What might happen to the people who are left behind?

_____

_____

3. **Reading Skill: Setting a purpose for reading** helps you focus your attention on what you are reading. What purpose did you set for reading the three poems?

_____

4. **Literary Analysis:** Complete this chart by explaining what each detail from the poems from "Out of the Dust" tells you about the poems' **cultural context**, or the ways of life and attitudes of farmers during the Dust Bowl.

Detail	Ways of Life and Attitudes
Dust blew away crops, covering items and people.	
Ma and Pa do not cry when their wheat crop is destroyed.	Farmers had to be tough and not show emotion.
Pa decides to plant again, but other families decide to move away.	

SUPPORT FOR WRITING AND EXTEND YOUR LEARNING

Writing: Writing a Research Proposal

Write a short **research proposal** for a report on how the Dust Bowl affected farmers in the 1930s. A research proposal is an outline or description of information you plan to research. Complete these steps to help you organize your proposal.

Title of the report: _____

List at least two sources for your report: _____

_____

_____

Explain what you will describe first in your report: _____

_____

Explain what you will describe last in your report: _____

_____

Listening and Speaking: Oral Presentation

Prepare an **oral presentation** on the effects of the Dust Bowl during the 1930s. Answer the following questions as you research the subject.

- When did the drought begin? When did it end? _____

_____

- What crops were grown in the area at the time? What crops, if any, are grown in the area now?

_____

_____

- What was the population of the area at the beginning of the drought? What was the population at the end of the drought?

_____

_____

Choice: A Tribute to Martin Luther King, Jr. • An Episode of War

READING SKILL

Before you start to read, it is a good idea to **set a purpose for reading**. Deciding on a purpose gives you a focus. Then, you can **adjust your reading rate** to go with the goal. When you adjust your reading rate, you choose a reading speed.

- When you read to learn new information, read *slowly* and carefully. Take time to think about what you read. Reread if you do not understand.

- When you read for fun, read as *quickly* as you like. Reread if something is extra interesting to you.

The chart below shows examples of reading rates. Fill in the blanks in the empty chart to show your reading plan for the selections.

Source	Magazine article on rock star	Source	Biography of John F. Kennedy	Source	
Purpose	Entertainment	**Purpose**	Research report	**Purpose**	
Reading Rate	Read quickly to find interesting details.	**Reading Rate**	Read slowly, selecting facts for your report.	**Reading Rate**	

LITERARY ANALYSIS

An **author's influences** are the things that affect his or her writing. History and culture play an important role in what an author writes.

You can better understand what you read if you know about an author's influences. Read about the author's life. Then, follow these steps when reading the text:

- Note details that show values or attitudes.

- Note historical figures or happenings that are included.

Choice: A Tribute to Martin Luther King, Jr.

Alice Walker

Summary The author describes Dr. King's successes with the civil rights movement. She explains how Dr. King inspired African Americans to appreciate their heritage.

Reading/Writing Connection

Complete the sentences below to describe an important news event that affected you.

1. The news that caused me to <u>react</u> strongly was _____.

2. A person who helped me <u>interpret</u> this event was _____.

3. This story caused me to <u>identify</u> _____.

Note-taking Guide

Use this diagram to recall the reasons that Alice Walker looks up to Martin Luther King, Jr.

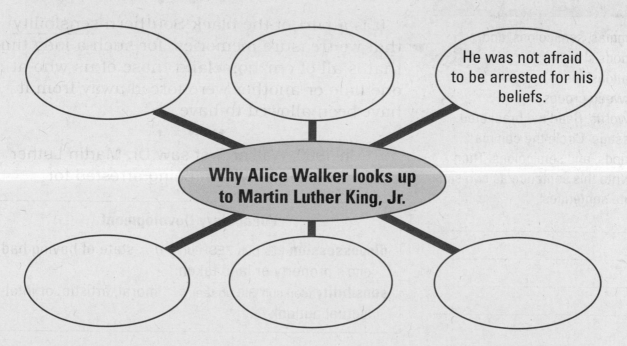

He was not afraid to be arrested for his beliefs.

Why Alice Walker looks up to Martin Luther King, Jr.

Describe a person you admire who leads, or has led, a fight for an important cause. What qualities do you admire in this person?

_____

_____

_____

Reading Skill

When you **set a purpose for reading**, you decide what to focus on as you read. Scan this page of text, and look closely at the first paragraph. What do you think your purpose will be in reading this text?

_____

_____

_____

Read Fluently

Commas, semicolons, and periods show relationships between groups of words. Read the bracketed passage. Circle the commas, periods, and semicolons. Then rewrite this sentence as two separate sentences.

_____

_____

_____

_____

Choice: A Tribute to Martin Luther King, Jr.

Alice Walker

This address was made in 1973 at a Jackson, Mississippi, restaurant that had refused to serve people of color until forced to do so by the civil rights movement a few years before.

◆ ◆ ◆

Walker begins by telling the story of her great-great-great-grandmother, a slave who walked with two babies from Virginia to Eatonton, Georgia, and describing the family cemetery in which generations of ancestors are buried.

◆ ◆ ◆

Yet the history of my family, like that of all black Southerners, is a history of <u>dispossession</u>. We loved the land and worked the land, but we never owned it; . . .

◆ ◆ ◆

Walker and others of the 1960s generation were compelled to leave the South to avoid having happy memories replaced by bitter recollections of brutal treatment.

◆ ◆ ◆

It is a part of the black Southern <u>sensibility</u> that we treasure memories; for such a long time, that is all of our homeland those of us who at one time or another were forced away from it have been allowed to have.

◆ ◆ ◆

In 1960, Walker first saw Dr. Martin Luther King, Jr. on television being arrested for

Vocabulary Development

dispossession (dis puh ZESH uhn) *n.* state of having had one's property or land taken

sensibility (sen suh BIL uh tee) *n.* moral, artistic, or intellectual outlook demonstrating in support of Hamilton Holmes and Charlayne Hunter,[1] who were attempting to enter the University of Georgia. Dr. King's calmness and bravery impressed her; his example changed her life.

◆ ◆ ◆

At the moment I saw his resistance I knew I would never be able to live in this country without resisting everything that sought to <u>disinherit</u> me, and I would never be forced away from the land of my birth without a fight.

He was The One, The Hero, The One Fearless Person for whom we had waited.

◆ ◆ ◆

Walker reminds listeners of the public acts of Dr. King: his speeches, his philosophy, his books, his preaching, his honors, and his deep concern for all displaced people. She also notes that people of color would not be permitted to eat in the restaurant in which she is speaking but for Dr. King's struggles. Walker also thanks Dr. King for an equally important, yet perhaps less obvious, gift.

◆ ◆ ◆

He gave us back our heritage. He gave us back our homeland; the bones and dust of our ancestors, who may now sleep within our caring *and* our hearing. . . .

He gave us <u>continuity</u> of place, without which community is ephemeral.[2] He gave us home.

Literary Analysis

An **author's influences** are the factors that affect his or her writing. List three things that influenced Walker in this essay.

_____

_____

_____

Reading Check

What does Walker say Dr. King gave her people? Circle three things.

Stop to Reflect

How do you think Walker's message affects or applies to modern readers?

_____

_____

_____

Vocabulary Development

disinherit (dis in HER it) *v.* to take away someone's property or rights as a citizen

continuity (kahn tuh NOO uh tee) *n.* state of continuing, without problems, interruptions, or changes

---

1. **Hamilton Holmes and Charlayne Hunter** students who made history in January 1961 by becoming the first two African Americans to attend the University of Georgia.
2. **ephemeral** (i FEM uhr uhl) *adj.* short-lived; fleeting.

Choice: A Tribute to Martin Luther King, Jr. **341**

Choice: A Tribute to Martin Luther King, Jr.

1. **Connect:** Walker made this speech in a restaurant that had refused to serve African Americans. What is important about this place?

_____

_____

2. **Interpret:** Walker saw Martin Luther King, Jr. arrested on television. What did she notice about the way he acted?

_____

_____

3. **Reading Skill:** Suppose that you are writing a report on Dr. King's accomplishments as a civil rights leader. You would need to find information about what he did to help African Americans. Would this speech be a good source of information for that **purpose**? Explain.

_____

_____

_____

4. **Literary Analysis:** Complete this chart to show how the **author's influences** affected her writing.

	Influences	Effect on Her Portrayal of Dr. King
Time and place of Walker's birth	Walker was born in pre-Civil Rights Era Georgia.	Walker could document the personal impact of Dr. King's actions.
Walker's cultural background		
Major news events		

SUPPORT FOR WRITING AND EXTEND YOUR LEARNING

Writing: Speech

A **speech** is meant to be read aloud to a group. Prepare a speech for the dedication of a local monument to Martin Luther King, Jr. Your speech should celebrate Dr. King's accomplishments and leadership in the civil rights movement. Use your notes from the prompts to write your speech.

- List three of Dr. King's values: _____

_____

- Explain three reasons why Dr. King should be remembered: _____

_____

_____

_____

- Explain why Dr. King's ideas are still important today: _____

_____

_____

Listening and Speaking: Role Play

Prepare a **role play** of an interview with a person who participated in a civil rights march. Use this chart to list the questions and answers you will use.

Questions	Possible Answers
1.	1.
2.	2.
3.	3.
4.	4.
5.	5.

An Episode of War

Stephen Crane

Summary A Civil War lieutenant is shot by a stray bullet. The other soldiers are worried for him. The doctors and medical staff act as if he is a bother. The lieutenant is ashamed that he was not shot in battle. His arm is removed. The lieutenant tells his family that missing an arm does not really matter.

Reading/Writing Connection

Complete this paragraph to describe how today's doctors and nurses try to make patients feel safe and secure.

Doctors and those who <u>assist</u> them try to _____.

They <u>communicate</u> as they work so that patients _____.

They try to <u>minimize</u> patients' worries about _____.

Note-taking Guide

Use this chart to record the attitudes of the different characters in "An Episode of War."

Characters	Attitudes	Reasons for Attitudes
Lieutenant		
Other soldiers	awed and sympathetic	
Surgeon		
Lieutenant's family		

An Episode of War

1. **Analyze:** The lieutenant was not shot in battle. He was dividing coffee when he was shot. How does this fact make you feel bad for him?

   _____

   _____

2. **Interpret:** The lieutenant's family cries when he returns with his arm amputated. He tells them, "I don't suppose it matters so much as all that." Why do you think he says this?

   _____

   _____

3. **Reading Skill:** Think about writing a research report about leadership in the Civil War. Would this text be helpful for that **purpose**?

   _____

   _____

4. **Literary Analysis:** Read the information about the author on page 1016 of the textbook. Fill in the chart to show the **author's influences** on his writing.

	Influences	Effect on "An Episode of War"
Crane's Interests	He was interested in the Civil War.	
Crane's Research		

SUPPORT FOR WRITING AND EXTEND YOUR LEARNING

Writing: Speech

Prepare a **speech** for the dedication of a local Civil War memorial. The memorial will honor those who died or were injured in the war. Begin by answering these questions:

- When did the Civil War take place? _____

- Did any Civil War battles take place near your community? _____
  If so, where and when? _____

- Did people in your community fight for the Union or the Confederacy?

  _____

- Why do you think those who fight in the Civil War, on either side, deserve to be honored?

  _____

  _____

Use your notes to help you write your speech.

Research and Technology: Newspaper Article

Write a **newspaper article** about the experience and cost of fighting in the Civil War. Make up statements that might have been made by the lieutenant in "An Episode of War."

What do you think the lieutenant would say about the kind of men with whom he served?	
What do you think the lieutenant would say about military hospitals?	
How do you think the lieutenant felt about having to live the rest of his life without an arm?	

Use the quotations from your chart in your newspaper article.

Transcripts

ABOUT TRANSCRIPTS

Transcripts are written records of speech. They use the exact words of the speakers. Transcripts provide a complete record of what was said at an event. They do not include opinions or rewording. People use transcripts to record:

- radio or television shows
- trials or government hearings
- interviews or oral histories
- debates or speeches

READING SKILL

Research involves looking up specific information. You might have to look at many documents to find what you need. You can **use the text structure** of a document to help you find the information you need. Transcripts have a special text structure. This chart lists the most common parts of transcripts.

Heading	This feature contains important information such as the date, topic, and time of the event.
Formatting	Each speaker is identified at the beginning of each line with capital letters, spacing, or special typefaces and colors.
Organization	An interviewer's or reporter's questions and comments identify the topics covered in the transcript. The text that follows each question or comment provides detailed information.
Brackets and Parentheses	These identify information that is not part of what was said. This can include source information or background information.

Build Understanding

Knowing these words will help you read this transcript.

paralyzed veterans (PAR uh lyzd VET uhr uhnz) *n.*   people who have been in the military and now have arms and/or legs that cannot move

paraplegics (par uh PLEE jiks) *n.*   people who have both legs paralyzed

spinal cord injuries (SPY nuhl KORD IN juh reez) *n.*   damage to the nerves that run from the brain down the back

Reading Transcripts

Transcripts are written records of speech. They are used in many different events. Look at this transcript. What type of event is it from?

_____

Reading Skill

You can **use the text structure** to understand transcripts. Look at the **heading** on this transcript. Circle the date the program aired and the name of the program. What was the program about on this specific day?

_____

_____

Reading Fluently

Reading transcripts can be confusing. Different people are involved, but you cannot see any of them. So, you have to keep them straight by looking at their names. You also have to remember how each person is involved in the discussion. Explain how each person below is involved in this radio show.

Bob Edwards: _____

Joe Shapiro: _____

Ken Seaquist: _____

MORNING EDITION,
NATIONAL PUBLIC RADIO

November 11, 2003

PROFILE: World War II veterans who founded the Paralyzed Veterans of America.

BOB EDWARDS, host: This is MORNING EDITION from NPR News. I'm Bob Edwards.

In February of 1947, a small group of World War II veterans gathered at Hines VA Hospital near Chicago. The fact that they were there at all was considered extraordinary. The men were paralyzed, living at a time when paraplegia was still an unfamiliar word and most people with spinal cord injuries were told they would die within a few years. But these wounded veterans had other ideas, so they came from hospital wards across the country to start a national organization to represent veterans with spinal cord injuries. Today on Veterans Day, NPR's Joseph Shapiro tells their story.

JOSEPH SHAPIRO reporting: The logo of the Paralyzed Veterans of America looks a bit like the American flag, except that it's got 16 stars, one for each of the men who started the PVA when they gathered at that first convention nearly 57 years ago. Today only one of those 16 paralyzed veterans is still alive. His name is Ken Seaquist. He lives in a gated community in Florida. . . . It's there that Seaquist sits in his wheelchair and flips through some yellowed newspaper clippings . . .

Mr. KEN SEAQUIST: Oh, here it is. OK.

SHAPIRO: . . . until he finds a photo. . . . The picture shows that convention. It was held in a veterans hospital just outside Chicago. A large room is filled with scores of young men in wheelchairs. Others are in their pajamas and hospital beds, propped up on white pillows.

Mr. SEAQUIST: There's Bill Dake. He came with us and then Mark Orr. Three of us came in the car from Memphis. Mark had one good leg, his right leg, and he was the driver of the car.

SHAPIRO: Ken Seaquist was a tall, lanky 20-year-old in an Army mountain ski division when he was wounded in Italy. He was flown back to the United States to a veterans hospital in Memphis. He came back to a society that was not ready for paraplegics.

Mr. SEAQUIST: Before the war, people in our condition were in the closet. They never went out hardly. They didn't take them out.

SHAPIRO: Few people had ever survived for more than a few years with a spinal cord injury. Infections were common and deadly. But that was about to change. David Gerber is a historian at the University at Buffalo. He's written about disabled veterans.

Mr. DAVID GERBER (University at Buffalo): With the development of antibiotics, which came into general use in World War II, there were many healthy spinal cord-injured veterans who were able to survive and begin to aspire to have a normalized life.

SHAPIRO: Gerber says neither the wounded veterans, nor the world around them at that time knew what to make of men who were seen as having gone from manly warriors to dependent invalids.

Mr. GERBER: The society is emphatically not ready for them, and nor is the medical profession. To this extent, it was often the paralyzed veterans themselves who were pioneers in the development of a new way of life for themselves.

SHAPIRO: Seaquist and the others set out to overcome the fear and pity of others. After Seaquist was injured, he never heard from his girlfriend. His mother's hair turned white in a matter of months. People stared when he went out in public. It was a time when a president with polio felt he had to hide the fact that he

TAKE NOTES

Reading Skill

The names of the speakers stand out in the **formatting** of the text. Circle the names of the three people who are talking on this page.

Note that a person's full name is given the first time the person talks. After the first time, names are written in shorter ways. Underline the name of a person who is talking for the first time on this page.

Reading Transcripts

Transcripts are the exact words spoken. This transcript is from an interview. Who are the people being interviewed? Skim through the whole transcript to find all of the names.

_____

_____

Reading Check

What two things does Shapiro say need to change? Circle the answers here and on the next page.

Transcripts are records of the exact words spoken. Summarize what Pat Grissom says he expected when he returned from the war.

_____

_____

_____

_____

This interview took place live on a radio station. Most of the people were not talking from written notes. Who do you think typed up this transcript?

_____

_____

According to Shapiro, how many soldiers had spinal cord injuries? Circle the answer.

used a wheelchair. Beyond attitudes, there was a physical world that had to change. When Seaquist arrived at the Memphis hospital, he could not get off the ward. There were steps in the way.

Mr. SEAQUIST: They had no idea of what they had to do for wheelchairs. So when we got there, they had to put in all these long ramps and this is what we were talking about. The ramping and just to get around the hospital and get out ourselves, you know; not having somebody help us all the time. We were an independent bunch.

SHAPIRO: There were about 2,500 soldiers with spinal cord injuries, most of them living in military hospitals around the country. Pat Grissom lived at Birmingham Hospital in California. He would become one of the first presidents of the PVA, but he was unable to travel from California to Chicago for that first convention. Grissom, too, had come back from war with little hope for his future.

Mr. PAT GRISSOM: I just suppose that we were going to live the rest of our lives either in the hospital or go to an old soldiers home. We were just going to be there taking medicine and if you got sick, they would try to take care of you and you'd have your meals provided and your future was the hospital or the old soldiers home.

SHAPIRO: At Birmingham Hospital, Grissom met a doctor who was about to become a pioneer in the new field of spinal cord medicine. Dr. Ernst Bors did a lot to improve the physical care of paraplegics. He also pushed the men at Birmingham to set goals for their lives, to go back to school, get jobs and marry. Bors and the veterans at Birmingham Hospital were the subject of a Hollywood film, _The Men._ The realistic and sympathetic portrayal helped the American public better understand paralyzed veterans. In the film, the kindly doctor in a lab coat is based on Bors. He urges on a wounded soldier in a white T-shirt, played by a young Marlon Brando.

(Soundbite of The Men)

Mr. MARLON BRANDO: Well, what am I going to do? Where am I going to go?

Unidentified Actor: Into the world.

Mr. MARLON BRANDO: I can't go out there anymore.

Unidentified Actor: You still can't accept it, can you?

Mr. MARLON BRANDO: No. What did I do? Why'd it have to be me?

Unidentified Actor: Is there an answer? I haven't got it. Somebody always gets hurt in the war.

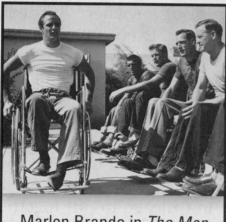

Marlon Brando in *The Men*

SHAPIRO: For Grissom and the other paralyzed veterans, there was something else that helped them go out into the world, a new technology. The introduction of automatic transmission meant that a car could be modified with hand controls for the gas and brakes. Pat Grissom.

Mr. GRISSOM: Oldsmobile came up with the hydromatic drive and they put on hand controls and they sent people out to start giving driving lessons to us and we started having visions of saving up enough money to get a car and then things were looking better all the time.

SHAPIRO: Ken Seaquist says driving opened up all kinds of possibilities, from going out to a restaurant with a bunch of friends to romance.

Mr. SEAQUIST: In Memphis, we had—our favorite place was called the Silver Slipper and they welcomed us with open arms and we had maybe 10, 12 wheelchairs going with our dates. Generally it

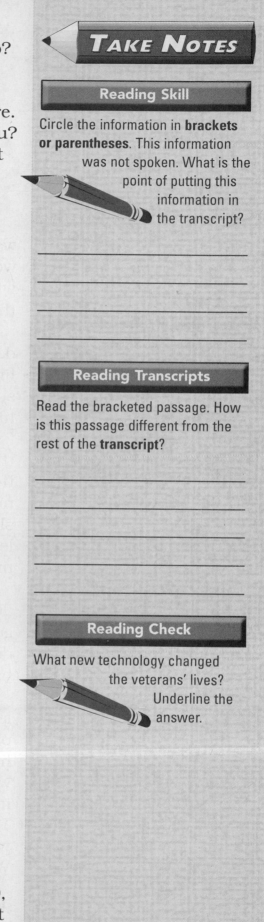

TAKE NOTES

Reading Skill

Circle the information in **brackets or parentheses**. This information was not spoken. What is the point of putting this information in the transcript?

_____

_____

_____

_____

Reading Transcripts

Read the bracketed passage. How is this passage different from the rest of the **transcript**?

_____

_____

_____

_____

_____

Reading Check

What new technology changed the veterans' lives? Underline the answer.

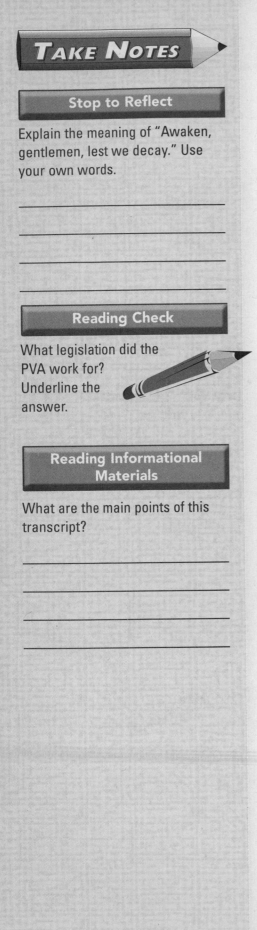

TAKE NOTES

Stop to Reflect

Explain the meaning of "Awaken, gentlemen, lest we decay." Use your own words.

_____

_____

_____

_____

Reading Check

What legislation did the PVA work for? Underline the answer.

Reading Informational Materials

What are the main points of this transcript?

_____

_____

_____

_____

Car modified with hand controls

was our nurses that we dated, 'cause, you know, we couldn't get out anywhere. We took the girls with us, you know. Eventually I married one of them.

SHAPIRO: Seaquist and his wife quickly had two daughters. And with a young family, he had to find work. He went to school and became a landscape architect. Ken Seaquist stopped seeing himself as an invalid and became a man with a future. So in 1947, he and the other founders of the PVA met in Chicago to put together a collective voice to express their dreams and what they needed to accomplish them. They came up with a slogan to get others to join, 'Awaken, gentlemen, lest we decay.' Ken Seaquist explains what it meant.

Mr. SEAQUIST: If they forget us, we're going to decay. We're going to be left in the closet. We've got to get out there and speak out, getting things done so we can roll around this country and have access to the whole country.

SHAPIRO: The PVA quickly won some important legislative victories in Washington: money for paralyzed veterans to modify automobiles and houses, money for medical care. Later they would help push for laws that would make buildings and streets accessible to wheelchair users. The PVA has continued to advocate for veterans with spinal cord injuries through every war since World War II.

Joseph Shapiro, NPR News.

THINKING ABOUT THE TRANSCRIPT

1. Why were veterans of World War II more likely to survive their injuries?

   _____

2. Why did the veterans form the Paralyzed Veterans of America?

   _____

   _____

READING SKILL

3. How does the **formatting** help you identify the comments by the veterans?

   _____

   _____

4. What about the **text structure** helps you locate the recording from *The Men*?

   _____

   _____

TIMED WRITING: EXPLANATION (20 minutes)

Paralyzed veterans face many stereotypes. Write a paragraph explaining why stereotyping can be hurtful.

• Identify examples of stereotypes from the transcript.

   _____

   _____

• Use these examples to explain why stereotyping can hurt people.

   _____

   _____

VOWEL SOUNDS IN UNSTRESSED SYLLABLES

In many words, the vowel sound in one or more syllables is not clear. These indistinct vowel sounds can cause spelling problems.

How Do You Spell "Uh"? Words like *dislocate* do not often cause spelling problems—you can clearly hear the vowel in each syllable. In many other words, though, the vowel in one or more syllables sounds something like "uh." This sound can be spelled with any vowel. For example, the *a* in *obstacle* sounds the same as the *i* in *hesitate*.

Study the word list, noting the spelling of vowels in unstressed syllables.

Practice Read the following paragraph. Circle any word that is misspelled. Then, write the misspelled word correctly on the lines.

Word List
medicine
multiply
evidence
category
discipline
episode
cemetery
oxygen
abandon
syllable

The unstressed syllubles in abanden and evadence always make me hesitate when I write the word. You can multeply my anxiety by ten when I see the words discipline and cematery. Is there medacine I can take that will help me spell these words? Evidunce shows that practicing the words will help me remember how they are spelled.

_____

_____

_____

_____

PART 2: TURBO VOCABULARY

The exercises and tools presented here are designed to help you increase your vocabulary. Review the instruction and complete the exercises to build your vocabulary knowledge. Throughout the year, you can apply these skills and strategies to improve your reading, writing, speaking, and listening vocabulary.

WORD ROOTS

The following list contains common word roots with meanings and examples. On the blank lines, write other words you know that have the same roots. Write the meanings of the new words.

Root	Meaning	Example and Meaning	Your Words	Meanings
-dict-	say or tell	*predict:* tell what might happen next		
-port-	carry	*support:* carry or hold something up		
-scrib-	write	*scribble:* write something quickly in a messy way		
-similis-	same	*similar:* alike in some way		

Root	Meaning	Example and Meaning	Your Words	Meanings
-spec-	look; see	*inspect:* look carefully at something		
-sum-	take; use	*assumption:* something that you think is true		
-vali-	strong; worth	*valid:* based on strong reasons or facts		
-ver-	truth	*verify:* make sure something is true		

PREFIXES

The following list contains common prefixes with meanings and examples. On the blank lines, write other words you know that begin with the same prefixes. Write the meanings of the new words.

Prefix	Meaning	Example and Meaning	Your Words	Meanings
con-	with; together	*concur:* agree with		
dis-	not	*disorganized:* not organized		
non-	without; not	*nonfat:* without fat		
pre-	before	*preview:* look before		

Prefix	Meaning	Example and Meaning	Your Words	Meanings
re-	again	*remake:* make again		
un-/an-/a-	not	*unbelievable:* not believable		

SUFFIXES

The following list contains common suffixes with meanings and examples. On the blank lines, write other words you know that have the same suffixes. Write the meanings of the new words.

Suffix	Meaning	Example and Meaning	Your Words	Meanings
-able/-ible	able to be	*movable:* able to be moved		
-ize/-yze	make	*publicize:* make public; tell people about		
-ly	in a way	*quickly:* done in a short amount of time		
-ment	act or quality of	*excitement:* feeling of being excited		

Suffix	Meaning	Example and Meaning	Your Words	Meanings
-ous	having; full of	*famous:* having fame; known and recognized by many people		
-sion/-tion	act or process of	*persuasion:* act of convincing someone		

USING A DICTIONARY

Use a **dictionary** to find the correct spelling, the meaning, the pronunciation, and the part of speech of a word. The dictionary will show you how the plural is formed if it is irregular. You can also find the word's history, or *etymology*, in a dictionary. Etymology explains how words change, how they are borrowed from other languages, and how new words are invented, or "coined."

Here is a sample entry from a dictionary. Notice what it tells about the word. Then, follow the instructions.

> **lemon** (lem´ ən) **n.**   [ME *lymon* < MFr *limon* < Ar *laimūn* < Pers *līmūn*] **1** a small, egg-shaped, edible citrus fruit with a yellow rind and a juicy, sour pulp, rich in ascorbic acid **2** the small, spiny, semitropical evergreen citrus tree (*Citrus limon*) bearing this fruit **3** pale yellow **4** [slang] something, esp. a manufactured article, that is defective or imperfect

1. Circle the *n.* in the dictionary entry. It stands for *noun*. Write what these other parts of speech abbreviations mean: *v.* _____, *adv.* _____, *adj.* _____ *prep.* _____.

2. Underline the origins of the word *lemon*. ME stands for Middle English, Ar stands for Arabic, and Pers. stands for Persian. What do you think MFr stands for? _____

3. Put a box around the pronunciation.

4. How many noun definitions does the entry have? _____

5. Which definition is slang? _____

6. Which definition of *lemon* is used in the following sentence? _____

The car that my dad bought turned out to be a lemon.

Activity: Use a dictionary to learn about the origins of these words.

1. literature _____ / _____ / _____
                pronunciation   main part of speech   original language(s)
_____ / _____
          1st meaning   other meanings

_____

_____

_____

2. language _____ / _____ / _____
                pronunciation   main part of speech   original language(s)
_____ / _____
          1st meaning   other meanings

_____

_____

Activity: Look up each of the following words in a dictionary. Then, write a definition of the word and a sentence using the word.

moment _____

_____

popular _____

_____

remedy _____

_____

blur _____

_____

lazy _____

_____

Use these word study cards to break big words into their parts. Write the word at the top of the card. Then, divide the word into its prefix, root, and suffix. Note that not all words have prefixes and suffixes. List the meaning of each part of the word. Next, find three words with the same root and write them on the card. Finally, write the word's part of speech and its definition. Use a dictionary to help you. One example has been done for you.

Word:	invisible	
Prefix	**Root**	**Suffix**
in: not	**vis:** see	**ible**-able to be

Root-related Words
1. vision
2. revise
3. visibility

Definition: invisible *adj.* not able to be seen

Word:		
Prefix	**Root**	**Suffix**

Root-related Words
1.
2.
3.

Definition:

WORD STUDY CARDS

Word:

Prefix	Root	Suffix

Root-related Words
1.
2.
3.

Definition:

Word:

Prefix	Root	Suffix

Root-related Words
1.
2.
3.

Definition:

Word:

Prefix	Root	Suffix

Root-related Words
1.
2.
3.

Definition:

analyze (AN uh lyz) *v.* study the parts of something
We *analyze* the details of the story to figure out the author's reason for writing it.

anticipate (an TIS uh payt) *v.* look forward to, expect
I *anticipate* that the character will join the team.

intention (in TEN shuhn) *n.* purpose; goal
The author's *intention* is to persuade.

predict (pree DIKT) *v.* make a logical assumption about future events
These clues help me *predict* what the character will do next.

revise (ri VYZ) *v.* correct, improve, or change
I *revised* my prediction because a new character entered the story.

A. True/False For each of the following, mark T or F to indicate whether the italicized vocabulary word has been used correctly in the sentence. If you have marked F, correct the sentence by using the word properly.

1. _____ You can *predict* how a story will end by paying attention to the author's clues.

2. _____ Rita *anticipates* the trip that she went on last week.

3. _____ When you *revise* an essay, you usually try to make it incorrect.

4. _____ The author's *intention* is to bore readers.

5. _____ When you *analyze* a story, you look at the plot details.

_____

_____

_____

_____

_____

_____

B. Use each word pair in an original sentence that illustrates the meaning of the academic vocabulary word.

analyze/situation _____

_____

anticipate/party _____

_____

intention/persuade _____

_____

predict/conclusion _____

_____

revise/errors _____

_____

C. Write new words that you come across in your reading. Define each word.

_____

_____

_____

conclude (kuhn KLOOD) *v.* decide by reasoning
What can you *conclude* from the details in the story?

differentiate (dif uhr EN shee ayt) *v.* show how things are different
It is not easy to *differentiate* between the two blue cars.

infer (in FER) *v.* draw conclusions based on facts
You can *infer* that the main character is very smart.

similar (SIM uh luhr) *adj.* alike
The twins Dee and Cary look *similar*, but not exactly alike.

unique (yoo NEEK) *adj.* having no like or equal
Although the stories have similar plots, they have *unique* themes.

A. True/False For each of the following, mark T or F to indicate whether the italicized vocabulary word has been used correctly in the sentence. If you have marked F, correct the sentence by using the word properly.

1. _____ What can you *infer* about the main character from the way he dresses?

2. _____ Ben can *differentiate* between books by describing how they are the same.

3. _____ Two pens that look exactly alike are *unique*.

4. _____ What can you *conclude* from the details in the story?

5. _____ Two *similar* books would be very different.

_____

_____

_____

B. Use each word pair in an original sentence that illustrates the meaning of the academic vocabulary word.

conclude/detail _____

_____

differentiate/novels _____

_____

infer/details _____

_____

similar/traits _____

_____

unique/characteristic _____

_____

C. Write new words that you come across in your reading. Define each word.

_____

_____

_____

accurate (AK yuh ruht) *adj.* free from error; correct; exact
Make sure that the facts are *accurate*.

bias (BY uhs) *n.* unfair preference or dislike for someone or something
He has a *bias* against anyone who is not an athlete.

cite (SYT) *v.* refer to an example or fact as proof
How many sources did you *cite* in your research report?

focus (FOH kuhs) *n.* the central point of a work
The *focus* of her essay is exercise.

focus (FOH kuhs) *v.* concentrate on one thing
Focus your attention on the example on the board.

support (suh PORT) *v.* provide evidence to prove or back up an idea
I can *support* my point with many facts and examples.

topic (TAHP ik) *n.* the subject
The *topic* of his essay was volcanoes.

A. Code Name Use the code to figure out each vocabulary word. Each letter is represented by a number or symbol. Write the word in the blank to help you remember how to spell it.

%	5	•	*	2	#	!	7	^	&	9	¶	£	$	3	¥	+	=	?	÷	4	¢	6	§	«	ç
a	b	c	d	e	f	g	h	i	j	k	l	m	n	o	p	q	r	s	t	u	v	w	x	y	z

1. # 3 • 4 ?   _____

2. ? 4 ¥ ¥ 3 = ÷   _____

3. ÷ 3 ¥ ^ •   _____

4. % • • 4 = % ÷ 2   _____

5. 5 ^ % ?   _____

B. Answer each question. Then, explain your answer.

1. Would drama be a good *topic* for a science paper? _____

_____

2. If an answer is *accurate*, are there mistakes in it? _____

_____

3. When you are trying to *focus* on homework, is it a good idea to watch

television? _____

_____

4. Would you expect someone with a *bias* to always be fair? _____

_____

5. Is it a good idea to *support* your ideas with facts and examples? _____

_____

C. Write new words that you come across in your reading. Define each word.

_____

_____

_____

_____

_____

_____

adapt (uh DAPT) *v.* change something to make it more suitable
Adapt the author's language to fit your own style of writing.

clarify (KLAR uh fy) *v.* explain; make clearer
A context clue can *clarify* the meaning of an unfamiliar word.

context (KAHN tekst) *n.* text surrounding an unfamiliar word
Study the *context* in which an unfamiliar word appears.

emphasize (EM fuh syz) *v.* stress
Emphasize the author's main points.

restate (ree STAYT) *v.* express the same idea in a different way
Restate the sentence in your own words.

A. Completion Complete each sentence that has been started for you. Your sentence completion should be logical and illustrate the meaning of the vocabulary word in italics.

1. The teacher tried to *clarify* _____

_____

2. A writer might *adapt* a story to _____

_____

3. It is a good idea to *restate* a poem so that _____

_____

4. If you look at the *context* surrounding an unfamiliar word, you may be

   able to _____

_____

5. One way to *emphasize* an important idea in writing is to _____

_____

B. Using the word pair, write an original sentence that illustrates the meaning of the academic vocabulary word.

emphasize/main point _____

_____

restate/words _____

_____

adapt/story _____

_____

context/unfamiliar _____

_____

clarify/difficult _____

_____

C. Write new words that you come across in your reading. Define each word.

_____

_____

_____

_____

_____

consequence (KAHN si kwens) *n.* result; outcome
The character's actions had horrible *consequences*.

evaluate (ee VAL yoo ayt) *v.* judge; determine the worth or strength of something
Evaluate the evidence carefully before making a decision.

impact (IM pakt) *n.* the power to produce changes or effects
Books can have an *impact* on government policy.

rational (RASH uhn uhl) *adj.* based on reason; logical
His conclusion was not *rational*; it was based on emotions.

valid (VAL id) *adj.* based on facts and strong evidence; convincing
A *valid* conclusion can be supported with evidence.

A. Completion Complete each sentence that has been started for you. Your sentence completion should be logical and illustrate the meaning of the vocabulary word in italics.

1. One *consequence* of a heavy rain might be _____

_____

2. A *valid* conclusion would _____

_____

3. A *rational* reason to go to bed early is _____

_____

4. One way that teachers *evaluate* students is _____

_____

5. Weather can have an *impact* on _____

_____

B. Using the academic word pair, write an original sentence that illustrates the meaning of the words.

consequence/terrible _____

_____

impact/strong _____

_____

rational/idea _____

_____

valid/conclusion _____

_____

evaluate/evidence _____

_____

C. Write new words that you come across in your reading. Define each word.

_____

_____

_____

_____

_____

_____

essential (uh SEN shuhl) *adj.* necessary

A summary should include only the *essential* ideas in a text.

identify (y DEN tuh fy) *v.* recognize; find and name

Identify the facts that answer your question.

organized (OHR guh nyzd) *v.* arranged in a logical order

The details of a summary should be *organized* in a way that makes sense.

revise (ri VYZ) *v.* change; adjust

As you read, you may *revise* your original purpose for reading.

sequence (SEE kwuhns) *n.* order

Retell important plot events in the correct *sequence*.

A. True/False For each of the following, mark T or F to indicate whether the italicized vocabulary word has been used correctly in the sentence. If you have marked F, correct the sentence by using the word properly.

1. _____ A telephone book should be *organized* in alphabetic order.

2. _____ When you *revise* an essay, you should not change anything.

3. _____ We will *identify* the dishes after dinner.

4. _____ A dictionary is an *essential* tool for an English student.

5. _____ If something is out of *sequence*, it is in the correct order.

_____

_____

_____

B. Answer each question. Then, explain your answer.

1. Is a television *essential* for life in the United States? _____

_____

2. Should words in a dictionary be *organized* in order of importance? _____

_____

3. What would be a logical *sequence* for events in a story? _____

_____

4. Why might you *revise* your essay? _____

_____

5. If you were asked to *identify* the main character in a story, what would

you do? _____

_____

C. Write new words that you come across in your reading. Define each word.

_____

_____

_____

_____

_____

WORDS IN OTHER SUBJECTS

Use this page to write down academic words you come across in other subjects, such as social studies or science. When you are reading your textbooks, you may find words that you need to learn. Following the example, write down the word, the part of speech, and an explanation of the word. You may want to write an example sentence to help you remember the word.

dissolve *verb* to make something solid become part of a liquid by putting it in a liquid and mixing it

The sugar *dissolved* in the hot tea.

_____

_____

_____

_____

_____

_____

_____

_____

_____

_____

_____

_____

_____

_____

_____

_____

_____

_____

_____

_____

_____

_____

_____

VOCABULARY FLASH CARDS

Use these flash cards to study words you want to remember. The words on this page come from Unit 1. Cut along the dotted lines on pages V25 through V32 to create your own flash cards or use index cards. Write the word on the front of the card. On the back, write the word's part of speech and definition. Then, write a sentence that shows the meaning of the word.

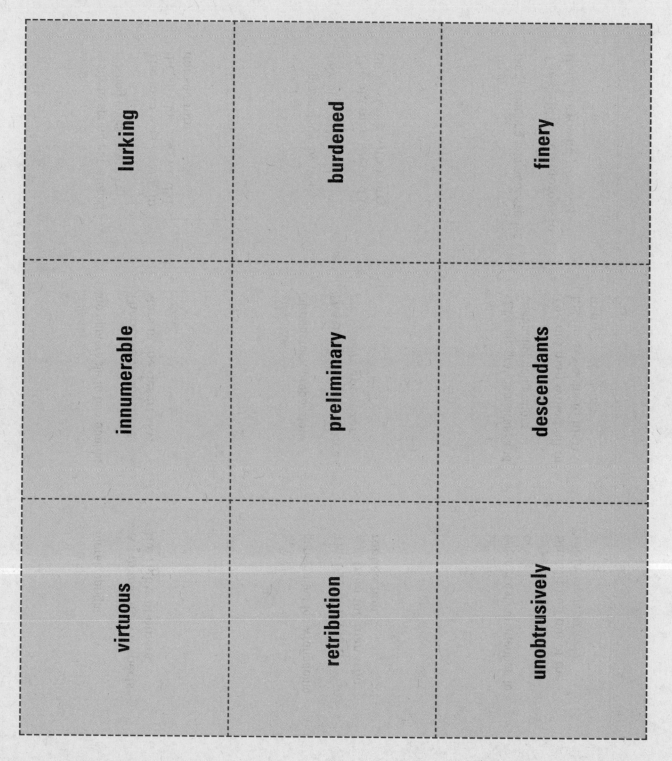

lurking	burdened	finery
innumerable	preliminary	descendants
virtuous	retribution	unobtrusively

verb
ready to spring out, attack; existing undiscovered

The man was *lurking* in the shadows so we did not see him.

---

adjective
weighted down by work, duty, or sorrow

The old man seemed to be *burdened* with worry.

---

noun
fancy clothing and accessories

The girls felt glamorous in their borrowed *finery*.

---

adjective
too numerable to be counted

There are *innumerable* stars in the desert sky.

---

adjective
introductory; preparatory

The dinner began with a *preliminary* appetizer.

---

noun
children, grandchildren, and continuing generations

The old man willed all of his possessions to his many *descendants*.

---

adjective
moral, upright

A *virtuous* man respects the rights of others.

---

noun
punishment for wrongdoing

The victim wanted *retribution* from the man who robbed him.

---

adverb
without calling attention to oneself

She slipped out of the room *unobtrusively*.

VOCABULARY FLASH CARDS

Use these flash cards to study words you want to remember. Cut along the dotted lines on pages V25 through V32 to create your own flash cards or use index cards. Write the word on the front of the card. On the back, write the word's part of speech and definition. Then, write a sentence that shows the meaning of the word.

VOCABULARY FLASH CARDS

Use these flash cards to study words you want to remember. Cut along the dotted lines on pages V25 through V32 to create your own flash cards or use index cards. Write the word on the front of the card. On the back, write the word's part of speech and definition. Then, write a sentence that shows the meaning of the word.

VOCABULARY FLASH CARDS

Use these flash cards to study words you want to remember. Cut along the dotted lines on pages V25 through V32 to create your own flash cards or use index cards. Write the word on the front of the card. On the back, write the word's part of speech and definition. Then, write a sentence that shows the meaning of the word.

VOCABULARY FOLD-A-LIST

Use a fold-a-list to study the definitions of words. The
words on this page come from Unit 1. Write the definition
for each word on the lines. Fold the paper along the dotted
line to check your definition. Create your own fold-a-lists
on pages V35 through V38.

sinister _____

_____

compliance _____

_____

tangible _____

_____

impaired _____

_____

rigorous _____

_____

inexplicable _____

_____

celestial _____

_____

exertion _____

_____

maneuver _____

_____

ascent _____

_____

Fold In →

VOCABULARY FOLD-A-LIST

Write the word that matches the definition on each line.
Fold the paper along the dotted line to check your work.

threatening harm or evil _____

agreement to a request _____

able to be perceived by
the senses _____

made weaker or less useful _____

very harsh or strict _____

not possible to explain _____

heavenly _____

energetic activity; effort _____

series of planned steps _____

the act of climbing or rising _____

Fold In ◄

VOCABULARY FOLD-A-LIST

Write the words you want to study on this side of the page. Write the definitions on the back. Then, test yourself. Fold the paper along the dotted line to check your answers.

Word: ______________________

____

Word: ______________________

____

Word: ______________________

____

Word: ______________________

____

Word: ______________________

____

Word: ______________________

____

Word: ______________________

____

Word: ______________________

____

Word: ______________________

____

Word: ______________________

____

Fold In ←

VOCABULARY FOLD-A-LIST

Write the word that matches the definition on each line.
Fold the paper along the dotted line to check your work.

Definition: ______________________________

____

Definition: ______________________________

____

Definition: ______________________________

____

Definition: ______________________________

____

Definition: ______________________________

____

Definition: ______________________________

____

Definition: ______________________________

____

Definition: ______________________________

____

Definition: ______________________________

____

Definition: ______________________________

____

Fold In ←

VOCABULARY FOLD-A-LIST

Write the words you want to study on this side of the page. Write the definitions on the back. Then, test yourself. Fold the paper along the dotted line to check your answers.

Word: _____

_____

Word: _____

_____

Word: _____

_____

Word: _____

_____

Word: _____

_____

Word: _____

_____

Word: _____

_____

Word: _____

_____

Word: _____

_____

Word: _____

_____

Fold In ←

VOCABULARY FOLD-A-LIST

Write the word that matches the definition on each line.
Fold the paper along the dotted line to check your work.

Definition: ______________________

____

Definition: ______________________

____

Definition: ______________________

____

Definition: ______________________

____

Definition: ______________________

____

Definition: ______________________

____

Definition: ______________________

____

Definition: ______________________

____

Definition: ______________________

____

Definition: ______________________

____

Fold In ←

COMMONLY MISSPELLED WORDS

The list on these pages presents words that cause problems for many people. Some of these words are spelled according to set rules, but others follow no specific rules. As you review this list, check to see how many of the words give you trouble in your own writing. Then, add your own commonly misspelled words on the lines that follow.

abbreviate	auxiliary	census	deficient
absence	awkward	certain	definitely
absolutely	bandage	changeable	delinquent
abundance	banquet	characteristic	dependent
accelerate	bargain	chauffeur	descendant
accidentally	barrel	chief	description
accumulate	battery	clothes	desert
accurate	beautiful	coincidence	desirable
ache	beggar	colonel	dessert
achievement	beginning	column	deteriorate
acquaintance	behavior	commercial	dining
adequate	believe	commission	disappointed
admittance	benefit	commitment	disastrous
advertisement	bicycle	committee	discipline
aerial	biscuit	competitor	dissatisfied
affect	bookkeeper	concede	distinguish
aggravate	bought	condemn	effect
aggressive	boulevard	congratulate	eighth
agreeable	brief	connoisseur	eligible
aisle	brilliant	conscience	embarrass
all right	bruise	conscientious	enthusiastic
allowance	bulletin	conscious	entrepreneur
aluminum	buoyant	contemporary	envelope
amateur	bureau	continuous	environment
analysis	bury	controversy	equipped
analyze	buses	convenience	equivalent
ancient	business	coolly	especially
anecdote	cafeteria	cooperate	exaggerate
anniversary	calendar	cordially	exceed
anonymous	campaign	correspondence	excellent
answer	canceled	counterfeit	exercise
anticipate	candidate	courageous	exhibition
anxiety	capacity	courteous	existence
apologize	capital	courtesy	experience
appall	capitol	criticism	explanation
appearance	captain	criticize	extension
appreciate	career	curiosity	extraordinary
appropriate	carriage	curious	familiar
architecture	cashier	cylinder	fascinating
argument	catastrophe	deceive	February
associate	category	decision	fiery
athletic	ceiling	deductible	financial
attendance	cemetery	defendant	fluorescent

foreign	minuscule	proceed	_____
fourth	miscellaneous	prominent	
fragile	mischievous	pronunciation	
gauge	misspell	psychology	
generally	mortgage	publicly	_____
genius	naturally	pursue	
genuine	necessary	questionnaire	_____
government	neighbor	realize	
grammar	neutral	really	_____
grievance	nickel	recede	
guarantee	niece	receipt	_____
guard	ninety	receive	
guidance	noticeable	recognize	_____
handkerchief	nuisance	recommend	
harass	obstacle	reference	_____
height	occasion	referred	
humorous	occasionally	rehearse	_____
hygiene	occur	relevant	
ignorant	occurred	reminiscence	_____
immediately	occurrence	renowned	
immigrant	omitted	repetition	_____
independence	opinion	restaurant	
independent	opportunity	rhythm	_____
indispensable	optimistic	ridiculous	
individual	outrageous	sandwich	_____
inflammable	pamphlet	satellite	
intelligence	parallel	schedule	_____
interfere	paralyze	scissors	
irrelevant	parentheses	secretary	_____
irritable	particularly	siege	
jewelry	patience	solely	_____
judgment	permanent	sponsor	
knowledge	permissible	subtle	_____
lawyer	perseverance	subtlety	
legible	persistent	superintendent	_____
legislature	personally	supersede	
leisure	perspiration	surveillance	_____
liable	persuade	susceptible	
library	phenomenal	tariff	_____
license	phenomenon	temperamental	
lieutenant	physician	theater	_____
lightning	pleasant	threshold	
likable	pneumonia	truly	_____
liquefy	possess	unmanageable	
literature	possession	unwieldy	_____
loneliness	possibility	usage	
magnificent	prairie	usually	_____
maintenance	precede	valuable	
marriage	preferable	various	_____
mathematics	prejudice	vegetable	
maximum	preparation	voluntary	_____
meanness	previous	weight	
mediocre	primitive	weird	_____
mileage	privilege	whale	
millionaire	probably	wield	_____
minimum	procedure	yield	

When you are reading, you will find many unfamiliar words. Here are some tools that you can use to help you read unfamiliar words.

PHONICS

Phonics is the science or study of sound. When you learn to read, you learn to associate certain sounds with certain letters or letter combinations. You know most of the sounds that letters can represent in English. When letters are combined, however, it is not always so easy to know what sound is represented. In English, there are some rules and patterns that will help you determine how to pronounce a word. This chart shows you some of the vowel digraphs, which are combinations like *ea* and *oa*. Two vowels together are called vowel digraphs. Usually, vowel digraphs represent the long sound of the first vowel.

Vowel Digraphs	Examples of Unusual Sounds	Exceptions
ee and *ea*	steep, each, treat, sea	head, sweat, dread
ai and *ay*	plain, paid, may, betray	plaid
oa, *ow*, and *oe*	soak, slow, doe	now, shoe
ie and *igh*	lie, night, delight	friend, eight

As you read, sometimes the only way to know how to pronounce a word with an *ea* spelling is to see if the word makes sense in the sentence. Look at this example:

The water pipes were made of *lead*.

First, try out the long sound "ee." Ask yourself if it sounds right. It does not. Then, try the short sound "e." You will find that the short sound is correct in that sentence.

Now try this example.

Where you *lead*, I will follow.

WORD PATTERNS

Recognizing different vowel-consonant patterns will help you read longer words. In the following sections, the V stands for "vowel" and the C stands for "consonant."

Single-syllable Words

CV – go: In two-letter words with a consonant followed by a vowel, the vowel is usually long. For example, the word *go* is pronounced with a long *o* sound.

In a single syllable word, a vowel followed only by a single consonant is usually short.

CVC – got: If you add a consonant to the word *go*, such as the *t* in *got*, the vowel sound is a short *o*. Say the words *go* and *got* aloud and notice the difference in pronunciation.

Multi-syllable words

In words of more than one syllable, notice the letters that follow a vowel.

VCCV – robber: A single vowel followed by two consonants is usually short.

VCV — begin: A single vowel followed by a single consonant is usually long.

VCe — beside: An extension of the VCV pattern is vowel-consonant-silent *e*. In these words, the vowel is long and the *e* is not pronounced.

When you see a word with the VCV pattern, try the long vowel sound first. If the word does not make sense, try the short sound. Pronounce the words *model*, *camel*, and *closet*. First, try the long vowel sound. That does not sound correct, so try the short vowel sound. The short vowel sound is correct in those words.

Remember that patterns help you get started on figuring out a word. You will sometimes need to try a different sound or find the word in a dictionary.

As you read and find unfamiliar words, look the pronunciations up in a dictionary. Write the words in this chart in the correct column to help you notice patterns and remember pronunciations.

Syllables	Example	New words	Vowel
CV	go		long
CVC	got		short
VCC	robber		short
V/CV	begin open		long long
VC/V	closet		short

MNEMONICS

Mnemonics are devices, or methods, that help you remember things. The basic strategy is to link something you do not know with something that you *do* know. Here are some common mnemonic devices:

Visualizing Create a picture in your head that will help you remember the meaning of a vocabulary word. For example, the first four letters of the word *significance* spell *sign*. Picture a sign with the word *meaning* written on it to remember that significance means "meaning" or "importance."

Spelling The way a word is spelled can help you remember its meaning. For example, you might remember that *clarify* means to "make clear" if you notice that both *clarify* and *clear* start with the letters *cl*.

To help you remember how to spell certain words, look for a familiar word within the difficult word. For example:

Believe has a *lie* in it.

Separate is *a rat* of a word to spell.

Your *principal* is your *pal*.

Rhyming Here is a popular rhyme that helps people figure out how to spell *ei* and *ie* words.

i before *e* — except after *c* or *when sounding like *a* as in neighbor and weigh.*

List words here that you need help remembering. Work with a group to create mnemonic devices to help you remember each word.

_____   _____

_____   _____

_____   _____

_____   _____

List words here that you need help remembering. Work with a group to create mnemonic devices to help you remember each word.

_____   _____

_____   _____

_____   _____

_____   _____

_____   _____

_____   _____

_____   _____

_____   _____

_____   _____

_____   _____

_____   _____

_____   _____

COMMUNICATION STRATEGIES

Use these sentence starters to help you express yourself clearly in different classroom situations.

Expressing an Opinion
I think that _____
I believe that _____
In my opinion, _____

Agreeing
I agree with _____ that _____
I see what you mean.
That's an interesting idea.
My idea is similar to _____'s idea.
My idea builds upon _____'s idea.

Disagreeing
I don't completely agree with you because _____
My opinion is different than yours.
I got a different answer than you.
I see it a different way.

Reporting a Group's Ideas
We agreed that _____
We decided that _____
We had a different approach.
We had a similar idea.

Predicting
I predict that _____
I imagine that _____
Based on _____ I predict that _____

Paraphrasing
So you are saying that _____
In other words, you think _____
What I hear you saying is _____

Offering a Suggestion
Maybe we could _____
What if we _____
Here's something we might try.

Asking for Clarification
I have a question about that.
Could you explain that another way?
Can you give me another example of that?

Asking for a Response
What do you think?
Do you agree?
What answer did you get?

VOCABULARY BOOKMARKS

Cut out each bookmark to use as a handy word list when you are reading. On the lines, jot down words you want to learn and remember. You can also use the bookmark as a placeholder in your book.

TITLE		**TITLE**		**TITLE**	
Word	**Page #**	**Word**	**Page #**	**Word**	**Page #**

VOCABULARY BOOKMARKS

Cut out each bookmark to use as a handy word list when you are reading. On the lines, jot down words you want to learn and remember. You can also use the bookmark as a placeholder in your book.

TITLE		
Word	**Page #**	
_____	_____	
_____	_____	
_____	_____	
_____	_____	
_____	_____	
_____	_____	
_____	_____	
_____	_____	
_____	_____	
_____	_____	
_____	_____	
_____	_____	
_____	_____	
_____	_____	

TITLE		
Word	**Page #**	
_____	_____	
_____	_____	
_____	_____	
_____	_____	
_____	_____	
_____	_____	
_____	_____	
_____	_____	
_____	_____	
_____	_____	
_____	_____	
_____	_____	
_____	_____	
_____	_____	

TITLE		
Word	**Page #**	
_____	_____	
_____	_____	
_____	_____	
_____	_____	
_____	_____	
_____	_____	
_____	_____	
_____	_____	
_____	_____	
_____	_____	
_____	_____	
_____	_____	
_____	_____	
_____	_____	

VOCABULARY BUILDER CARDS

Use these cards to record words you want to remember. Write the word, the title of the story or article in which it appears, its part of speech, and its definition. Then, use the word in an original sentence that shows its meaning

Word: _____ Page _____

Selection: _____

Part of Speech: _____

Definition: _____

_____

My Sentence _____

_____

Word: _____ Page _____

Selection: _____

Part of Speech: _____

Definition: _____

_____

My Sentence _____

_____

Word: _____ Page _____

Selection: _____

Part of Speech: _____

Definition: _____

_____

My Sentence _____

_____

Use these cards to record words you want to remember. Write the word, the title of the story or article in which it appears, its part of speech, and its definition. Then, use the word in an original sentence that shows its meaning

Word: _____ Page _____

Selection: _____

Part of Speech: _____

Definition: _____

_____

My Sentence _____

_____

Word: _____ Page _____

Selection: _____

Part of Speech: _____

Definition: _____

_____

My Sentence _____

_____

Word: _____ Page _____

Selection: _____

Part of Speech: _____

Definition: _____

_____

My Sentence _____

_____

VOCABULARY BUILDER CARDS

Use these cards to record words you want to remember. Write the word, the title of the story or article in which it appears, its part of speech, and its definition. Then, use the word in an original sentence that shows its meaning

Word: _____ Page _____

Selection: _____

Part of Speech: _____

Definition: _____

_____

My Sentence _____

_____

Word: _____ Page _____

Selection: _____

Part of Speech: _____

Definition: _____

_____

My Sentence _____

_____

Word: _____ Page _____

Selection: _____

Part of Speech: _____

Definition: _____

_____

My Sentence _____

_____

V5

Use these cards to record words you want to remember. Write the word, the title of the story or article in which it appears, its part of speech, and its definition. Then, use the word in an original sentence that shows its meaning

Word: _____ Page _____

Selection: _____

Part of Speech: _____

Definition: _____

My Sentence _____

_____

Word: _____ Page _____

Selection: _____

Part of Speech: _____

Definition: _____

My Sentence _____

_____

Word: _____ Page _____

Selection: _____

Part of Speech: _____

Definition: _____

My Sentence _____

_____

(Acknowledgments continued from page ii)

HarperCollins Publishers, Inc.
Excerpt from *An American Childhood* by Annie Dillard. Copyright © 1987 by Annie Dillard.

Hill and Wang, a division of Farrar, Straus & Giroux, LLC
"Thank You, M'am" by Langston Hughes from *Short Stories.* Copyright © 1996 by Ramona Bass and Arnold Rampersad. "Your World" by Georgia Douglas Johnson from *American Negro Poetry.* Revised edition copyright © 1974 by the Estate of Arna Bontemps. First edition copyright © 1963 by Arna Bontemps. All rights reserved.

Holiday House, Inc.
"January" from *A Child's Calendar* by John Updike. Text copyright © 1965, 1999 by John Updike. All rights reserved. Reprinted by permission of Holiday House, Inc.

Estate of Dr. Martin Luther King, Jr. c/o Writers House LLC
"The American Dream" by Dr. Martin Luther King, Jr. from *A Testament of Hope: The Essential Writings* of Martin Luther King Jr. Reprinted by arrangement with the Estate of Martin Luther King Jr., c/o Writers House as agent for the proprietor, New York, NY. Copyright © 1968 Martin Luther King Jr., copyright © renewed 1996 Coretta Scott King.

Alfred A. Knopf, Inc.
"The 11:59" by Patricia C. McKissack. From *The Dark Thirty,* illustrated by Brian Pinkney, copyright © 1992 by Patricia C. McKissack. Illustrations copyright © 1992 by Brian Pinkney. "Harlem Night Song" by Langston Hughes from *Selected Poems Of Langston Hughes.* copyright © 1994 by The Estate of Langston Hughes. Used by permission of Alfred A. Knopf, a division of Random House, Inc.

Liveright Publishing Corporation
"Runagate Runagate" Copyright © 1966 by Robert Hayden, from *Collected Poems of Robert Hayden,* edited by Frederick Glaysher. Used by permission of Liveright Publishing Corporation.

Robert MacNeil
"The Trouble with Television" by Robert MacNeil condensed from a Speech, November 1984 at President Leadership Forum, SUNY. Copyright © 1985 Reader's Digest and Robert MacNeil.

Eve Merriam c/o Marian Reiner Literary Agency
"Thumbprint" from A Sky Full of Poems by Eve ...rriam, Copyright © 1964, 1970, 1973 Eve ...riam. Copyright renewed 1992 Eve Merriam, ... Dee Michel and Guy Michel. Reprinted by ...ssion of the author.

... Scott Momaday
...rld" by N. Scott Momaday from *The Gourd* ... Reprinted by permission.

...ublic Radio
...ld War II veterans who founded the ...erans of America" from *National* ...*November 11, 2003.* Copyright ...l Public Radio. All rights reserved. ...mission.

North Carolina Ferry Division
"North Carolina Ferry System Schedule" from *NC Dot Ferry Division And Public Information Office.* Reprinted by permission.

Naomi Shihab Nye
"Hamadi" by Naomi Shihab Nye from *America Street.* Copyright © 1993 by Naomi Shihab Nye. Reprinted by permission.

Oxford University Press, Inc.
"Summary of the Tell-Tale Heart" by James D. Hart from *The Oxford Companion To American Literature.* Copyright © 1941, 1948, © 1956, 1965, 1983 by Oxford University Press, Inc. Reprinted by permission.

Pantheon Books, a division of Random House, Inc.
"Coyote Steals the Sun and Moon" from *American Indian Myths and Legends* edited by Richard Erdoes and Alfonso Ortiz, copyright © 1984 by Richard Erdoes and Alfonso Ortiz.

Pearson Education, Inc., publishing as Prentice Hall
"The War in Vietnam" from *The American Nation* by Dr. James West Davidson and Dr. Michael B. Stoff. Copyright © 2003 by Pearson Education, Inc., publishing as Prentice Hall. Used by permission.

G.P. Putnam's Sons, A Division of Penguin Young Readers Group, A Member of Penguin Group (USA) Inc.
"Describe Somebody," and "Almost a Summer Sky" from *Locomotion* by Jacqueline Woodson, copyright © 2003 by Jacqueline Woodson. Used by permission of G.P. Putnam's Sons, A Division of Penguin Young Readers Group, A Member of Penguin Group (USA) Inc.

Random House, Inc.
"Raymond's Run" by Toni Cade Bambara, copyright © 1971 by Toni Cade Bambara, from *Gorilla, My Love. The Diary of Anne Frank* by Frances Goodrich and Albert Hackett, copyright © 1956 renewed by Albert Hackett, David Huntoon & Frances Neuwirth in 1986. Used by permission of Flora Roberts, Inc.
CAUTION NOTICE: Professionals and amateurs are hereby warned that *THE DIARY OF ANNE FRANK* is subject to a royalty. It is fully protected under the copyright laws of the United States of America and of all countries covered by the International Copyright Union (including the Dominion of Canada and the rest of the British Commonwealth), the Berne Convention, the Pan-American Copyright Convention and the Universal Copyright Convention as well as all countries with which the United States has reciprocal copyright relations. All rights, including professional/amateur stage rights, motion picture, recitation, lecturing, public reading, radio broadcasting, television, video or sound recording, all other forms of mechanical or electronic reproduction, such as CD-ROM, CD-I, information storage and retrieval systems and photocopying, and the rights of translation into foreign languages, are strictly reserved. Particular emphasis is laid upon the matter of readings, permission for which must be secured from the Author's agent in writing.

Marian Reiner, Literary Agent
"Concrete Mixers" from *8 A.M. Shadows* by Patricia Hubbell. Copyright 1965, 1993 by Patricia Hubbell. Used by permission of Marion Reiner for the author.

Maria Teresa Sánchez
"Old Man" by Ricardo Sánchez from *Selected Poems.* Used by permission of Maria Teresa Sánchez for the Estate of Dr. Ricardo Sánchez.

Scholastic, Inc.
From *Out of the Dust* ("Debts," "Fields of Flashing Light," and "Migrants") by Karen Hesse. Published by Scholastic Press/Scholastic Inc. Copyright © 1997 by Karen Hesse. "An Hour with Abuelo" from *An Island Like You and Other Stories of the Barrio* by Judith Ortiz Cofer. Published by Orchard Books/Scholastic Inc. Copyright © 1995 by Judith Ortiz Cofer.

Argelia Sedillo
"Gentleman of Río en Medio" by Juan A.A. Sedillo from *The New Mexico Quarterly, A Regional Review, Volume Ix, August, 1939, Number 3.*

The Society of Authors
"Silver" by Walter de la Mare from *The Complete Poems Of Walter De La Mare 1901–1918.* Copyright © 1969. Used by permission of The Literary Trustees of Walter de la Mare and the Society of Authors as their representative.

Sprint
"Instructions for an Answering Machine" from *Sprint User's Manual for Tapeless Digital Answering System with Time/Day SP-818.* Used by permission of Sprint.

Estate of Jackie Torrence
"Brer Possum's Dilemma" retold by Jackie Torrence from *Homespun: Tales From America's Favorite Storytellers* by Jimmy Neil Smith. Copyright © 1988 by Jackie Torrence. Reprinted by permission of the Estate of Jackie Torrence.

Vital Speeches of the Day
From "Sharing in the American Dream: the task may seem staggering" by Colin Powell from *Vital Speeches, June 1, 1997, V63 N16, P484(2).* Copyright © 1997 Colin Powell. Copyright © 1997 Vital Speeches.

W. W. Norton & Company, Inc.
"Water Names" from *Hunger* by Lan Samantha Chang. Copyright © 1998 by Lan Samantha Chang.

Walker & Company
From "The Baker Heater League" by Patricia and Fredrick McKissack from *A Long Hard Journey: The Story Of The Pullman Porter.* Copyright © 1989 by Patricia and Fredrick McKissack. All rights reserved. Used with permission of Walker & Company.

Richard & Joyce Wolkomir
"Sun Suckers and Moon Cursers" by Richard and Joyce Wolkomir. Copyright © 2002 by Richard & Joyce Wolkomir. Reprinted with the authors' permission.

Note: Every effort has been made to locate the copyright owner of material reproduced on this component. Omissions brought to our attention will be corrected in subsequent editions.

PHOTO AND ART CREDITS